New Trends
& Generations
in African Literature

T0323732

African Literature Today

'one of the best authoritative journals of African literature today . . .' *Matatu*

'a journal consistently immersed in all the ongoing issues of African literature . . .'
World Literature Today

Editor: Eldred Durosimi Jones
* 1, 2, 3, and 4 Omnibus Edition
  5 The Novel in Africa
  6 Poetry in Africa
  7 Focus on Criticism
  8 Drama in Africa
* 9 Africa, America & the Caribbean
*10 Retrospect & Prospect
  11 Myth & History

Editor: Eldred Durosimi Jones
Associate Editor: Eustace Palmer
Assistant Editor: Marjorie Jones
  12 New Writing, New Approaches
*13 Recent Trends in the Novel
*14 Insiders & Outsiders
1–14 were published from London by
Heinemann Educational Books and from
New York by Africana Publishing
Company

The new series is published by
James Currey Publishers and Africa World Press
*ALT 15 Women in African Literature Today
*ALT 16 Oral & Written Poetry in African Literature Today
*ALT 17 The Question of Language in African Literature Today
*ALT 18 Orature in African Literature Today
*ALT 19 Critical Theory & African Literature Today
*ALT 20 New Trends & Generations in African Literature

*Copies of back issues marked with an asterisk may be purchased from your bookseller or direct from James Currey Ltd

Future Issues

Place a standing order with your supplier for future issues

ALT 21 Childhood in African Literature
Childhood is a frequently recurring theme in African literature which runs through all the genres: poetry, the novel, drama and autobiography. Camara Laye's *The African Child* and Wole Soyinka's Aké have taken their place as classics in this kind. Deadline for the submission of articles has passed.

ALT 22 Exile & African Literature
Articles are invited on the influence of exile (including the African diaspora) on the literature of Africa and its significance in the work of particular writers. Deadline for the submission of articles December 1995.

ALT 23 will focus on South Africa. With the end of political apartheid, South Africa once more enters the mainstream of world literature. Articles are invited on major developments in South African literature, the role of writers and institutions such as publishing houses, theatre groups etc. in the struggle against apartheid. Deadline for the submission of articles June 1996.

Before embarking on articles contributors are advised to submit proposals to the Editor, Professor Eldred Durosimi Jones: Fourah Bay College, University of Sierra Leone, Private Mail Bag, Freetown, Sierra Leone. Unsolicited articles are welcome, but will not be returned unless adequate postage arrangements are made by the contributors.

All articles should be well typed, double spaced on A4 paper with a wide margin. References to books should include the author or editor, place, publisher, date and the relevant pages.

Contributors must keep a spare copy in case of loss in transit.

New Trends & Generations in African Literature

A review
Editor: ELDRED DUROSIMI JONES
Assistant Editor: MARJORIE JONES

JAMES CURREY
LONDON

AFRICA WORLD PRESS
TRENTON N.J.

James Currey
an imprint of Boydell and Brewer Ltd,
PO Box 9, Woodbridge, Suffolk IP12 3DF, UK
and 668 Mount Hope Avenue, Rochester NY 14620-2731, USA
www.jamescurrey.com
www.boydell and brewer.com

Africa World Press, Inc.
PO Box 1892
Trenton
NJ 08607

A catalogue record is available from the British Library

ISBN 978–0–85255–520–0 (James Currey paper)
ISBN 978–0–86543–506–3 (Africa World Press cloth)
ISBN 978–0–86543–507–0 (Africa World Press paper)

Transferred to digital printing

Typeset in 10/11pt Melior Colset Pte. Ltd., Singapore

Contents

Editorial Article
New Trends
& Generations

Eldred D. Jones

Modern African literature developed during the period of contact with non-African (European) peoples and their languages, the bulk of it coming just before and since independence. Political independence usually generated such a change of focus as to define the beginning of a new period in the literary history of each country. Pre-independence literature was largely characterized by concern with the African's plight in relation to European influence and consisted of protest against domination, calls for unity against the oppressor and assertions of the African's right to self-determination. It asserted the validity of African concepts and systems and was often romantic and sentimental.

Political independence enjoyed only a brief period of celebration, if any at all (Wole Soyinka's *A Dance of the Forests* did not linger over romantic celebration) before writers and thinkers were alerted to new dangers. Exploitation had not after all disappeared with political independence; only the exploiters had changed. Writers had been the leaders of protest under colonialism, politicians and writers being often the same persons. Independence separated this identity and the writers in their examination of their experience under independence found themselves increasingly alienated from the politicians, often becoming their victims. The targets of protest changed from the colonial invader to the inheritors of their power. It is thus possible to distinguish in the literatures of most countries pre-independence from post-independence literature but only as trends rather than a sudden dramatic break.

A significant development since independence has been the increasing importance of women writers and the consequent focus on women's situation in society, their pre-occupations with family and work, and their attempts to free themselves from the trammels of tradition. Flora Nwapa, one of the pioneers in this field, died in 1993 bringing to an end a career which also almost defines a trend. Although she declined the title of feminist, her writings are among the most serious attempts to present the concerns of African womanhood. Mariama Bâ who died in 1981 had similarly drawn attention to the position of a woman in an Islamic society but women writers have not been exclusively concerned with women's affairs. Eno Obong's *Garden House* is as much concerned with politics and the performance of men in it as it is with the position of women in society. As Lilyan Kesteloot also points out in her article in this number, Aminata Sow Fall, Awa Keita and Khady Sylla break out of the limited concerns of women into the wider field of national life and politics, a field more usually associated with their male counterparts.

War is another phenomenon that produces a sufficient change in focus to mark new trends and schools of literature. In Zimbabwe and Kenya, and in so far as the struggle against apartheid can be called a war, in South Africa, war was telescoped into independence so that post-war and post-independence coincide. War in Nigeria came well after independence and marked off a new influence so that the term post-civil war can be used by Chréacháin to identify a period in Nigerian literary history. A comparison however, between post-war Nigerian literature on the one hand, and post-war/post-independence literature of Zimbabwe and Kenya on the other, shows many similarities; the gap between politicians and writers being equally wide, and the disillusion and futility of war being equally bitter. Both sets of writers come down on the side of the ordinary people against their oppressors.

Even in countries where independence was achieved with comparative ease and without bloodshed, a similar literature of protest against the misuse of independence by corrupt political systems has arisen. In francophone Africa, literature has moved from the optimistic assertions of the validity of African values and celebration of its innocent virtues to the novels of disillusion and disenchantment of the 1970s and 1980s. Nwachukwu-Agbada sees three generations of poets while Awodiya similarly identifies three generations of playwrights in modern Nigerian literature. While trends and schools may be identified the new voices are as committed to their social responsibilities as their predecessors had been. They are committed to the cause of the ordinary people and have put themselves in the firing line in their opposition to powerful forces who they see as betraying the people in whose name and by whose sacrifice wars were fought and independence won.

Political events in Africa sometimes move with bewildering speed. When Duma Ndlovu wrote in 1986: '... there will be change in the country, sooner than most people think' even he would hardly have thought that less than a decade later political apartheid would have crumbled. South African writers will now have to emerge from the dominating theme of apartheid into a closer examination of humanity in a 'free' society. The speed with which events happen is similarly demonstrated by the fact that yet another military regime has overtaken the three mentioned in Chréacháin's article. The military phenomenon has provided Nigerian writers with a succession of sub-periods in their literary history.

African literature continues to be intensely political and seems destined to remain so for some time. The writers are in the thick of the fight for the true liberation of their countries, a position which is still fraught with dangers.

Eldred D. Jones

Turning Point in the Francophone/African Novel: The Eighties to the Nineties

Lilyan Kesteloot *

tr. Saidu Bangura, Dept of Modern Languages, Fourah Bay College

It is interesting to see the efforts critics make in their attempt to grasp and to define what has been happening among writers in recent years. B. Mouralis contrasts authors belonging to 'the classical age of the African novel' with those of today who aim at underlining the absence of structure and the essentially 'formless' character of the world they present in their works. Suzanne Gasster and Locha Mateso refer to novels which are 'epics in reverse' or 'counter-epics' in which the characters defeated by their own stories become anti-heroes projected into a world which they no longer understand. A. Chemain, for his part, is struck by the rising violence in the accounts and examines their significance: a symptom of the aggravating conflicts of post-colonial society or a salutary catharsis that portends a renaissance? In the case of Séwanou Dabla, what is striking is the confusion in values, the absurdity of a dislocated universe.

What then has happened to that Africa that is supposedly without a history? Barely 30 years ago black writers in three continents indulged in prophetic proclamations under the influence of Négritude, proliferating accusations, demands and great hopes! Of course, as early as the seventies, attention was drawn to the opening phases of a literature of 'disenchantment' (a term coined by J. Chévrier) which, after pointing out the aftermath of independence the beneficiaries of which expected miracles, aptly described the illusion/disillusion process. African novelists and playwrights, Francophone as well as Anglophone, reacted very quickly and echoed the deviations of indigenous politicians, the ridiculous aspects and contradictory morals of the new bourgeoisie, the disappointments and difficulties of the people whose

*The editors gratefully acknowledge the assistance of Lulu Wright of the Department of Modern Languages, Fourah Bay College, in the editing of this article.

condition only worsened rather than improved. But how can one put it? There was always Hope! Novels like those of Francis Bebey, *Le Fils d'Agatha Moudio* or *La Poupée Ashanti*, W. Sassine's *Saint Monsieur Baly*, those of Sylvain Bemba, *Les Cargonautes*, or *Les Monimambou* by Guy Menga, those of Aminata Sow Fall like *La Grève des Battu* or *L'Appel des arènes*, those of Seydou Badian or Pascal Couloubaly, all revealed the torments of African life but also its joys, even if one was far from the paradise promised in electoral campaigns. *Le Soleil des indépendances* by Kourouma, though radically pessimistic remained tempered by the constant humour which ran through it and masked its profound tragedy, a humour that was not yet destructive. The last work in this series was *Le Pleurer-rire* by H. Lopès, whose title expressed perfectly the dosage of bitter-sweet which was for almost twenty years the recipe for the post-colonial African novel. This corresponded more or less to the mitigated replies Africans gave to the banal, daily question – 'How are things?' – 'Un peu seulement' ('Not so bad'), the Cameroonian would say; 'doni-doni' ('so-so'), would come from the Malian; and 'Sènègalaisement' ('Senegalish'), the Dakarois would say, meaning, 'not wonderful but bearable'!

And then suddenly they can no longer bear it. The tone changes. In quick succession appear *Le Bel Immonde* and *Shaba 2* by Mudimbe, *L'Etat honteux*, *L'Anté-peuple*, *Lorsa Lopez* by Soni Labou Tansi, *Les Cancrelats* and *Les Méduses* by Tchicaya, *Le Récit du cirque* by Fantouré, *Toiles d'araignées* by Ibrahim Ly, *Le Zéhéros* by W. Sassine, *Le Temps de Tamango* and *Les Tambours de la mémoire* by Boubakar Boris Diop, *Routiers des chimères* by Ibrahima Sall, *La Latrine* by Severin C. Abega, *Les Ecailles du ciel* by Tierno Monemembo, *Sahel! sanglante sécheresse* by Alpha Diarra, *Le Bal des caïmans* by Yodi Karone, *Au Bout du silence* by Laurent Owondo ... Silence in fact! No more laughter. Or then laughter becomes leering, sneering, groaning – a real avalanche of narratives reminiscent of the writing in days gone by (1939), of Césaire the visionary. The critic is tempted here to call upon the poet who would no doubt be better able to find words to describe the hallucinatory universe which, in the works of our novelist, replaces that indulgently long-suffering Africa where humour and shrewdness always enable the hero to get out of difficult situations. The hero is suppressed or ridiculous, a roving character humiliated, in stories in which the colours (if one were to paint them) range from blood red (wars, murders, repressions) to muddy (corruption, prostitution, drugs); from ash grey (like the life of Ayi Kwei Armah's The Man in *The Beautyful Ones Are Not Yet Born*) to pitch black like the life of the child in the novel of L. Owondo or S. Abega).

Everything happens as if the writers could no longer restrain themselves from exhuming, with a violence unheard of, the fall-out from those rotten regimes which act like cancers infecting in turn all levels of the society which they gangrene. According to their inspiration and ability, in realistic mode, but more often hallucinatory even delirious, they vent forth through their writing a reality that borders on nightmare. But whatever the mode of expression, the text ends up in madness, death or stupor. The recurrence of this type of narrative is in the process of giving rise to a new school which could be called 'The African Absurd'. These novels have in fact a metaphysical dimension which goes beyond their main topic and which can be measured by the profound malaise which they emit. They provoke anguished questioning not only of the current politico-social situation in Africa or the adventure of the black race, but just man, humanity and its degree of deterioration. For in these depressing narratives, North and South are inextricably intermingled not by the actual presence of Europeans (this is becoming increasingly rare in the modern novel) but by the purulence of prisons where there is torture, industries that pollute (as in *Les Ecailles du ciel*), cities and shanty towns, money for which people poison, kill and sell themselves. Does all this not originate from the West?

So we find after a lapse of forty years this feeling of an absurd universe that existentialist writers expressed so forcefully for European post-war generations: a world without justice, without an ultimate purpose, without laws if not that of the strongest, the law of the bomb and the gun. Sartre and Camus then accused an indifferent God. African writers no longer accuse anyone; they are crying out in a vacuum, and this is sinister. This 'African Absurd' however is less heir to the existentialists of 1945 and the French new novel than to South American novelists like Cortàzar, Asturias or García Marquez. Their 'under-developed' world is nearer to the African urban environment and to the misery of the rural areas. One can also identify the influence of Anglophone Africans like Ayi Kwei Armah, Ngũgĩ and Soyinka.

Furthermore, our writers find in these a literary bias that is relevant to modern thinking, and permits them to depart from the mould of the nineteenth-century French novel or that of the oral tale. Thus to the disorder of a chaotic universe, a narrative characterized by divers accidents will correspond. We have already highlighted the eclipse of the 'exemplary' hero, a phenomenon accentuated by the degradation or the caricature of secondary characters. One notices breaks in the logic of conduct or situations; or yet again, the almost total suppression of action (for example in the writings of Laurent Owondo) which produces a stagnant account, an obsessive meditation on a being slowy ensnared in silence between the sea and the ghetto. Or else in an alternative treatment, the action evaporates into a lived/dreamt delirium which becomes pure surrealistic discourse, a perfect allegory no doubt, of non-relatable events, as for instance in *Les Sept Solitudes* and *Lorsa Lopez* by Soni Labou Tansi – the ultimate in abstruse homology of text and subject matter. But at this point you reach the limit of experience; the text itself has become unintelligible and loses all interest apart from the fact that it symbolizes totally that incongruous, atrocious disgusting society, and constitutes the only reality comparable to 'the absurdity of a dissertation now empty, in which words have ceased to designate and signify, and become a mere conglomeration of slogans'.

However, according to the authors, this loathsome reality contains threats and angry outbursts, and therefore surviving traces of life; or else it is only the bleak magma of a universe struck by entropy and in the process of disintegration, a stage prior to a salutary apocalypse about which novelists moreover, have no clear idea either. For all the points of reference have been broken. One can no longer invoke the great communist evening, nor expect aid from the USSR and redemption from the Revolution. The Négritude ideology no longer inspires novelists, and nor does the dream of the American way of life. They have become very reserved, indeed silent, on political theories, be they left- or right-wing. Ethics are derided whether traditional or rationalist, the human race is no longer innocent; the family has changed into parasites; the village has ceased to be an authority of reference and the refuge of the socially displaced, as happened in *Maïmouna* by Abdoulaye Sadji or *Africa ba'a* by Rémy Médou Mvomo.

On the other side, a degree no longer guarantees employment and religions are incapable of re-orienting the urban masses consumed by needs multiplied by imported gadgets; this 'garbage' society from the West and its process of internal deconstruction is marvellously portrayed by Pape Pathé Diop in his parable novel. Novels of the African absurd are thus witnesses to every kind of deviation and perdition. But beyond this ideological drifting, one can examine the literary significance of these books. Where are African writers heading? The effort expended on writing is indisputable. 'Before, I used to narrate now I am writing,' said Henri Lopès in describing this more sustained emphasis on style, the text becoming the ultimate attempt to understand (or escape from) intolerable reality. The writer no doubt, no longer is victim of the illusions of the not too distant past, a fact I have already pointed out in connection with poets. 'I do not seek to change society ... novels will not change the world ... but what I do not like, I denounce . . . I write in order not to sink; we live in a situation where everyone owes it to himself to have his own life-buoy, and as for me, I cling on to my books.'

We may compare such modesty with declarations on the power of the word, 'a miracle weapon' capable of transforming the world; another thing one notices and this is new, is a halt to speculations on the power of the word, on the incantation of witchcraft, on the magical and at the same time pedagogical dimension of African literature. Our novelists no longer want to be seen as moralists, mouthpieces, catalysts of their peoples as was still the wish of Cheikh Hamidou Kane or Seydou Badian Kouyate, taking their cue from pronouncements by Alioune Diop and the two Congresses of black writers and artists. Writing is freeing itself from its former constraints: militancy, prophecy, education, *vox populi*, in a word, all that was conventionally referred to as literature of commitment. In short, the design of the African writer is taking on individual characteristics and recoiling on its ego. The best examples of this tendency are *L'Ecart* by V.Y. Mudimbe, and *Giambatista Viko* by M. Ngal. But with Mudimbe, this tendency begins to focus on metaphysical anguish and more so in *Shaba 2* where it is affirmedly paramount; and this, while leaving with the reader the choice of deciding whether such a horrific story is the result of divine grace or the absurdity of the human condition.

Thus the novelist is freeing himself from collective tasks for more personal objectives and a more intensive search for style. This search in turn is giving rise to modifications, then to turbulence in the narrative structure of the novels. Mohamadou Kane has clearly highlighted in his thesis, *Roman et tradition*, the analogy between the structure of oral narrative and written romantic narrative: in particular, the linear aspect of the action, the unfolding of continuous chronology and the outline of the journey, the psychological shallowness of the characters and the frequent recourse to dialogue, as far as the didactic side of the novel which recalls the social function of the traditional tale. But now with the new African novel, all these parameters are being overturned: the propensity of dialogue overflows into narration, to produce a mock orality (Alioune Tine), the narrative loses its chronological flow so as to make leaps forward and backward in time as well as in space: time of present action, projected future, resurging past, return to the present, time split in half in the minds of other narrators, time lived/time dreamt, in short, choice food for lovers of Genette and the accidents of diagesis?

Locha Mateso states the position like this:

> Everything depends on the way in which one conceives the relationship between writers and the world through the

medium of symbols. These writers challenge the contract of expression which traditionally governed this relationship ... there is a break with normative writing ... narratives divested of their linear form, oralised much in demand for exogenous breaks with context and destruction of the effect of the real. ... With its redundant qualifications and its repetitions that mimic the structure of conversational language, the novel is settling down into permanent syntactic fluctuation.

We shall have to admit after this diagnosis, that the era of the story-novel is approaching its end, and that other criteria are necessary in order to appreciate the force of post-1980 novels. Yes, the novelists have really broken their mould, and we can expect all the surprises of Pandora when we open a 'black' novel of the new school today.

The Novel of Manners

However, parallel to this avant-garde movement, the production of that straightforward novel of manners still continues, where people merely evoke – without any visionary ambition and without stylistic adventure – everyday Africa preferably in its micro-circles. Ch-Ndao's *Excellence vos épouses* or *Marabout de la sécheresse* as well as the novels of Francis Bebey cited above are excellent examples of this genre. The majority of the novels by women can be placed within this category: Aminata Sow Fall, Mariama Bâ, Catherine Ndiaye, Ken Bugul, Nafi Diallo, A. Rawiri, Simone Kaya, Régine Yaou, Philomène Bassek, Maïga Ka, Flora Nwapa in Nigeria, Grace Ogot in Uganda, Rebecca Njau in Kenya, all re-create with varying degrees of talent the pangs of marriage, together with love, jealousy, competition, adultery, neglect, barrenness, then children, tensions and ruptures. Within the context of the tradition/modernism conflict, they tackle the problems of traditional beliefs and practices, the feminine condition, the extended family and its constraints. Some like Aminata Sow Fall and Awa Keita, escape from the specific feminine universe. *L'Ex-père de la nation*, by the former, is a novel on political manners, which could well have been written by a man; Awa Keita also talks about politics: meetings, speeches, militant fraternity. Khady Sylla on her side, explores the interferences of the real and the imaginary, of which writing is the meeting point.

Worthy of mention also is the fictionalized account by a very young girl, Aïcha Diouri, which deals with the fall and rise of a drug addict in *La Mauvaise Passe*. The memoirs of a young prostitute which Mamadou Samb, a teacher, has published under the title *De*

Pulpe et d'orange should be read. Drugs and prostitution are two favourite themes in the novel of manners of the eighties testifying to the spread of these social evils. The most accomplished novel depicting the world of young drug addicts is Abasse Ndione's *La Vie en spirale*. For the other aspects of social life we may cite G. Oupoh and J.M. Adiaffi. Asse Gueye is widening the still narrow path of the detective novel, followed by Moussa Konate with *L'Assassin* and M.S. Keita with *L'Archer bassari*. Moussa Konate is however better known for dramatic works which portray a painful childhood, such as *Fils du chaos*. Within the same category fall the cruel short stories of Maurice Bandaman's *Une Femme pour une médaille* and Tanella Boni's *Une Vie de crabe*.

As can be seen, current social novels no longer hesitate to 'depoeticize' traditional society only lately held sacred in works like *L'Enfant noir* or *L'Aventure ambiguë*. But was Amar Samb not the precursor of this neo-realism with his *Matraqué par le destin*, a novel so badly received in the seventies? The novel of manners is tending towards a sometimes suffocating naturalism as exemplified by Mpoyi Buatu's *La Reproduction*, and the works of Emongo Lomomba, Ilboudo and S. Okoumba.

Finally, alas! the developing prison novel which has become a category bestriding the novel of manners and the novel of the absurd. All these works, *Prisonnier de Tombalbaye* by Antoine Bangui, *Detained* by Ngũgĩ wa Thiong'o, *Toiles d'araignées* by Ibrahim Ly, *The Man Died* by Wole Soyinka – these analyse in detail the miseries, the horrors of black prisons, where politics are most often confused with 'common rights'. South African novels similarly portray white prisons – apparently they match each other for human rights violation.

The Regional Novel

We shall now glance in a third direction in order to understand a type of novel more deeply rooted in a particular locality and a specifically rural one which aims at an in-depth exploration of the peasant mind, and at times takes over from ethnology. Its preoccupations are limited to the village level and it stands aloof from national or international politics. It is written in a sober, very controlled, often classical prose. Its object is to conjure up the 'Africa of the bush' confronting itself. At the head of this movement which I would term regionalist, we should note Olympe Bhêly-Quénum, who for that matter has always fitted into this perspective, with *Le Chant du lac*, *Un Piège sans fin* and especially, *L'Initié*.

The didactic novel of Massa Makan Diabate, *Comme une Piqûre de guêpe*, and also *L'Assemblée des Djinns* are true documents on western Mali as is his trilogy on the barber, the butcher and the lieutenant of Kouta. The novels of Tidiane Dem and of Amadou Koné are themselves very much tied to the Savannah. And the world of *Au Seuil de l'irréel* and *Le Temps des Bilakoro* takes its rhythm from this, far from the stress of the big city. If one considers *Le Cap des chèvres* by Weynde Ndiaye, one discovers the life of a little village perched on the ocean front where a marvellous serenity exists side by side with the petty electoral intrigues of the place. There too Dakar seems to be ten thousand kilometres away. Clochemerle dictates its own pace of life. Every character is a person and he matters to the community. *Le Silence de la forêt* by E. Goyemidié is quite a simple almost timeless story, a look by one ethnic group at another, the Bangas at the Pygmies, at first consciousness of differences, then growing experience of communication, respect and love.

In this view of Africa in essence, emerges the beautiful work of Jean Pliya, *Les Tresseurs de corde*, where real questions are asked, questions in tune with villagers and handled by them. Ab Lam and K. Noaga also treat these rural concerns. At last a new generation of Malagasy writers such as Charlotte Rafenomanjata, Michèle Rakotoson, M. Raharimanana are directing their attention towards the socio-cultural investigation of the great Island. Needless to say this vein is fruitful. It produced in France authors like Giono, Pagnol, Mistral, the Georges Sand of *La Petite Fadette* and the beautiful Norman stories of Barbey d'Aurevilly.

No claim is made here to have exhausted the whole range of categories of Francophone African novels. There are, for example, novels of adventure, novels of love, novels of initiation, and so on. The concern has been only to highlight the principal trends that are evident in the writings of recent years, and their relation to the political and social evolution of Africa.

WORKS CITED

[This Bibliography was compiled with the kind assistance of Dr John Conteh-Morgan of the Ohio State University, Columbus, Ohio]

Abega, Severin C. *La Latrine*. Dakar: Nouvelles Editions Africaines, 1988.
Bandaman, Maurice. *Une Femme pour une médaille*.
Bangui, Antoine. *Prisonnier de Tombalbaye*. Paris: Hatier, 1984.
Bebey, Francis. *Le Fils d'Agatha Moudio*. Yaoundé: CLE, 1967. *La Poupée Ashanti*. Yaoundé: CLE, 1973.
Bemba, Sylvain. *Le Dernier des Cargonautes*. Paris: L'Harmattan, 1981.
Bhêly-Quénum, Olympe. *Le Chant du lac*. Paris: Présence Africaine, 1965.

Un Piège sans fin. Paris: Stork, 1960. *L'Initié.* Paris: Présence Africaine, 1979.

Boni, Tanella. *Une Vie de crabe.* Dakar: Nouvelles Editions Africaines, 1990.

Buatu, Mpoyi. *La Reproduction.* Paris: L'Harmattan, 1986.

Ch-Ndao. *Marabout de la sécheresse.* Dakar: Nouvelles Editions Africaines, 1979. *Excellence vos épouses.* Dakar: Nouvelles Editions Africaines, 1983.

Couloubaly, Pascal. *Les Angoisses d'un monde.* Dakar: Nouvelles Editions Africaines, 1980.

Dem, Tidiane. *Masseni: roman.* Dakar: Nouvelles Editions Africaines, 1977.

Diabate, Massa Makan. *Comme une Piqûre de guêpe.* Paris: Présence Africaine, 1981. *L'Assemblée des Djinns.* Paris: Présence Africaine, 1985. *Le Lieutenant de Kouta.* Paris: Hatier, 1979. *Le Coiffeur de Kouta.* Paris: Hatier, 1983. *Le Boucher de Kouta.* Paris: Hatier, 1982.

Diarra, Alpha. *Sahel! sanglante sécheresse.* Paris: Présence Africaine, 1981.

Diop, Boubakar Boris. *Le Temps de Tamango.* Paris: L'Harmattan, 1981. *Les Tambours de la mémoire.* Paris: Nathan, 1987. rpt. Paris: L'Harmattan, 1990.

Diouri, Aïcha. *La Mauvaise Passe.* Dakar: Editions Khoudia, 1990.

Fantouré, A. *Le Récit du cirque.* Paris: Buchet/Chastel, 1976.

Goyemidié, E. *Le Silence de la forêt.* Paris: Hatier, 1984.

Kane, Cheikh Hamidou. *L'Aventure ambiguë.* Paris: Julliard, 1960.

Kane, Mohamadou. *Roman et tradition.* Dakar: Nouvelles Editions Africaines, 1982.

Karone, Yodi. *Le Bal des caïmans.* Paris: Karthala, 1980.

Keita, M.S. *L'Archer bassari.* Paris: Karthala, 1984.

Konate, Moussa. *L'Assassin.* Paris: Présence Africaine, 1981. *Fils du chaos.* Paris: Présence Africaine, 1985.

Koné, Amadou. *Les Frasques d'Ebinto.* Paris: Hatier, 1980. *De la chaire au trône.* Paris: Radio-France Internationale, 1975. *Jusqu'au seuil de l'iréel: chroniques.* Dakar: Nouvelles Editions Africaines, 1976. *Le Respect des morts.* Paris: Hatier, 1980. *Les Liens.* Abidjan: CEDA, 1980.

Koné, Amadou. *Jusqu'au Seuil de l'irréel: chroniques.* Dakar, Nouvelles Editions Africaines, 1976. *Le Temps des Bilakoro.*

Kourouma, A. *Le Soleil des indépendances.* Montréal: Le Presse de l'Université de Montréal, 1968.

Laye, Camara. *L'Enfant noir.* Paris: Plon, 1953; Paris: Presses Pocket, 1976.

Lopès, H. *Le Pleurer-rire.* Paris: Présence Africaine, 1982.

Ly, Ibrahim. *Toiles d'araignées.* Paris: L'Harmattan, 1982. rpt. 1985.

Mateso, Locha. *La Littérature africaine et sa critique.* Paris: ACCT, Karthala, 1986.

Médou Mvomo, Rémy. *Africa ba'a.* Yaoundé: CLE, 1969.

Menga, Guy. *Les Nouvelles Aventures de Moni-Mambou.* Yaoundé: CLE, 1975.

Monemembo, Tierno. *Les Ecailles du ciel.* Paris: Editions du Seuil, 1986.

Mudimbe, V.Y. *Le Bel Immonde.* Paris: Présence Africaine, 1976. *L'Ecart.* Paris: Présence Africaine, 1979. *Shaba 2: Les Carnets de Mère Marie-Gertrude.* Paris: Présence Africaine, 1989.

Ndiaye, Weynde. *Le Cap des chèvres*. Dakar: Editions Khoudia, 1990.

Ndione, Abasse. *La Vie en spirale*, Dakar: Nouvelles Editions Africaines, 1984.

Ngal, M.M. *Giambatista Viko ou le viol du discours africain: recit.* Lubumbashi: Editions Alpha-Omega, 1975. Also published in Paris by Hatier in 1984.

Ngũgĩ wa Thiong'o. *Detained*. London: HEB, 1981.

Noaga, Kollin. *Le Retour au village*. Issy-les-Moulineaux: Eds. Saint-Paul.

Owondo, Laurent. *Au Bout du silence*. Paris: Hatier, 1985.

Pliya, Jean. *Les Tresseurs de corde*. Paris/Abidjan: Hatier; CEDA, 1987.

Rakotson, Michèle. *Dadabé, et autres nouvelles*. Paris: Karthala, 1984.

Sadji, Abdoulaye. *Maïmouna: Petite Fille noire*. Paris: Présence Africaine, 1965. rpt. 1980.

Sall, Ibrahima. *Routiers des chimères*. Dakar: Nouvelles Editions Africaines, 1982.

Samb, Amar. *Matraqué par le destin*. Dakar: Nouvelles Editions Africaines, 1973.

Samb, Mamadou. *De Pulpe et d'orange*. Dakar: Nouvelles Editions Africaines, 1973.

Sassine, W. *Saint Monsieur Baly*. Paris: Présence Africaine, 1973. *Le Zéhéros*. Paris: Présence Africaine, 1985.

Sow-Fall, Aminata. *La Grève des Battu ou les déchets humains*. Dakar: Nouvelles Editions Africaines, 1979. *L'Appel des arènes*. Dakar: Nouvelles Editions Africaines, 1982. *L'Ex-père de la nation*. Paris: L'Harmattan, 1987.

Soyinka, Wole. *The Man Died*. London: Rex Collings, 1972.

Tansi, Soni Labou. *L'État honteux*. Paris: Editions du Seuil, 1981. *L'Anté-peuple*. Paris: Editions du Seuil, 1983. *Les Sept Solitudes*. Paris: Editions du Seuil, 1983. *Lorsa Lopez*. Paris: Editions du Seuil, 1985.

Tchicaya U Tam'si. *Les Cancrelats*. Paris: Albin Michel, 1980. *Les Méduses*. Paris: Albin Michel, 1982.

History & Radical Aesthetics: A Study of Festus Iyayi's *Heroes*

Fírinne Ní Chréacháin

The Nigerian Civil War, which ended exactly twenty years ago, has inspired a considerable number of literary works, mainly novels by Ibo writers who experienced the war at close quarters over an extended period from inside the secessionist enclave. Festus Iyayi's novel, *Heroes*, which was awarded the Commonwealth Writers' Prize in 1988, differs somewhat from most of these works, not only in the lateness of its arrival and its non-Ibo origins, but much more on account of the broader nature of its concerns. Writing as a non-Ibo from outside the war arena proper, Iyayi's interest in the war stems less from a need to express and come to terms with his personal experience of the war, as is the case with most of the other novelists, than from a desire to use the war to expose the workings of certain forces in Nigerian society, forces which he considers as prevalent today as they were twenty years ago.

Iyayi's first novel, *Violence*, which was published in 1979 and explores the relationship between casual labour and indigenous entrepreneurs in contemporary Benin City, immediately won its author a place among the new generation of radical Nigerian writers. His second novel, *The Contract*, also set in Benin, exposes the economics of the oil boom and the decadence of the class which fattened on it. Iyayi is a well-known intellectual and activist whose artistic production is an integral part of his political practice. He was National President of the Academic Staff Union of Universities in the mid-1980s, and was subsequently dismissed from his lecturing post at the University of Benin, and detained by State Security.

The relationship between the historical event and its fictional representation, situated as it is in the vast mine-pitted terrain of 'realism' is a complex one. In this study of *Heroes*, our analysis will focus on just one dimension: the use of history by the radical artist as a means of intervening in the making of history. We shall examine how Iyayi has selected and shaped particular past events with a view to raising the consciousness of present-day Nigerians and ultimately encouraging them to play an active part in determining the course of history in the future. We shall try to show the way in which Iyayi's treatment of the Civil War is determined both by the course that Nigerian history has taken since the war ended, and by his concern for the future of his society.

Iyayi's novel is set in the then Mid-Western State, and is based on two well-known and important episodes in the early stage of the war. In the opening chapter, Benin City, which, like the rest of the state, had been 'overrun' by the Biafrans, is recaptured by the Federal army. Historically, this event took place in September 1967, and is referred to by Olusegun Obasanjo, in his account of the war, *My Command*, as 'the turning point of the war' (p. 34), since it helped to prevent the Biafran advance on Lagos and the West. The second episode, which took place some three weeks later, is the disastrous failed attempt by the Federal army to cross the River Niger at Asaba and seize Onitsha, a failure which was one of the causes of the long-drawn out nature of the war thereafter. This Federal fiasco, in which hundreds of lives, both Federal and Biafran, were lost, provides a climax for the novel.

The protagonist of *Heroes*, Osime Iyere, is a young journalist in Benin City. His ideological development from his initial populist nationalism to class-consciousness is a direct product of his experience of the two historic events mentioned above. Osime's original faith in the rightness of the Federal cause is shaken by the brutality of the Federal troops during the recapture of Benin City. A couple of weeks with the rank-and-file at the Asaba front, risking his life alongside the ordinary soldiers on Asaba bridge, while the Commanding Officer rushes off to join in the wedding celebrations of the Head of State in far-away Lagos, completes Osime's ideological reorientation: he realizes that the war has less to do with problems of tribalism and the need to preserve national unity, as the dominant ideology had led ordinary Nigerians to believe, than with the political ambitions of rival factions within the ruling class, 'the greed of those in power for more power' (p. 64).

Osime realizes that the truth about the war can only be expressed within the terms of a totally new problematic: not the problematic of conventional history, formulated in terms of famous generals and conquered territories, but one which would seek answers to more fundamental questions like 'Whose war? Which war? Why war?' (p. 113). He determines that his own account of the war will reveal the ruling-class interests for which ordinary Nigerians lost their lives, and do justice to the real heroes, the rank-and-file, the 'unknown soldiers' (p. 87).

The task that Iyayi explicitly sets himself in *Heroes* has much in common with that of the radical historian: to expose the ideological bias of bourgeois historiography and, by adopting the perspective of the exploited majority, to reveal the class interests that are the motive force of history. This project is expressed with remarkable economy in the novel's title; the single word, 'heroes', connotes both the generals who are the leading figures of bourgeois historiography, and the 'unknown soldiers' who replace them in the radical version. Iyayi is equally explicit in stating the purpose of radical history and radical art. The exposure of ruling-class self-interest helps to liberate the exploited from the dominant ideology, and ultimately to mobilize them against the ruling class. As Osime tells the soldiers, 'I want you to know the truth, and knowing the truth helps until there are so many who know the truth that you can do something about it' (p. 32).

I would now like to examine the novel from two related angles: to look at Iyayi's radical version of history against the back-drop of those versions produced by the dominant ideology, and secondly, to examine his 'manipulation' of certain historical facts in terms of his aesthetic and ideological aims.

The novel itself explicitly invites an intertextual approach. In a key passage, one of the 'unknown soldiers' tells Osime: 'After this war, many generals will write their accounts, in which they will attempt to show that they were the heroes of the war.... They will tell the world that they single-handedly fought and won the war. The names of soldiers like Otun, Emmanuel, Ikeshi and Yemi will never be mentioned.' (p. 86). Twenty years later, Iyayi's readers are of course in a position to vouch for the validity of Sergeant Audu's prediction; several such accounts by well-known public figures did appear after the war. We shall focus here on Obasanjo's *My Command*, not because Iyayi would seem to have had this specific version in mind, but precisely because of its representative nature in terms of the dominant ideology that *Heroes* seeks to counter. Iyayi's purpose is clearly to attack trends, not specific individuals.

General Obasanjo was the Chief Engineer of the Army Corps of Engineers during the early years of the war, and later Divisional Officer of the Third Division responsible for the final push which brought the war to an end in 1970. In 1976, he became Head of State after the assassination of Murtala Mohammed in an abortive coup, and in 1979, his government handed power back to civilians.

Obasanjo is one of several historical figures mentioned by name in the novel. Indeed, the little incident in which his name features encapsulates Iyayi's aim to rewrite history. Osime the journalist arrives at the war front at Asaba and asks a corporal to lead him to Obasanjo. The man replies: 'Who? I don't know him. Never heard of him. Is he a soldier?' (p. 91). In case we might have missed the point, Osime repeats his request to another soldier a few pages later, with identical results. This then, is an example of the generals who would claim that 'they single-handedly fought and won the war'! For the reader familiar with Obasanjo's own account, Iyayi's mischievous little dig at the general has an added resonance; apart from the egocentric title of his work, *My Command*, Obasanjo, while not going quite so far as to say he won the war single-handedly, certainly seems convinced that without him it would never have ended. He also claims to have visited the front at Asaba numerous times (p. 35), and prides himself on his excellent relationship with the rank-and-file (p. 76). Iyayi's little Obasanjo scene has turned history (or the dominant version thereof) upside down, and in this history from below, it is the generals who have never been heard of, who are the real 'unknown soldiers'.

What emerges above all from a comparison of the Obasanjo version of history with that of Iyayi is the extent to which the two texts concur in the data they include, and how this agreement in choice of detail only serves to underscore their fundamental ideological differences. For instance, Iyayi's description of the people's joyous welcoming shouts of 'One Nigeria' as the Federal troops march victoriously into Benin City (p. 8) is echoed in Obasanjo's account (p. 41). But whereas Obasanjo sees the people's response as just one more piece of evidence to justify his own role and to prove to readers the rightness of the Federal cause, Iyayi's protagonist will soon have to swallow his own joyous shouts and to subject to scrutiny the ideological exploitation of the idea of national unity by elements of the ruling class to hoodwink ordinary Nigerians into sacrificing their lives in a war which would bring them nothing.

Both authors also deal with the treatment of the Ibos in Benin after the recapture of the city by the Federal army. For Obasanjo, the Federal officer, the 'flushing out' of 'rebels' hiding in houses in Benin is a routine affair, passed over in a subordinate clause (p. 39). In Iyayi's hands, there is nothing routine about the brotherly courage of the Bini man who hides his Ibo friends in his

roof, nor about the callousness of the Federal troops who laugh
as they shoot the ceiling to pieces and watch the blood of their
fellow Nigerians come dripping down (p. 16). It is ordinary
Nigerians like the Bini man who know the real meaning of national
unity, Iyayi seems to be saying.

Similarly, the execution of Ibo civilians mistakenly branded as
spies, which is for General Obasanjo no more than an 'unfortunate
event' (p. 39) is turned by Iyayi into one of those unforgettable
scenes which shock so deeply that they leave an indelible mark
on the reader's consciousness (p. 56). This ability to shock the
reader into a new understanding of reality is a hallmark of Iyayi's
work, already very much in evidence in *Violence*.

Nowhere is the divergence of perspective more marked than in
the handling by the respective writers of the reaction of the rank-
and-file to the war, a reaction often expressed in desertion and
self-inflicted wounds, in an effort to avoid being sent into battle.
In *Heroes*, on the eve of the fateful Asaba–Onitsha crossing, the
hated new Divisional Commanding Officer, Brigadier Otunshi, a
fictive character, harangues his troops concerning such activities.
Otunshi wants to take Onitsha at all costs, in order to present the
victory to the Head of State at the latter's wedding ceremony in
Lagos the following day:

> . . . to win, to take the city, to get the wedding present, we need
> discipline. Our soldiers are not disciplined. Many of them are
> cowards. See how they shoot themselves in their hands or legs.
> But I intend to have this discipline and you are going to help
> me enforce it. Thus, as a first step, any soldier with hand or
> leg wounds will henceforth face the firing squad. They will be
> summarily executed (p. 149).

In this passage, Iyayi might be accused of caricaturing the
military establishment. But, reading Obasanjo's factual account,
the fiction, while certainly over-simplified, seems almost like
an understatement. Not only did Obasanjo, like his unpopular
fictional counterpart, execute all deserters and cases of self-
inflicted wounds, he describes repeatedly, and with evident satis-
faction, the lengths to which he went to bring all such offenders
to book (pp. 57, 77, 89). It is true that, while the fictive Otunshi
dispenses summary 'justice', Obasanjo sees a need to justify the
executions by having such wounds 'scientifically' diagnosed by an
army doctor. But the difference is one of degree, not of essence.

While Obasanjo admits that self-inflicted wounds constituted
fifty per cent of the casualties in his own division (p. 57), his ruling-

class perspective prevents him from asking why the rank-and-file should indulge in this on such a massive scale. What matters to him is that incidents of this nature, if unchecked, could seriously affect the outcome of the war. In his eyes, the executions are justified quite simply in terms of their efficacy in reducing the number of offences (p. 89). Iyayi, on the other hand, rewriting history from below, makes articulate the silences in Obasanjo's text. In the company of Iyayi's protagonist, the journalist Osime, we share the rank-and-file's rotten stinking quarters, sleep like them on bare mattress-less bed-springs, and listen to them as they express their weariness, their anxiety about their far-away families that they are given no leave to visit, their courage, and the way they are betrayed by their officers who, on the rare occasions when they do set foot on the battle-field, make sure to beat a hasty retreat as soon as danger threatens (p. 88). Reading Iyayi, we confront the source of phenomena like self-inflicted wounds and desertion in the conditions of existence of the rank-and-file, and not in cowardice and indiscipline, as Iyayi's Brigadier Otunshi would have us believe, and which would appear to be less the hallmarks of the rank-and-file than of their so-called 'superior' officers.

We also follow Osime to the cocktail parties which seem to be a much more central part of the officers' lives than is the battle-field, and watch them, their glittering wives and girlfriends by their sides, eat and drink to satiation. Iyayi's choice of the journalist-protagonist facilitates our movement between the two poles, and the bottle of whisky that Osime manages to sneak from the officers' table for his friend Sergeant Kesh-Kesh in the soldiers' miserable quarters is a poignant symbol of the class contradictions which underpin the situation at the warfront, and the society as a whole (p. 144).

To give Obasanjo his due, he also deplores the endless social whirl in which the officers indulge (p. 89), and tries to stamp out certain malpractices, like the withholding of wages in the hope that men would die in action before collecting their money (p. 86), to which Iyayi also refers (p. 122). But what Obasanjo cannot admit, and this is precisely what Iyayi's version succeeds in conveying, is that such malpractices are not aberrations; they are typical of the behaviour of the ruling class, expressing the essence of their relationship with those they exploit. At best Obasanjo's approach is reformist; he is satisfied to clean up the system and make it work, and his confidence that the reader will see his actions as beneficial to the whole of society, and not just to his own class, is typical of the ruling class and of the way the dominant ideology functions.

At its worst, Obasanjo's account displays the sort of insen-
sitivity which characterizes the ruling class and enables it to live
with its conscience. Where Iyayi's dialectical approach exposes
the contradictions within the army, which in turn mirror the class
nature of the larger society, Obasanjo never gets beyond a bits-
and-pieces empiricism which, while it enables him to observe, for
example, that the rank-and-file go for years without leave and die
without their wages, also enables him to execute them without a
qualm when they balk at such conditions.

The inter-textual approach is useful in that it allays any
sneaking suspicion on the part of the reader that the picture of
the ruling class that *Heroes* presents is distorted in line with
Iyayi's ideological bias. Reading the dominant versions, one
realizes that there was no need for Iyayi to fabricate anything.

One reason why Iyayi, writing in 1986, chooses to focus on
events of twenty years earlier, should be apparent by now. The
war provides an opportunity to examine the class interests which
Iyayi sees as the real motive force of Nigerian history, and a
concrete, familiar context within which to help his readers to
disentangle these interests from the ideological overgrowth which
tends to conceal them from view. For Iyayi, the army is the
society in microcosm, and the generals are just one group in a
long list of exploiters, which also includes the politicians, the
businessmen, the traditional rulers, the religious leaders and even
the professors, and which repeats itself over and over through the
length of the novel like a bedevilled litany.

Thus, in attacking the generals, Iyayi attacks the ruling class.
But the novel also calls into question the role of the military
per se. When Iyayi explicitly evokes in the reader echoes of texts
like *My Command*, he is making some very precise comments on
the role of the military in Nigerian history, and making them from
this side of history, from the point of view of the present. In other
words, in *Heroes*, we see that the historical novel is determined
as much by what has happened *since* as by what happened *then*.
Iyayi's attack on the generals can only be understood if set in the
context not just of the role of the military during the war itself,
but also of all that they have come to represent to Nigerians by
the time of writing the novel twenty years later.

When the war began, Nigeria was a beginner in terms of
military rule. By the time *Heroes* appeared in 1986, Nigerians
were experiencing their sixth military regime, and the current
leader, General Babangida, had declared his intention of staying
in power for another six years. The military, originally welcomed
by many in 1966 as a 'corrective' alternative to the politicians of

the First Republic, had, beginning with Gowon, and with the noteworthy exception of Murtala Mohammed, gradually lost most of their credibility and come to be seen less as an alternative to the politicians and more as politicians with guns at their disposal.

The return to the past therefore serves something of the same purpose for Iyayi as it does for Achebe, albeit in a different context: retelling the tale of the war is a means of showing 'where the rain began to beat us' in terms of military rule. Reminding readers of the shortcomings of the military during the war is another way of inviting people to ask what the current crop of soldiers are doing to prove that they are any better than their predecessors.

Perhaps the best example *Heroes* provides of the role played by the *since* as opposed to the *then* in the historical novel is Iyayi's treatment of Murtala Mohammed. This brings us to the second part of our analysis, where we shall examine two major deviations from historical 'fact' in the climax of the novel. As we have already noted, the historical event which features in the novel's climax is the Federal attempt to cross the Niger at Asaba and capture Onitsha in the second week of October, 1967. This unsuccessful exercise was masterminded and led by Murtala, who was Commanding Officer of the Second Division at the time. But in the fictive rendering, Iyayi has Murtala recalled to Lagos before the disastrous crossing, and has him replaced by the fictive Brigadier Otunshi. The second deviation from fact is Iyayi's anachronistic use of the wedding of the Head of State, General Gowon, which coincides in the novel with the Asaba disaster in 1967, whereas in reality it took place eighteen months later, in April 1969.

The freedom to adapt reality and history in accordance with the dictates of the artist's vision is a recognized aspect of artistic licence. What is not always so readily admitted, especially by critics of 'art for art's sake' tendencies, is that deviations from historical fact are part of the meaning of the artistic work. The disappearance of Murtala from *Heroes* before the fateful events at Asaba, and the juggling with the date of Gowon's wedding, constitute striking departures from historical fact in a novel which otherwise emphasizes its fidelity to history and reality through the extensive use of the names of real people and places, and of well-known historical events. Both deviations offer insights into Iyayi's artistic practice and his ideological purpose.

Murtala's career during the Civil War was neither particularly outstanding nor entirely blameless. During the recapture of the Mid-West, his name was associated with bank theft in Benin, and his insistence on the Asaba–Onitsha crossing, carried out against advice from Lagos and with such tragic consequences, could be seen as rash and irresponsible. Yet, in striking contrast to all the other well-known military figures mentioned by name in the novel, Murtala emerges in *Heroes* under a wholly positive light. Whereas the rank-and-file have 'never heard of' Obasanjo, they speak of Murtala as 'an excellent officer. A fine soldier, Very dedicated and honest. One of the very best' (p. 125). The fictive Otunshi takes all the blame for Asaba, and even for the Benin banks escapade.

Clearly, if Iyayi has used his artistic licence to salvage Murtala from the military scrap-heap, in a novel where Obasanjo, as we have seen, is mercilessly cut down to size, and Ojukwu and Gowon are depicted on the run together before the wrath of the united Nigerian masses (p. 169), it is on account of what Murtala came to mean to Nigerians later, during his brief '200 days' in office from July 1975, when he led a successful coup against Gowon, to his assassination early the following year. By 1975, the Gowon regime was notorious for its flamboyance and corruption, the seeds of which are already exposed in Iyayi's description of the military during the war. Murtala, when he came to power, took a number of steps against the corruption of the ruling class and in favour of the masses which, together with his whole-hearted support of the MPLA in Angola and the nationalization of several imperialist ventures at home, accounts to a large extent for his widespread popularity.

Murtala's popular appeal has increased rather than diminished since his death; his elevation to the status of folk-hero must be seen in terms of the need for a myth to sustain the popular imagination in the face of the hardships experienced by the Nigerian masses under all subsequent regimes, both military and civilian. It is therefore not only out of genuine respect for his undeniable achievements, but in recognition of his hold over Nigerian readers, that Iyayi singles him out for unqualified approval. Iyayi is aware of Murtala's effectiveness as a whip to lash at all other Nigerian leaders. He knows that merely to call Murtala's name in Nigeria is to speak volumes against the ruling class in general, and against the three subsequent military regimes, including, of course, the current one.*

But it is when we consider the second deviation from historical fact in the novel's climax that the full aesthetic and ideological meaning of Murtala's disappearance from the novel emerges. The second departure from history advances the date of Gowon's wedding to make it coincide with the Asaba tragedy. Murtala's

---

*Another military regime has since succeeded. Ed.

replacement, the fictive Brigadier Otunshi, dispatches the Federal soldiers across the bridge, and, assuming victory, promptly rushes off to the wedding.

The replacement of the 'very dedicated and honest' Murtala by a fictive character refered to by the rank-and-file as a 'real mean bastard' (p. 122), and the shifting of Gowon's wedding date must be taken together, as essential ingredients in the radical artist's rendering of the Asaba scene. In removing the popular folk-hero, Murtala, from a scene which might have tarnished his image and confused the reader's responses, in placing the blame for Asaba on an obnoxious fictive figure whose disregard for the lives of his men and concern for his own frivolous enjoyment are typical of the ruling class and the military leadership, and in synchronizing the events at Asaba with Gowon's wedding, which took place with even more pomp and flamboyance than Iyayi suggests, as hundreds were still dying on the front in 1970, and which came to symbolize to Nigerians all the callousness of a corrupt regime, Iyayi brings to the climax of his novel a unity of tone and a feeling of necessity which a factual account cannot provide.

The result is the intense and dramatic sequence on Asaba bridge, to which, as we read, we feel all the rest of the novel has been leading us. The novel's whole project – the rewriting of history, the exposure of the social contradictions, the unmasking of the ruling class – now explodes upon us as we huddle in the dark on the bridge with Osime the journalist. A few yards away, the bridgehead has been racaptured by the 'enemy' and is about to be blown up. Sergeant Kesh-Kesh and his men, with their usual courage and professionalism, fight on, buoyed up by the hope that their Commanding Officer will soon return to the scene with reinforcements. But we, the readers, know that Otunshi is already half-way to Lagos, his thoughts probably more full of the champagne that will flow at the wedding than of the blood of the slain Federal soldiers which runs together with that of the Biafrans into a single symbolic pool on Asaba bridge (p. 196).

Without Iyayi's art, the battle of Asaba bridge might be seen as just one more unfortunate episode in the war. The death of hundreds of rank-and-file soldiers could be taken for granted in the circumstances. Such is the empiricist reasoning of bourgeois history. In Iyayi's hands, the fate of the soldiers is locked together with the wedding: if the rank-and-file are sent into battle, if hundreds of soldiers on both sides must die, it is for a reason – to satisfy Otunshi's whim to add a further flamboyant touch to Gowon's already unseemly nuptial festivities. Iyayi's Asaba bridge is not just one more unfortunate episode in the war, it contains the essence of the Nigerian dialectic, that the masses must sacrifice their lives to satisfy the greedy whims of the ruling class.

Iyayi has modified the details, but articulated the essence which lies beneath the clumsy, contingent nature of historical fact. Central to his art is the judicious use of the *typical*, of what people will recognize as characteristic of the society, in terms of events and of the agents shaping them. For Iyayi, the Asaba–Onitsha crossing, in which hundreds of ordinary Nigerians from all over the country lost their lives but which brought no benefit to the Nigerian masses, is clearly such an event. Similarly typical is Gowon's wedding. Iyayi knows that Gowon's wedding is capable of stirring the memories of Nigerians of his own generation, of re-awakening old resentments against the ruling class and the upper echelons of the military which are part of it. For those too young to remember the war, the artistic combination of the Asaba tragedy and the wedding provides a paradigm which makes sense, not only of a war they did not experience, but of the cruel realities of their own lives today.

Murtala has to be removed from the Asaba scene precisely because his historical role in it cannot be perceived by the reader as typical of the revolutionary figure he later became. History fails to provide the typical agent of the Asaba tragedy, so fiction creates him, in the person of the villain Otunshi. Murtala, the only leader in recent Nigerian history whom Nigerians recognize as having taken really radical steps to change the unjust system, is thus freed to serve in the novel as a positive inspiration to Iyayi's readers to join in the struggle for which Murtala died and to which Iyayi's artistic rendering of history contributes.

WORKS CITED

Iyayi, Festus. *Violence*. Harlow: Longman, 1979. *The Contract*. Harlow: Longman, 1982. *Heroes*. Harlow: Longman, 1986.
Obasanjo, Olusegun. *My Command*. London: Heineman, 1980.

Men & Women: Gender Issues in Tsitsi Dangarembga's *Nervous Conditions* & *She No Longer Weeps*

Rosemary Moyana

In *Nervous Conditions*[1] and *She No Longer Weeps*,[2] Tsitsi Dangarembga has portrayed men and women who are antagonistic towards each other. Women in particular have been portrayed differently from those in earlier Zimbabwean literature in English.[3] The woman's voice here is new and revolutionary, so that by the time we finish reading *She No Longer Weeps*, we are definitely stunned by Martha's solution to the problem she faces in her relationship with men. That ending also reminds us of Ngũgĩ wa Thiong'o's stunning ending to his novel *Devil on the Cross*[4] in which we see Wariinga, a woman who perhaps is brutalized less than Martha (because at least she retains parental support in spite of her illegitimate pregnancy while Martha gets thrown out of the home), finally defy law, custom and authority to mete out justice to her offender, seducer and symbol of her oppression in exactly the same form that Martha does to Freddy in *She No Longer Weeps* (p. 59). This indeed, is a new woman.

The ending of *Nervous Conditions* also heralds the birth of a new woman as Tambudzai, the narrator, says,

> Quietly unobtrusively and extremely fitfully, something in my mind began to assert itself, to question things and refuse to be brainwashed, bringing me to this time when I can set down this story. It was a long and painful process for me, that process of expansion ... whose events stretched over many years and would fill another volume ... (p. 204)

What is being described here is a process of becoming. Treva Broughton has correctly observed that *Nervous Conditions* 'is a hopeful book, both in its sense of impending change ... and in the scope and subtlety of its critique of gender relations within and beyond the boundaries of race and class.'[5] The women in both the play and the novel clearly undergo some struggle and they emerge as different persons at the end. It is the nature of this struggle and change which we need to analyse and to understand so that we can appreciate the kind of new woman created by Dangarembga in her two works; so that we can understand why we say that that woman's voice is new and revolutionary.

About her own writing, the author has said: 'I deal with women who break away from oppression but find themselves caught in a guilt trap . . .'[6] When we begin with this statement to unravel meaning from her novel and play, we discover that the author 'has put masculinity in question by the very fact of asserting the rights of women and the claims of femininity. It is not only masculinity which is being questioned here . . . it is also tradition in a patriarchal society.'[7] Thus, at the end of the novel, the author, through Tambu, makes clear what her preoccupation has been all along: '. . . the story I have told here, is my own story, the story of four women whom I loved, and our men, this story is how it all began' (p. 204).

For the novel, it all begins with Tambu's announcement that 'I was not sorry when my brother died. Nor am I apologising for my callousness, as you may define it, my lack of feeling' (p. 1). Indeed, it is a strange declaration. Yet not so strange when we, once again, consider what she says at the end about asserting herself, questioning and refusing to be brainwashed. These statements reveal a process of resistance brought about by the antagonism that exists between men and women in the novel and in the play. Hence, the focus is on gender issues in both works.

Perhaps we should define what we mean by *gender* if we are to proceed on a common premise. We can define the word in three ways:

1. as the body;
2. as our social roles of male and female;
3. as the way we internalize and live out these roles.[8]

For our purposes, all three definitions interact at different times as we apply them in the analysis of the characters in the novel and play. Yes, there are men and women here, biologically and we can apply Sigmund Freud's dictum that 'anatomy is destiny'.[9] For the male characters in *She No Longer Weeps*, this dictum is especially pertinent because that is what they believe in, fanatically. But in the novel, the female and male roles interchange at certain times: men feeling emasculated and behaving accordingly; some women, namely the Aunts, becoming part of the patriarchy and sitting at patriarchal meetings; others feeling so nervous that they lack confidence in themselves and therefore cannot express their opinion where gender issues are raised. All these interchanges can be explained through our understanding of definitions two and three above, and here we are free to reject Freud's absolute dictum in favour of Erickson's when he argues that 'anatomy, history and personality combine to form one's destiny....'[10] He is refering to the social roles and the way they are internalized and lived out by each individual. To further emphasize this point, Easthope has correctly asserted:

> Every society assigns new arrivals [i.e., new borns] particular roles, including gender roles, which they have to learn. The little animal born into a human society becomes a socialised individual in a remarkably short time.... This process of internalizing is both conscious and unconscious....[11]

The above statement is pertinent and is applicable to Dangarembga's characters especially in the novel which we shall analyse closely later. Carol McMillan has also expressed the same view as she says:

> The thrust of feminist argument has ... for the most part, rested on the belief that since (apart from reproduction) there are no important differences between the sexes, nothing can justify a segregation of their roles. Any differences which may exist are said to be fostered *culturally* by forcing women to concentrate their activities exclusively in the domestic sphere [emphasis mine]. This in turn leads to the development of supposedly feminine traits such as self-sacrifice and passivity, which has the added consequence of inhibiting the development in women of their potential as rational, intellectual and creative beings.[12]

With this theory in mind then, let us now briefly analyse both the male and female characters in the two works, beginning with the novel, to demonstrate the nature of the women's struggle which brings about the revolutionary change in them. We will also see whether, indeed, all these female characters get caught in a guilt trap in their attempt to extricate themselves from the undesirable social conditions.

The women in the novel, particularly Tambudzai, Nyasha and Lucia rebel against their expected social roles. There is a concerted effort to make Tambu accept her lot; to subdue her 'wild', 'unnatural', unbridled spirit. When the family can only afford fees for one child (ironically, the fees are raised by the mother through the sale of vegetables and other produce), it is Nhamo, the boy who gets the opportunity to continue with school. Tambu has to stay at home and of course, her father thinks that she should not mind. After all, he asks, 'Can you cook books and feed them to your husband?' Then he advises, 'Stay at home with your mother. Learn to cook and clean. Grow vegetables.' (*Nervous Conditions*, p. 15). Her mother goes even further in her efforts to socialize the child to her difficult feminine role in the home with:

> This business of womanhood is a heavy burden.... How could it not be? Aren't we the ones who bear the children? When it is like that you can't just decided [sic] today I want to do this, tomorrow I want to do that, the next day I want to be educated! When there are sacrifices to be made you are the one who has to make them. And these things are not easy. You have to start learning them early, from a very early age. The earlier the better so that it is easy later on. Easy! As if it is ever easy. And these days it is worse, with poverty of blackness on one side and the weight of womanhood on the other. Aiwa! What will help you, my child, is to learn to carry your burdens with strength. (p. 16)

This is the kind of self-sacrifice and passivity that Carol McMillan is talking about which is being fostered on Tambudzai in the name of tradition and culture.[13] Nhamo, her brother (a typical example of a 'new arrival' or 'newly born' who gets socialized into his role in a very short time and plays that role with excellence), rubs it in when he adds that wanting to go to school will not help. 'It's the same everywhere. Because you are a girl.... What did you expect? Did you really think that you could send yourself to school?' (p. 21). It is after this conversation that Tambu says her 'concern for [her] brother died an unobtrusive death'. On her yearning to go to the airport to meet Babamukuru who is coming from England, Tambu's father disciplines her; calls her aside and implores her to curb her 'unnatural inclinations: it was natural for [her] to stay at home and prepare for the homecoming,' she is told (p. 33).

These are the kinds of ideas that bombard Tambudzai at an early age; ideas which she struggles to challenge throughout her childhood. While her father, mother and brother try to instil in her the womanly virtues 'seen as a mixture of timidity, tenderness, compliance, docility, softness, innocence and domestic competence',[14] she rebels against such gender apartheid by struggling to find her own money to educate herself through growing maize and selling it to raise her own fees which she succeeds in doing as she gets a £10 donation in the city, enough to educate her through primary school. This is the education which will change and revolutionize her life as she will be able to create her own economic base in future.

If we follow her story throughout the novel, we will find many examples of attempts to socialize Tambudzai at an early age into her feminine role which would in turn force her or train her to be uncreative and docile; the kind of qualities exhibited by Netsai, her younger sister whose character she analyses as pliable: ... the type that will make a sweet, sad wife' (p. 10). Netsai sees nothing wrong in strapping a baby to her back and carrying Nhamo's luggage while the latter walks on home, unencumbered!

Finally, Nhamo, who is a negation of Tambudzai, physically gets eliminated from the story through death (rather shrouded in mystery) in order to make way for Tambu's continuation with education beyond standard three and standard six to secondary school at Sacred Heart where we leave her at the end of the story. Her struggle and experiences throughout the novel result in her earlier declaration that she feels no sorrow after her brother's demise, neither does she apologize for such seeming callousness. The author endorses this brave articulation through her device of eliminating Nhamo at an opportune moment.

We did say that Nyasha and Lucia are the other rebellious women in the novel. Nyasha has problems with her father because of what he interprets to be her non-conformity. Babamukuru, her father, tries to subdue her by forcing her to eat all her food, by physically assaulting her. She returns her father's blows and rebels against the forced diet by vomiting all that she has eaten and therefore, suffers from anorexia and finally, a nervous breakdown. She is extremely mature for her age and analyses issues in a very rational manner (e.g. pp. 78; 159ff). Yet she suffers for these mature ideas as they are judged to be 'unnatural' by her father.

As for Lucia, she remains unmarried but becomes pregnant by her boyfriend, Takesure, whom she calls a cockroach and believes that 'cockroaches are better. They are easy to chase away, isn't it?' (p. 153). By remaining unmarried she symbolically refuses to fall into the traditional, socialized, expected role. She defies the men in the novel: Babamukuru, Jeremiah, Takesure, etc. She defies Babamukuru's order to leave her brother-in-law Jeremiah's home where her sister is married and lives a miserably poor life. Her resilience manifests itself throughout and when Takesure talks nonsense about her, she simply grabs his ear and pinches hard! (pp. 143–88). Finally, when Lucia decides to leave, it is on her own terms and in fact, she goes to the Mission to look for employment and to attend an adult literacy class, preparing for further emancipation through education.

These are the women who refuse to be compartmentalized into their chiselled up roles. They question, struggle, and become liberated in different ways – Tambu and Lucia achieving their own independence, while Nyasha finds it difficult to cope with the demands of a patriarchal world complicated by alienation caused by western education acquired abroad and lack of good parental guidance. The outlet for her is, sadly, a nervous breakdown.

At the beginning of this discussion we did say that Dangarembga puts masculinity in question by the very fact that she asserts the rights of women. At this point then, let us analyse the very embodiment of this masculinity. Babamukuru is the living symbol of masculinity and therefore, patriarchy in this novel. He is the epitome of this culture – he is domineering, benevolent; the provider for his own and his extended family: but callous, unthinking, unimaginative, uncreative though hard-working in a stilted way. The author treats masculinity as the source of oppression, not only for the women, but also for what we shall call the emasculated male (to be dealt with later). Masculinity is manifested in such manly virtues as 'courage, endurance, physical stamina, wiliness, [sound] judgment, and a corresponding [and] complementary conception of what is right for women'.[15] Whether in the form of father, husband or brother, masculinity is seen as oppressive and Babamukuru is the man at the centre of this oppression. Indeed, he does not mind that position since he enjoys being treated as 'the origin for everything, the light we all need to see by, the air we have to breathe'[16] and the benefactor we all cannot do without! Several examples abound in the novel to support this view (see, for example, pp. 30–1; 120–48; 158–9).

His over-domineering masculinity, however, emasculates his less successful brother (and nephew, Takesure), who literally cannot do anything else but wait for provisions and deliverance from poverty from Babamukuru (see pp. 14–15; 30–1; chapter 20). In chapter 20, Jeremiah's improvidence is explained by resorting to the supernatural and to show how ridiculous these men's ideas are, Babamukuru suggests that a church wedding be held for him and his wife as a cure for his problems as an alternative to traditional cleansing with herbs.

Another emasculated character, Takesure, is brought to Jeremiah's home to help with work, but ends up doing nothing of the sort. Both he and Jeremiah cannot control Lucia in the way they are used to (because her personality exudes self-confidence). So Takesure blames her for his misfortunes (p. 145). The climax in Jeremiah's lethargy is reached when even the homestead's huts fall while the two just drink on and watch. It takes Tambudzai and Lucia to fix the roofs and of course, Babamukuru thanks Jeremiah for the job, and the latter happily and unashamedly takes that full credit. For it is unthinkable that women could do such work!

These men are emasculated because they no longer have a good self-image. They are overshadowed by Babamukuru's terrible efficiency. As Jeane Block argues, 'sexual identity means ... the earning of a sense of self that includes a recognition of gender secure enough to permit the individual to manifest human qualities that our society ... has labelled [manly].'[17] Jeremiah and Takesure have lost this 'sense of self' and 'gender security', and hence, we have called them emasculated males masquerading their roles. These are the men (including Nhamo and Babamukuru) to whom Tambu refers at the end of the novel when she says she tells her story, that of the four women she loved and 'our men'. It is legitimate for her to say that, because her life and that of the other women is tangled up with the life of these men.

There is Maiguru, after all, who is a living symbol of nervousness and fear. She is so engulfed by the fear of her husband that she suffers silently under his yoke for a long time instead of the two of them being companions and friends. The man is so unfriendly that when the wife and children greet him in the evening, he merely grunts inaudibly. So everything Maiguru does, even reprimanding Nyasha, is done in order to please or appease Babamukuru (for example, the case of Nyasha's book, pp. 81–5; also, pp. 137–9; 140–3). She even speaks in baby language to him: 'my daddy-yo', etc.

When she is called upon by other women to take a stand against the patriarchy, she declares that it is not her concern. She has thus been integrated into passively upholding the patriarchy's oppressive system the way oppressed people help uphold their oppressive systems. Later on though, she explodes as the pressure mounts and reaches boiling point. She complains to her husband about her ill-treatment – she never receives her salary, it all goes to Babamukuru – and runs off to her brother (pp. 172–5)! She is the type Dangarembga refers to in her comment about women and the guilt trap, especially if we take into account Nyasha's comment and analysis of her character on p. 175. As for the Aunts, they are clearly part of the patriarchy and although ineffective in that role, they too prop up the system.

This discussion leads logically to our consideration of the characters in the play, *She No Longer Weeps*. The protagonist, Martha, starts off as a girl who is in love, willing to live with her boyfriend Freddy and is knitting for her expected baby. The male characters in this play, Freddy, Joe and Lovemore, are so terribly male-chauvinist as to be repulsive. They delight in abusing women so much that by the time one finishes reading the play, a word like *bitch* rings offensively through one's ears! Here is a typical example of Freddy's abuse of Martha:

> ... You want to know? ... a bitch. Only a bitch would do that. You are a bitch Martha. Never forget that. No man will ever want you. Even if I hadn't spoilt you. You wear trousers like a man, you drink like a man, you argue and challenge men as though you were not a woman yourself. What you don't know is that that education of yours is good for only one thing ... it lets you earn money. That's the only reason why men like women like you, otherwise you are useless. But even that education of yours is gone now ... pregnant. You are finished. Women like you have no place in Zimbabwe. (p. 9)

Later Lovemore, Martha's new boyfriend, asks how many 'rape' or 'wife beating' cases she dealt with at work.

Frankly I find the male characters in this play more of caricatures. The way they enact their role as men is typical of those who believe that 'anatomy is destiny'. They denigrate, humiliate and insult women in a manner that is unreasonable. Martha's father and Babamukuru of *Nervous Conditions* are carved from the same stone, as are Maiguru of that novel and Martha's mother in the play, except that the latter is more cruel and callous. Both are a bundle of nerves. As parents they are all incompetent; they worry more about public opinion than the welfare of their daughters. Thus, Martha's parents prefer to send her away to her uncle so that the father can go on preaching with honour (pp. 33; 38). The hypocrisy here is glaring.

The other female characters in the play, Mrs Mutsika and Mrs Chiwara who run a club for single mothers are no better. So that in the final analysis, they too are victims of the patriarchal society from which they cannot extricate themselves. Although they try to help other women who have been victimized, they fail to articulate the issues convincingly and they end up insulting Martha instead. Their situation is similar to that in the novel where Tambu's mother and others try to protest against the injustices of the patriarchy (pp. 137–41), yet feel too afraid to direct their anger to the correct place. They find a scapegoat in Maiguru and Tambu's mother champions this tirade of insults against her! Yet we should remember that she is the one woman who suffers tremendously under the heavy weight of womanhood; to the point where she adopts a fatalistic attitude as she asks Lucia:

Does it matter what I want? Since when has it mattered what I want? So why should it start mattering now? Do you think I wanted to be impregnated by the old dog [her husband, Jeremiah]? Do you think I wanted to travel all this way across this country of our forefathers only to live in dirt and poverty? Do you really think I wanted the child for whom I made the journey to die only five years after it left the womb? Or my son to be taken from me? So what difference does it make whether I have a wedding or whether I go? It is all the same. What I have endured for nineteen years I can endure for another nineteen, and nineteen more if need be. Now leave me! Leave me to rest. (p. 153)

Maybe the only way she redeems herself is towards the end when she correctly identifies the cause of Nyasha's nervous breakdown as being 'the Englishness' of her parents and their whole way of life (pp. 202-4). Otherwise such a fatalistic attitude to life is self destructive, and there is absolutely no need for it.

The crucial issue the author seems to be addressing in both the play and novel is centred on the debate of whether or not, 'given equal educational and occupational opportunities, women will in fact prove themselves in the world of "reason"'.[18] Martha certainly proves that she is equal to anyone in her law profession, male or female, and her new material conditions are a proof of this success. We can actually see Martha as the grown up Tambu, having charted her way determinedly against all overwhelming odds, through to completing her education and professional training, and therefore, acquiring the kind of emancipation and independence she needed. The experiences both girls have had to endure harden them to the point where Martha can 'no longer weep' and Tambu can no longer feel apologetic for feeling no sorrow after her brother's death; it was a good riddance!

On the question of how to deal with the likes of Freddy, symbols of patriarchal, maniacal oppression, Martha's solution is simple – like Wariinga's solution – *kill them!* which she does without flinching and without fear of reprisals; something similar to what Tambu does, in spirit, to Nhamo.

The portrayal of women in the two works is complex but one thing that emerges unequivocally is the fact that women must deal squarely with their social problems. Young girls must also struggle for their advancement, educationally or socially, the way Tambudzai does. She is an inspiration to those who find themselves having to leave school because there is not enough money to educate both boys and girls in the family, especially under Zimbabwe's Economic Structural Adjustment Programme (ESAP) in 1992. The stabbing of Freddy at the end of *She No Longer Weeps* should be interpreted symbolically rather than literally. Those women who struggle without giving up hope, herald the impending change that Broughton is talking about: change in attitude for both men and women as they evaluate and re-evaluate their social roles towards society and towards each other. It is in this way that the two works differ in their portrayal of woman from earlier Zimbabwean literature in English. Few portray men and women in such glaring antagonism with women ending with the upper hand. In Dangarembga, gender issues are dealt with controversially.

NOTES

1. Tsitsi Dangarembga, *Nervous Conditions* (Harare: Zimbabwe Publishing House, 1988). References to this text will be by page number.
2. Tsitsi Dangarembga, *She No Longer Weeps* (Harare: The College Press, 1987). References to this play will be by page number.
3. See discussion of some of these women in Rudo Gaidzanwa, *Images of Women in Zimbabwean Literature* (Harare: The College Press, 1985).
4. Ngũgĩ wa Thiong'o, *Devil on the Cross* (London: Heinemann, 1982): 254.
5. Treva Broughton, excerpts in Publisher's blurb to Tsitsi Dangarembga's *Nervous Conditions*.
6. Fiona Lloyd, Margaret Waller, Tisa Chifunyise, Ann Holmes, Laiwan, *Zimbabwean Women in Contemporary Culture, 1992 Diary-Notebook* (Harare: The Zambabwean Women in Countemporary Culture Trust, ZWICCT, 1992) page opposite 11–17 May 1992 of *Diary-Notebook*.
7. Anthony Easthope, *What a Man Gotta Do?* (London: Paladin Grafton Books, 1986): 1.
8. Easthope: 2–3.
9. Jeane H. Block, *Sex Role Identity and Ego Development* (London: Jossey-Bass Publishers, 1984): 2.
10. E.H. Erickson, *Identity: Youth and Crisis* (New York: Norton, 1968), quoted in Jeane H. Block, *Sex Role Identity and Ego Development*: 2.
11. Easthope: 3.
12. Carol McMillan, *Women, Reason and Nature: Some Philosophical Problems with Feminism* (Oxford: Basil Blackwell, 1982): ix.
13. McMillan: ix.
14. Brenda Almond, 'Women's Right: Reflections on Ethics and Gender' in Morwenna Griffiths and Margaret Whiteford, *Feminist Perspectives in Philosophy* (London: MacMillan, 1988): 42.
15. Almond: 42.
16. Easthope: 12.
17. Block: 1.
18. McMillan: x.

Ken Saro-Wiwa:
Maverick Iconoclast
of the Nigerian Literary Scene

N.F. Inyama

The Nigerian literary scene has witnessed the emergence of a good number of new writers in the last one and half decades. Among the more frequently-mentioned names in literary circles are Festus Iyayi, Tanure Ojaide, Isidore Okpewho, Femi Osofisan, Ifeoma Okoye. Ken Saro-Wiwa belongs to this circle of the more notable crop of new authors.

Ken Saro-Wiwa was born in 1941 into the Ogoni tribe, one of the ethnic groups which make up Nigeria's oil-rich Rivers State. He was educated at Government College, Umuahia (Okigbo and Achebe are among the school's other star-author products), and the University of Ibadan, where he read English and where he also acquired a reputation as a very good actor. His academic training and acting experience have had definite influences on his writing.

If Saro-Wiwa is something of a literary late bloomer when compared to Achebe, Soyinka, Okigbo, Clark, for example – all Ibadan products – it is partly because shortly after graduating in 1965, the Nigerian crisis period (roughly 1965 to 1970) drew him into roles which he never envisaged for himself. First, he was the administrator of Bonny, which was recaptured by Nigerian Federal troops at the early stages of the civil war. Later he was a state commissioner in the Rivers State government. In these roles he gained personal experiences of the civil war and insights into the wider politics of Nigeria, much of which he has recorded in his war memoir, On A Darkling Plain[1] and which have also made him a vocal and committed campaigner for minority rights.

After leaving government service in 1973, Saro-Wiwa went into private business, founding a publishing company along the way, Saros International Publishers, which has published all his works so far. But this period of political, administrative and commercial activity certainly contributed to the delay in his publishing or paying full attention to his creative works.

Since publishing his war novel *Sozaboy* in 1985, however, Ken Saro-Wiwa has proved to be among the most prolific of Nigeria's new authors. Apart from *Sozaboy*, and the war memoir mentioned earlier, he has published two satirical novels, two volumes of short stories, books of short plays, narrative versions of his long-running and highly successful television comedy series 'Basi and Company', and some children's books. He has also published a collection of war poems, *Songs in a Time of War* (1985). This article will focus primarily on his novels and short stories.

That his own company publishes his works is neither an indication of overriding narcissism, nor of a failure to meet other publishers' standards of quality and competence, for Saro-Wiwa has a very high level of literary awareness and competence. Certain faults and weaknesses exist in his works, inevitably, but the overall picture is of a writer with a definite sense of plot, irony, and dialogue, as well as of a writer who is conscious of the functions of language both as a narrative vehicle and a definer of characters' images in a literary work. Nearly every Nigerian newspaper and magazine has reviewed one or other of his works, and he has attracted wide critical and scholarly attention.

Another preliminary observation on Saro-Wiwa's literary development is the fact that although he only started publishing recently, there is evidence – especially from the short stories – that the stories have had a long period of gestation. These indications are confirmed through historical and linguistic references and will be explored more fully later.

Saro-Wiwa's first novel *Sozaboy* is also probably his most challenging work in critical terms. It is a record of the war experiences (the Nigerian civil war) of a naive youth, Mene. Before joining the army, the protagonist was an apprentice to a lorry driver, making daily trips from his village, Dukana, to the nearest township, Pitakwa. During a break in their daily routine of work Mene meets a pretty girl, Agnes, in a palm wine bar in the city, who had run back from the crisis in Lagos. The two discover that they come from the same village, and not too long afterwards, get married. Meanwhile the reverberations of the national crisis come closer and closer and reach even somnolent and complacent Dukana. Partly to escape the harassments from over-zealous youthful civil defenders and the intimidating behaviour of marauding soldiers, but essentially out of a naive misperception of the nature of soldiering in war time, Mene joins the Biafran army. After a period of training, he and his company are deployed to defend the riverine approaches to Biafra. Not long after, they are overrun by the enemy and he is eventually taken prisoner. But he is spared from execution when his captors decide to employ him as one of their drivers. One day he abandons the vehicle and goes off in search of his mother and his wife who had fled their village when the fighting reached there. In the process he suffers some more harrowing experiences and narrow escapes, including a betrayal by his own village chief, now a refugee, but feeding fat and growing rich on food meant for his starving people. The war comes to an end as abruptly as it had begun for the hero, and after another fortuitous escape he returns to Dukana, only to learn that Agnes and his mother had in fact died during an air-raid, that the people of Dukana think that he is a ghost, since they were convinced that he too had died, and blame the cholera epidemic among them on his ghostly presence. His informer warns him to go away, since the Dukana villagers have resolved to 'bury him properly' in order to lay his death-bearing ghost. Thus, he leaves, homeless, friendless and confused.

In *Sozaboy* Saro-Wiwa boldly confronts three critical areas of fiction writing: language, point of view and plotting. The area of language has attracted the most critical interest, and the reason is clear: Saro-Wiwa breaks with precedence and writes in what he calls 'rotten English', and which he defines as

> a mixture of Nigerian pidgin English, broken English and occasional flashes of good, even idiomatic English. This language is disordered and disorderly. Born of a mediocre education and severely limited opportunities, it borrows words, patterns and images freely from the mother-tongue and finds expression in a very limited English vocabulary. To its speakers, it has the advantage of having no rules and no syntax. It thrives on lawlessness and is part of the dislocated and discordant society in which Sozaboy must live, move and have his being.

He further declares, 'Whether it throbs vibrantly enough and communicates effectively is my experiment'.[2]

Critics seem to agree that this experiment is successful, that this 'rotten English' not only suits the narrator's level of education (he is a primary school leaver) but also, according to Theo Vincent, 'is an artistic realisation of the eponymous hero's dislocated consciousness of his new vision of himself'.[3] Abiola Irele says that the

> choice of idiom here goes beyond a mere experiment and fulfills a function that is essential to the meaning of the novel. This is

no longer, as with Okara's *The Voice*, or Tutuola's novels, a personal dislocation of the structure of English to suit a generalised African mode of expression, but a creative handling of an existing language, a collective property whose sinews reflect areas of strength characteristic of a Nigerian – that is *national* – mode of expression.[4]

In this sample of 'rotten English', Mene ('Sozaboy', 'soldierboy') is describing a boat patrol:

So now we begin paddle the canoe small small through the swamp and creek. By the time we get to the river, day have break well well. We still paddle the canoe. Bullet say we must to be careful because plenty of our sozas have already dead in this patrol business. We did not go too far. We saw no any enemy at all. But we hear gun shooting from far. When they shoot the bullet will land inside the water. One time the bullet just pass over my head *Heeeuun! Heeeun!* I just fall inside the canoe. So I ask Bullet What all this nonsense mean. So he said that the enemy is also on patrol. And if he can shoot and kill us, he will shoot and kill us. And if we can shoot and kill them, we too must to do so. When I hear of shoot and kill, fear begin catch me small. Then I said to myself that nobody can kill me because I must return to Dukana with plenty rope. Then the enemy begin to shoot again. And Bullet return the fire. He fire them many times. He fire till he no get fire for inside him gun. The other boys begin to fire too. They fire plenty. But I myself, I was only looking at them like *mumu*, I did not even fire one time. My hand just no move. So as all the fire have finished, we just turn the canoe, return to the camp. (p. 106)

One of the more striking and positive aspects of Saro-Wiwa's linguistic experimentation is that he possesses enough artistic control to sustain the tone and idiom for the entire length of the book. An additional achievement is that the author manages somehow not to lose the seriousness of import of certain scenes and incidents to what might initially appear to be a linguistic parody. For instance, Mene's brutal experiences still strike the reader with deep horror, even in this level of expression. It is also this linguistic level or medium which stamps a distinctive personality on Mene, the narrator, and also exposes the naive quality with which the author endows him. The author therefore remains faithful to his definition of his 'rotten English' and largely succeeds in making it work as a narrative medium. At no time, indeed, does the reader lose a consciousness of the grimness of the war situation that is being described.

In spite of these achievements however, the most obvious problems for the non-Nigerian or non-West African reader would still
emanate from the linguistic area. Certain expressions or phrases
are rather obscure, and even as slang, they appear to belong to
a generation of slang usage more current in the early sixties than
in the seventies or eighties. Were the reader to even consult the
four-page glossary of obscure expressions at every point of baffle-
ment he might end up with a halting narrative and halting comprehension. However, the reader who is familiar with this kind of
linguistic usage in English-speaking West African streets would
see Saro-Wiwa's bold and risky experiment as quite successful.

But language is only one level of judgement for any work of
literature, even if it is a first novel. The levels of judgement
become even more elaborate and critical when the author has
chosen as his theme the most tragic of human aberrations – war.
Attitudes, prejudices and points of view are projected through
characterization and plot; the author's selection of narrative
details and description of experience could reflect more of his
own point of view and attitude to his subject matter than those
of his characters. In a novel with a first-person narrative point
of view, such as *Sozaboy*, the crucial challenge for the author is
to convince the reader that the opinions and perceptions which
are expressed or implied by the naive or unreliable narrator are
credibly his, and not those of an intrusive author hiding behind
the mask of a naive character.

In *Sozaboy* Saro-Wiwa battles with this technical challenge by
determinedly sustaining the naive image of his protagonist. Mene
is remarkably, even incredibly naive. He perceives events and
incidents at a surface or literal level. He is easily carried away,
and when notions get into his head he acts on them as though they
were reality. Agnes is the first girl in his life and he is quickly
overwhelmed by her relatively sophisticated romantic adven-
turousness. In no time at all he marries her. His joining the army
in war time and putting his life at obvious risk is precipitated by
nothing more serious than his wife's wish for a 'soza husband who
can defend her when trouble come' (p. 59), and a childish notion
that he will rise fast in the ranks and return to protect his Dukana
kinsmen from the harassments of war-time soldiers. In training at
the military camp, what impress him most are the parades, road
marches and the singing. The possibility of danger and death do
not even come into his consciousness. If he associates war with
death at all, it is the enemy's death, not his. He even imagines that
this 'Mr Enemy' is one individual. When he finally gets to the front
he is totally bewildered by the ugly reality, which he cannot come
to terms with – digging trenches, sleeping in them, going for days

without food. This naive image and misperception is climaxed with Mene and his trench mates being taken in by the 'friendliness' of an enemy agent whom they welcome to their trenches and naively give vital information. Not long afterwards, their position and their camp are overrun by the enemy and Mene is eventually taken prisoner.

Although the sustenance of Mene's image as a naive narrator may be one of the novel's main technical achievements, it also creates one of its principal problems in relation to point of view. The reader might question the credibility of Mene's naive or credulous image, especially when one notes that he is quite intelligent, having failed to go beyond primary six only because of his mother's poverty. Again, unlike his other Dukana stay-at-home kinsmen, he makes a daily trip to the nearest township, is familiar with the ways of the city (he meets Agnes in a bar) and sees a lot more of the world than the average Dukanan. Besides, he is perspicacious enough to identify the wasteful, wretched, complacency of his townsmen and to see through the self-serving deceitful ways and contemptible obsequiousness of the village chief, Birabe. Above all, the hero is mature enough to obtain a professional driver's licence, and no one is surprised when he marries his Agnes. In other words, he has become an adult member of society, with a certain level of education in addition. To expect the reader therefore to believe or accept the extreme naivety of the protagonist-narrator is to demand too much suspension of the reader's disbelief. It is difficult, for example, to accept that Mene is so young and ingenuous as not to know that a war front is not a mere comfortable bedroom, that it carries dreadful dangers, or that a soldier (especially after he has been trained) should not clamber out of his trench (he calls it 'pit') and stand up to look at the enemy's trenches. Mene does not even appear to know what has caused the war – except that some fellow called 'Enemy' has stopped salt from getting to Dukana in sufficient quantities.

But an insistent and even intrusive authorial viewpoint tries to override these apparent contradictions by pressing the reader to accept that Mene and his fellow soldiers are innocents dragged, zombie-like, into a precarious adventure by a nebulous conspiracy. This viewpoint is reaffirmed, I think, by statements made by two other characters in the novel. The character who later metamorphoses into 'Manmuswak', the enemy agent who deceives Mene and his mates, is heard at the early stages of the story to say of the impending war, 'Well, I don't think it is good thing or bad thing. Even sef I don't want to think. What they talk, we must do. Myself, if they say fight, I fight. If they say no fight, I cannot fight. Finish' (p. 17). Another soldier whom Mene meets in a Biafran prison camp says he 'joined the army because I like as the sozas were marching and singing and wearing fine fine uniform and boot. The one I like most is the cap. Even for the cap alone, I can join army one hundred times' (p. 163). Yet, this particular naive man has a wife and children.

Authorial perspective presents war as an unmitigated and senseless tragedy, distinguished only by a relentless succession of gratuitous brutalities, which principally befall the protagonist, Mene. The war that is experienced by our hero-narrator lacks the slightest veneer of nobility of action or heroism. This tends somehow to reduce the reader's sympathy for the hero, since he appears to have no real quality to enable him to challenge his situation. He is like one adrift and events control him, rather than the other way round. Perhaps, again, the author intends that in this respect Mene should be seen as representing the helpless many who are in no position to dictate the turn of events in war time. However, the unrelieved cruelties described in the novel appear to me to offer a rather limited perspective on the nature of war, showing more of an authorial bias than the reality of the protagonist's experience.

Significant characters and incidents are few. One character 'Manmuswak' – is difficult to understand. His role is undefined. One does not discover what he really is – double agent, mercenary, or wandering madman. He does not illuminate anything, merely dogging the protagonist like ill-fate. He plays a *deus ex machina* role that is not altogether credible, unless again the author means him to be seen as representing some of the more bizarre emanations of a war situation.

Ultimately, *Sozaboy* will survive as a work of art mainly on the success of its bold experiment with language. This, I think, is a considerable achievement for a first novel.

In *Prisoners of Jebs* (1990) Saro-Wiwa returns to conventional satire and language. As a satirist he scores excellent marks, employing with adroitness the literary devices of ridicule, humour, deliberate exaggeration, and so on. His knowledge of the Nigerian, even African, environment is all-encompassing, and this makes it possible for him to people his satirical world with characters from all tiers of Nigerian and African society – politicians, military top brass, contractors, sycophants, tribalists, journalists, members of the judiciary, drug traffickers and more.

The concept of a 'Jebs Prison' is as farcical as it is allegorical. The Organization of African Unity decides to build an élite prison for the most prominent prisoners from each member-country.

There they would be made to think out solutions to the continent's myriad problems. The Nigerian government, known for its vain-glorious and spendthrift ways, would finance its construction and subsequent maintenance. In due course an off-shore island is created through sand-filling and Jebs Prison built. The prisoners arrive from various African countries, but principally from the West African sub-region. But right from the beginning, the 'Nigerian factor' of corruption predominates. The contract for the construction of the artificial island is awarded to a Dutch firm 'at twice the price they had offered to do it. This was the Nigerian interpretation of the term "double Dutch"' (p. 2); the actual prison construction contract is awarded to 'a Mr Popa of Popa Construction Company ... [who] did not own a wheelbarrow nor ... a kobo in the bank' (p. 3). Later, Popa becomes an inmate of the prison, having spent much of the contract money to acquire a chieftaincy title, thus falling foul of a short-lived reformist government in Nigeria. The Prison Director is a non-Nigerian, but under the self-serving attention of Chief Popa, he soon becomes accomplished in Nigerian ways, especially the trick of making millions of Niara 'disappear'.

Having created his allegorical setting, his Lilliput, Saro-Wiwa proceeds, Swiftian fashion, to excoriate Nigerian society. The dominant tone is one of acerbic humour: the reader is encouraged to laugh, but not to overlook the serious issues of ethnic domina-tion, corrupt judiciary and governments, armed robbery, ill-educated journalists (symbolized by Peter Dumbrok), wastage and stealing of public funds (the Prison Director), the toleration of filthy environments (the Prison itself) and the irrelevance of much of the African military set-up (the 'snoozing generals' arrive at Jebs and promptly fall asleep).

Fate and events on the Nigerian scene, and the African con-tinent generally, stock Saro-Wiwa's satirical arsenal. An exag-gerated celebration of a minor football cup victory, wasteful overspending on a continental meeting, the suspicious escape from custody of a drug-pusher or an armed robbery suspect, the loss of his money bags to foreign thieves by an African president, the unguarded utterances of prominent politicians, the geo-political ambitions of Gaddafi, an unfavourable review of his book – all these are turned to satirical advantage by the author. This trait also makes the story appear too topical in content; but most successful satires reflect the contemporary events of their times – so long as the satire is anchored to the basic or enduring foibles of the particular society that generates it, and the satirist is able to maintain a certain allegorical distance. Saro-Wiwa,

I think, meets these criteria in his satire, and as long as the traits he lampoons are present in Nigerian society, the novel will retain a considerable timeless flavour.

It is to his enduring credit and an indication of his vibrant sense of humour that the author does not even spare himself. At a point in the story, the Prison Director asks Pita Dumbrok who the dreaded Ken Saro-Wiwa was: '. . . Peter confirmed that indeed he knew Mr Saro-Wiwa, by ill-repute if nothing else. "He is a mean, spiteful little wretch, and so small you wouldn't find him among a colony of soldier ants. He's learning to be a satirist"' (p. 103).

This quality, also, might excuse some of the more glaring personal references or attacks in the satire, a trait which has been criticized by some reviewers. For instance, Pita Dumbrok whom he presents as a moronic journalist who arrives at Jebs Prison, and is captured and put in a cage by the Director, is a pseudonym for one Peter Okute who had described *Sozaboy* as having a 'silly plot'. For most of the story he is left in the cage where, to every question, he answers 'silly plot, silly plot!' In the end, however, Pita undergoes an educational reform under the aegis of a magical Guinean professor (*à la* Soyinka's professor), and when the professor makes the prison disappear to save it from an impending attack by Nigeria, Pita Dumbrok is the only one who escapes. Later in the sequel to *Prisoners of Jebs*, Pita emerges as the hero, an intellectually inquisitive and socially conscious and inspired journalist, dreaded by a corrupt and fascistic government which eventually eliminates him with a parcel bomb.

The humour notwithstanding, however, the authorial vision of his society is pessimistic and could be summarized in the statement the Prison Director makes about his Nigerian prisoners: 'The prisoners from other parts of Africa are fairly polite. They give me no trouble. But the Nigerians are the most contentious, the most troublesome, the most greedy, the most venal, the most vicious group of people God ever put together in any corner of the world' (p. 35). This is decidedly Swiftian, and echoes that moment when, after Gulliver had described his nation's ways and institutions to the Brobdingnagian king, the latter picks him up and says: 'My little friend Grildrig . . . I cannot but conclude the bulk of your natives to be the most pernicious race of little odious vermin that nature ever suffered to crawl upon the surface of the earth' (Book II, chapter 6).

What Saro-Wiwa's satire refuses to do is to pretend that the ills of Nigerian society are merely skin-deep and transient; it refuses to promote a false optimism about a future that will correct itself without a reformed, penitent populace. Acute

authorial sensitivity to the peccant lapses of his society accounts
for the fairly frequent harshness of tone. What Saro-Wiwa said
of the social goals of his television series 'Basi and Company'
could well apply to *Prisoners of Jebs* and its sequel, *Pita
Dumbrok's Prison* (1991): 'We were creating an awareness of
our predicament. This was the most important thing. We are in
trouble as a nation. And unless people realise this, they would
not be able to change their habits'.[5] To create the necessary
awareness, Saro-Wiwa through his satire makes himself society's
gadfly, an iconoclast with little respect for corrupt sacred cows
of a complacent populace. In *Pita Dumbrok's Prison*, the sequel
to *Prisoners of Jebs*, Saro-Wiwa continues his satirical examination of his society. But *Pita Dumbrok's Prison* is in many ways a
different kind of novel from *Prisoners of Jebs*. Where *Prisoners
of Jebs* is somewhat episodic, and the incidents are farcical and
designed to provoke loud laughter, the second novel is much more
organic and has a story with a clear-cut plot line.

Having escaped from Jebs Prison just before it is conjured away
to safety by the Guinean professor-magician, Pita Dumbrok is
rescued by men of the invading Nigerian navy. On his return
to his newspaper, he is encouraged to write about his experiences
during the one year he spent in the prison. But after only two
instalments, the serialization is stopped by government authorities. Jebs has become the subject of international controversy
and a source of embarrassment to the local military junta which
denies the existence of such a place. Meanwhile, a female journalist, Asa, has gone on a journey to verify Pita's bizarre tale.
She confirms the truth and begins writing her own report in
her newspaper. Soon, this too is stopped, and in anger she
resigns from her job. Thereafter, she and Pita go underground,
having sensed that both of them face some danger from the
authorities. Matters are further complicated by Pita's publication
of pamphlets which draw his countrymen's attention to their
desperate situation of poverty, exploitation, and so on.

In the meantime, the beautiful Asa falls in love with him and
they marry. His idealism nullifies for her his lack of money and
physical handsomeness. This development further angers the
navy commander and the chief of the secret police, the former
because he loses his position as Asa's lover, and the latter
because his efforts to seduce Asa fail woefully. Thereafter, every
effort is made to do away with Pita, since he had become a 'threat'
to 'state security'! Ultimately, someone sends him a parcel bomb
which kills him. The only hope for the survival of his idealism lies
with the disconsolate Asa, who is also expecting his child. Two

other journalists who go in search of the prison, Andizi and Biney, also lose their lives, but the reader takes consolation in the shooting of the navy commander and the chief of the secret police by Captain Ita, who rebels against his being used as a tool to destroy Pita Dumbrok.

The story is told in the form of recollections by the various key characters, presumably assembled by Asa after their deaths, (Pita, Captain Ita, and Andizi), somewhat resembling the narrative structure of Achebe's *Anthills of the Savannah*. In *Prisoners of Jebs* the satire is intended to provoke loud and contemptuous laughter, but the satire in *Pita Dumbrok's Prison* arouses in the reader a strong sense of social tragedy. The archetypal confrontation between truth and falsehood, vision and ignorance, idealism and stagnation, freedom and dictatorship, is replayed within a contemporary ethos or context. The tragic outcome of this confrontation is almost predictable: truth and idealism and other virtues are often crippled or destroyed by evil dictatorship.

An initial reading of *Pita Dumbrok's Prison* creates a deceptive suspicion of thinness of plot or of digressionary development. But ultimately the reader comes to an awareness of a thematic unity that is reinforced by its allegorical structure and complexity.

Furthermore, although topical events appear to impinge strongly on the novel's content, what sustains it as a credible work of literature is the fact that Saro-Wiwa has not merely presented an artless assemblage of raw Nigerian life. Quoting Theo Vincent again,

> Jebs Prison looms as a chimera, Nigeria, and a protean metaphor. Its tantalising enigma is at the root of the many-layered possible interpretations of the work. The conception here and the big shadow which the prison casts over Nigeria – which is sometimes the prison also – reminds us of the penchant of 18th century satirists in English and European Literature who used this technique to lambast the foibles of their own societies.[6]

The quest motif intensifies the novel's allegorical dimension. The journeys which Pita, Asa, Andizi and Biney make are journeys of awareness. By passing through the seven islands on their way to search out Jebs, Andizi and Biney come into contact with inhabitants whose behaviours represent one or other of Nigeria's deadly sins – tribalism, religious strife, the ascendancy of ignorance, corruption, and so on. The author's powerful, almost despairing awareness of the problems of his society is thus captured in memorable and enduring images.

Saro-Wiwa's two volumes of short stories testify to the variety of his creative range. *A Forest of Flowers* (1986) contains nineteen stories and *Adaku and Other Stories* (1969) eighteen. In both collections the author abandons experimentation with language, and when he is satirical, the loud laughter of *Prisoners of Jebs* has been replaced with a wry, subdued, and sardonic humour, but one that is not less damning than the former. Characters are engaged in significant emotional, physical and psychological encounters, and in the course of probing these issues the author's presentations, necessarily compressed because of the demands of the literary form, often rise beyond mere competence and acquire a poignant profundity.

These stories probe varied worlds – from rural and urban environments to the most secret recesses of the inner mind. *A Forest of Flowers* is divided into two sections: 'Home Sweet Home', (the title of the first story in this section), and 'High Life', (the title story of the second section).

The first section deals with the 'forest' – a metaphor for the rural, forest-bound world of Dukana (Mene's home town in *Sozaboy*). The flowers that bloom in this forest village are *fleurs de mal*, of ignorance, superstition, filth and stagnation. These form the thematic link between the stories. In the eight stories which are set in Dukana, Saro-Wiwa refuses to shield these negative elements under a fake, romanticized, rural innocence. The much-vaunted African rural world of peace and harmony is revealed to harbour the most bizarre and pernicious vices: greed, envy and sheer cruelty. The notion of a caring, mutually-protective rural populace is belied by the frequency with which the people of Dukana allow their ignorance to overtake and overwhelm them and find expression in the crassest of cruelties, inflicted with horrifying implacability on one or other of their members. Three of the eight stories deal with death, but two are murders which the people inflict on their innocent victims. In 'A Family Affair' a family feels that it has been disgraced by the actions of one of its members who has gone mad. They bury him alive in spite of his protests:

> The voice persisted ever so faintly, ever so insistently, even as they covered the grave with the wet earth and huge logs of wood. Then when they heard no more sounds, when they felt sure their troubles had been buried deep in the bowels of the earth, they looked at each other, turned upon their heels and picked their silent way through the secretive forest back to Dukana. (p. 33)

In 'The Bonfire' a 'progressive' son of Dukana dies from diabetes in a place several hundred miles away from Dukana, but the Dukanans decide that some envious person at home had magically overcome the distance and killed him by remote control. On the day of his burial they declare one Nedam the culprit, drag him into his hut, lock him in, and set the hut on fire:

> And now came a horrendous clamour of human screams, a shriek of anguish and terror which rose above the bonfire. As the house burned, the youth of Dukana formed themselves into a ring round it to ensure that their victim did not escape. The huge flames leapt up and burned fast and soon there was nothing but ash and mud and a vile sooty smoke which spiralled upwards into the sky.
>
> And the youths, without a word, hurriedly disappeared in different directions. (p. 39)

Nedam's crime is that he is not given to sitting idly with others and gossiping, rather preferring to spend his time in the heart of the forest, where he owns a palm plantation, but which they know nothing of. He is different, and therefore dangerous.

The tragedies which the stories embody are evident even in their ironic titles. Thus in 'A Family Affair' the family relinquishes its role as protector of the weak and afflicted member, but rather turns his destroyer; the bonfire in 'A Bonfire' is not of celebration. In 'Home Sweet Home' a young mother of twins is exiled and her babies are destroyed. A young girl in 'The Divorcee', failing to produce children after three years of marriage is unceremoniously returned to her mother (who dutifully returns the bride price) without any compensations for her services to her husband and his family. The efforts of the Dukana populace to frustrate the impending visit of the sanitary inspector in 'The Inspector Calls' are equally ridiculous. They prefer to remain in their filth and squalor which the author describes in every grimy detail. The overwhelming and depressing emphasis is on the crushing weight of negative and destructive rural conservatism.

The second part of A Forest of Flowers deals with city dwellers. Although the stories are not as substantial in their tragic import as those in the first part, the scenes and characters are as cheerless as those in the rural environment. The city (whether Lagos or Port Harcourt) merely shows the other side of the same bad coin, in which women are maltreated by their husbands and society ('Night Ride', 'A Caring Man'), where new types of violence exist ('Garga'), where dedicated and honest men are the laughing stock of their corrupt colleagues ('The Stars Below'), and new

forms of cheating and chicanery are practised ('Acapulco Motel').
Modern cosmopolitan Nigeria does not appear to be much
different from superstitious Dukana; rather, the city gives the
village a negative complementarity which anchors the author's
perception of a different, ugly reality. For example, the description of the physical environment of Lagos in 'The Stars Below'
echoes the physical environment of Dukana, with its filthy,
disease-ridden, nauseating, surroundings:

> Big, luxurious cars belching forth thick suffocating smoke sat
> satirically beside dirty, ill-looking houses where people swarmed
> like maggots. The open market which spread monstrously below
> him was a confused mix of dirt, noise and bright colours. The
> babble of voices emanating from there was like the gulping rab-
> ble of frogs squatting in a mucky swamp.

That is where the tragedy essentially lies. The 'modern' city has
merely transferred the negative aspects of the village to a new
location. Nothing has changed or improved.

Adaku and Other Stories gives the reader a mixed perspective
on life and society. Two things are notable, however: the historical
range is broadened to reveal the well-spring of the author's
creativity. Events range from pre-colonial to the colonial and the
immediate post-colonial era. Stories like 'The Empire Builders',
'The Old Man's Fine', 'Sorcerers and Magicians' and 'Africa Kills
Her Sun' testify to the truth of this assertion.

The second and the more important fact is that the author
concentrates extensively on the fate of women in their relationships with men. In *A Forest of Flowers* a few of the stories
explored this theme, but in *Adaku and Other Stories* more than
half of the stories deal exclusively with issues in women's lives,
or issues which involve them in other contexts.

Particularly significant in the above regard are 'Judge',
'Dilemma', 'Reconciliation' and 'Her Last Duty'. Each of these
stories focuses on the victim status of women, the ease with which
the men they trust and sacrifice themselves for abuse and betray
them. At the same time the author draws the reader's attention
to the ironic complicity of the women in their victimization – their
seeming inability to learn from previous experience or their child-
like trust in token gestures of reconciliation which soon collapse
again.

For a writer whose first novel was only published in 1985,
Saro-Wiwa has shown a remarkable level of productivity and
artistic competence, at least by recent Nigerian standards. His
general thematic perspective also makes his writings immediately
relevant to his society.

In spite of the many points in his favour, however, certain lapses exist in his work. He will need ultimately to reduce, or do away altogether with obscure slang and expressions which need explanatory glossaries. He will also need to abandon certain clichés and stylistic habits. For instance, his characters rarely laugh; rather, they are perenially 'in stitches'. Sometimes, too, statements are repeated almost word for word within a short space. For example, in *A Forest of Flowers* (p. 55) 'The dead man lay on a bamboo mat in the bedroom, his face covered with a black, dirty cloth. The women sat around him weeping'. Three pages later, 'The dead man lay on the bamboo mat in the bedroom, his face covered with a black, dirty cloth. The women sat around him weeping, chasing away the flies.' Sometimes, too, there is a shift in tenses, especially in his narrative adaptations of his television drama 'Basi and Company', which distorts narrative progression badly. In such sudden and unnecessary shifts, the narrative language begins to sound like stage directions.

In general, however, Saro-Wiwa has come into the world of creative writing with very few of the awkward errors of language or artistic perspective of the new writer. His promise – in terms of quantitative productivity and artistic maturation, and the potential for its fulfilment – is immense.

NOTES

1. Ken Saro-Wiwa, *On A Darkling Plain* (Port Harcourt: Saros International Publishers, 1989). All his other works are published by the same company. Dates of publication of works cited in this article are included immediately after the first mention of the work.
2. Author's note to the text.
3. Quoted on the book's back-cover.
4. Abiola Irele, 'The Fiction of Saro-Wiwa (1)', Lagos: *The Guardian*, 17 Jan. 1987: 13.
5. Interview in *Topnews* 14 (1988).
6. Theo Vincent, 'The Rehabilitation of Pita Dumbrok', Lagos: *The Daily Times*, 8 January 1992: 187.

Land, War & Literature in Zimbabwe: A Sampling

Eldred D. Jones

Independence and majority rule came to Zimbabwe through a bitter war fought by the indigenous people against the alien invader who had expropriated their land, demeaned their culture and enslaved their bodies. The achievement of political power restored Africans to nominal control over their lives and land but lives which had been scarred by the horrors of war and a land which had been desecrated and which was still largely expropriated. The newly won power also brought about its own struggles and opened up divisions even among those who had fought together for the recapture of the spirit of the land and people. Post-war Zimbabwean writing examines the meaning of the liberation achieved through the sacrifices of the combatants and the plight of the ordinary people, often caught in the middle, the inheritors of the victory.

At the end of Yvonne Vera's *Nehanda* one is surprised that the novel has covered only 118 pages, such is its range in terms of time and the depth of the communal experience which it explores. Although it is dominated by the life of one woman, Nehanda, with whose birth it opens and whose defiant encounter with Browning in her prison cell ends the linear narration, the novel is really concerned with the spirit of the people which stretches back into time and is inextricably linked with the land itself which in turn enshrines the spirits of the ancestors. This spirit of the land is the source of the people's strength which will ensure their survival against the powerful forces unleashed against them by the colonial invader:

> The voice comes from within them from the cave, from below the earth, and from the roots of trees. The voice awakens the dead part of themselves, and they walk with new beliefs, with renewed wisdom. Purged of their fears, they are prepared to live and to die. (p. 81)

The clash of civilizations, of Europe and Africa, and the inevitable consequent conflict has been portrayed over and over in African literature since Achebe's *Things Fall Apart*, but rarely with such subtlety and art as in this novel. The total lack of common ground between the colonialist invader and the owners of the land, is exemplified in terms of the contrast between the place of the spoken word which is alive, flexible and humane on the one hand as against the fixed rock-like inhumanity of the printed word in the form of a treaty, in the two cultures:

> The paper is the stranger's own peculiar custom, a trick he employs against time. Among ourselves, speech is not like rock. Words are as malleable as the minds of the people who create them. (p. 40)

The intentions of the invaders are equally alien; they have come seeking gold to start with but their ultimate aim is to deprive the people of their land and hence of their spirit, self-respect and independence. By employing the technique of multiple role-playing, Yvonne Vera dramatizes the conflict by making Ibwe speak both as the white man, the messenger of his people, and the chief who embodies all their values thus reflecting some of the ambivalences created by the contact of civilizations, even within single individuals. By refusing to sit with the people, the white man's contempt for them emerges but his absence puts Ibwe into the role of mediator, a role into which Africans find themselves forced by this contact. Ibwe is transformed momentarily into the white man:

> They watch as Ibwe's shoulders and neck become hunched into a more forward posture. His stomach protrudes, and his arms hang oddly. He takes a few awkward, plodding steps, and when someone laughs, his aggressive stare makes the audience shrink back. . . . His jaw has moved forward, so that the words, when he continues speaking, seem to force their way out of his mouth. The people understand that the white man is now standing before them.
> 'I will give you guns, and teach you to pray to my God . . .'
> (p. 38)

But the basic integrity of the people is asserted and is realized in another transformation of Ibwe:

> Although he is a short man, the people see a tall man standing before them, majestic in bearing. He carries a staff which he waves ceremoniously to decorate his speech. When Ibwe continues speaking, it is in the voice of their own chief. (p. 39)

He has become the voice of the resistance. The clash is inevitable and the novel proceeds inexorably to the rebellion of the people inspired by the prophetess, Nehanda, under the military leadership of Kaguvi, and the carnage and destruction that result.

One of the distinctive features of this novel is the art with which dreadful events are portrayed so that the full depth of horror is conveyed without the goriness of detail. From the top of a tree 'the boy' (his anonimity generalizes the experience) who had been observing the surrounding landscape with its human activity – his sisters returning with water-pots from the stream – witnesses the destruction of home and life in one awful moment. Mother, Aunt and children lie dead while he chokes with the smoke of the burning village and a destitute boy walks forlornly into the hills no doubt to join his fatther as a freedom fighter.

Yvonne Vera writes with a conviction born of close observation. As Nehanda, then a little girl approaches the river, she observes the sounds produced by its different features:

> The lulling sound tells her where the river is deep and treacherous, the fast rippling gurgles tell her of the rapids over which it freely tumbles and that muffled thudding is its width, which is where the people cross to the opposite bank. (p. 15)

The clouds, mountains, animals, even insects – particularly the insects – are equally finely observed and portrayed:

> The grasshoppers hold to the grass with wings made wet by the dew, and they cannot fly. They bite into the stems, waiting for the rays of the sun. While they await the moment of their release, they wave their antennae in search of their future selves. (p. 77)

The novel proceeds with a number of interlocking narratives. The story of Nehanda's life and her development into the spirit of the people, is intertwined with Vatete's foreboding tale of the abducted child. This foreboding is realized in the clash heralded by the arrival of Browning and Smith. The liberation of the spirit of the people is pictured through the life of Mashoko/Moses who emancipates himself from his demeaning domestic service under Browning and returns to his cattle, respectability and rebellion: 'I am proud of my people. I am going back to the wisdom of my people' (p. 74). The novel moves with assurance backwards and forwards through these intertwining narratives emphasizing throughout the lack of comprehension of African values by the invading whites, and the threat that they pose to the integrity of the tradition of the Africans.

While *Nehanda* mainly set the scene for the ensuing conflict, Nevanji Madanhire's *Goatsmell* focuses on the post-war failure of the two main tribes of Zimbabwe to come to terms with each other and work for a common purpose. This failure amounts to a betrayal of the sacrifices made in the cause of liberation, responsibility for this betrayal being firmly laid at the door of the Zimbabweans themselves, the alien invader only peripherally appearing in the treatment.

The central issue in the liberation struggle was land: land which had been expropriated and which was to be returned to its original owners; the land which was the source of the people's belief in themselves, whose productivity sustained them and whose occasional aberrations through drought or other natural disaster spelt deprivation. Associated with the land are its physical features, its agricultural products, its cattle, the source of myth and spiritual sustenance, and the basis of belief. It is portrayed in all its magnificence when the hero Musiiwa strays from his fellow herdsboys, into a cave with prehistoric war paintings and other artefacts of the past. There is even a surviving piece of ancient pottery which becomes a recurring symbol in the novel. It is described here wholly preserved, its art work intact: 'It was intact and beautifully decorated. Its necklace was a chevron pattern with beads gracing it' (p. 40). When the cave is later revisited in a dream sequence the ceramic pot had disintegrated: '... it had turned into shards. Dirty shards. Its necklace had disappeared' (p. 133). The rock paintings had similarly been obliterated not by any deliberate act of vandalism but by a careless indifference to or unawareness of their existence and significance: '... someone had lit a fire below the pictures and the smoke had blackened the walls leaving the pictures invisible' (p. 133).

It is from this vantage point of the past that the land is described in all its integrity:

> I could see the north rising in the sky: Gotagota, Bumi and Mavuradonha. Below to the left, lying majestically like a lion that has fed well, Chizarira Hills. And from the east in the direction of the ocean, Nyanga, Vumba and Chimanimani Mountains that carried the sky on their bald head. ... I instinctively folded my lips and blew. The whistle came from deep down in my gut. At first it was shrill and high-pitched and then it thickened and became deep. The mountains shook and the earth trembled. I stopped and watched. I saw rodents and the beasts. They were emerging from the bowels of the earth. (pp. 40–1)

This was the land that was first expropriated by the white man, the remaining scraps of which were fought over by brother and brother and which after independence was further filched from the people by their politicians like the chef, the archetype of the venal politician. The politicians had lost their way in their greed:

> Our leaders have forgotten the Leadership Code which they themselves had drafted. They owned several farms each while the masses did not have enough land. They were bent on self-aggrandizement. Most had fleets of buses bearing the names of their relatives. The whole nation had veered off the road to Socialism. (p. 119)

Set within this background of the great betrayal of the revolution, which was fought for the liberation of the land, is the rivalry between Shona and Ndebele and the ruinous disunity which pointed to a bleak future for the country. The disunity and intense rivalry make it impossible for the two star-crossed protagonists, Musiiwa and Katazile, to come together symbolizing in their own, the fate of the two tribes. Their two fathers who ironically were leaders of 'Unity Talks' and who came to blows outside the House of Parliament also dramatized the seeming impossibility of a united country. On his way to hospital having been savagely beaten by Katazile's Ndebele kinsmen, Musiiwa reflects bitterly:

> 'What is the meaning of all this? Is this what we died for? Is this what the monument called Heroes' Acre stands for? I thought of all the great heroes. . . . Yes, they had all died not to liberate us. But to make us pummel each other with logs because we spoke different languages. Because we lived in different regions.' (pp. 72–3)

The war had failed to truly liberate and unite the people. Musiiwa with the help of Katazile now seek liberation and unity through art – surely a forlorn hope! His search takes two directions: he himself is a modern, largely abstract artist and his picture, Goatsmell, whose meaning is almost miraculously understood by Katazile across the tribal divide, seems to hold a momentary hope that unity could come through art. But this is only the spiritual unity of two individuals which does not transfer itself to their respective peoples. The other direction of the search is through the dance: Musiiwa theorizes that in the origins of the different tribal dances is an underlying unity, a rediscovery of which would lead to a supra-tribal unity. But his effort to realize this through the establishment of a cultural centre ends in a débâcle. The two lovers at the end of the novel find even personal union unrealizable. They look back at the wreck of their ideals, and incidentally the physical wreck that Musiiwa had become, and see no future for themselves and by implication, for the unity and progress of the nation:

> She looked at my wheelchair. My crutches. My legs. Me as a whole. She said softly, 'Musiiwa, is there any hope?' I said quietly, 'No, There is no HOPE.' (p. 135)

Goatsmell is conceptually ambitious and bravely faces the plight of post-independence Zimbabwe. It is however flawed by the overloading of its hero, Musiiwa, who provides the narrative voice, and because he is portrayed without irony his own naivety (a fault with which he charges his friends) affects the novel as a whole. It is scarcely credible that the young man could be a great artist, a brilliant academic, could research, write and publish a book, spearhead and execute an artistic project which involves lobbying reluctant permanent secretaries for funds, and building an arts centre while managing an undergraduate course as well as a drink problem. The language too, largely Musiiwa'a voice, and possibly an attempt to reproduce undergraduate speech – a mixture of American and English cliché – slackens the pace and seems inadequate to carry the weighty things which the novel essays. Expressions like 'it took my breath away', 'the well never ceased to give me the creeps', 'I shot from rags to riches', 'I missed a beat', 'Did I add insult to injury ...?' 'The people entrusted to run the centres had been sitting on their laurels', 'I did not leave any stone unturned', 'Then I threw a spanner in the works', 'the next time we raise our eyes we have gone down the drain', 'nipping this fragmentation of our dear country in the bud' – the full list is quite extensive – contain nuggets from English composition classes which, however, dull rather than sharpen the impact. And when in a moment of high sexual excitement the hero breaks into a mental recitation from 'the song of King Solomon': 'How beautiful you are, darling! How your eyes shine with love behind your veil ...' (p. 94) (compared with, say, the lines quoted above (p. 50, 52) from *Nehanda*) this seems like a capitulation into cliché. Features like these diminish in *Goatsmell* the organic wholeness, the union of matter and manner which characterizes *Nehanda* and an earlier work, Chenjerai Hove's *Bones*.

From the very first pages, *Bones* reeks with the smells, throbs with the rhythms, and reflects the total environment of the rural setting – landscape, animals, plants and above all, the human beings, particularly the warmth, the broad humanity and the life of suffering of its central character, Marita, through whose eyes much of the story is revealed.

One of the difficulties of writing about one civilization in the language of another is that of avoiding the associations which one civilization has imposed upon the language which has to be used to describe a completely different manner of life. English comes to Africa, particularly literary English, having grown out of a certain type of architecture, landscape and a highly, industrialized and mechanized situation to be used in a novel like *Bones* to describe a rural people working at a low level of material existence, working almost as slaves in the farm of a foreign dominator; people who defecate behind ant-hills in bushes only feet away from their gossiping neighbours who are totally unaware of their presence; people who hunt the animals they eat but with a reverence for their environment which makes it a sin to kill what you cannot eat – in contrast to the white farmer, Manyepo (the invader), who takes his gun into the forest, kills many animals indiscriminately and photographs them dying to make pictures for his walls, leaving their carcasses to rot or for the jackals to eat.

Chenjerai Hove has adopted a highly poetic style heavy with the images of the countryside, textured with the proverbs, aphorisms and wisdom of the people. He has also sought to reproduce the feel of the language with an imitation (or reproduction) of some of its features such as its rhetorical repetitions and inversions. The language which is for the most part sustained by the wealth of the imagery, flowing dense and compact, only occasionally declines into cliché as when 'the boy next door' pops in from the romantic paraphernalia of the other civilization or 'you must be joking' interrupts the characteristic idiom.

The technique of narration employed is that of the 'stream of consciousness', 'interior monologue' or what I prefer to call 'thought flow' sometimes expressed in speech and sometimes unexpressed in the mind of the character. There is very little authorial intervention and therefore hardly any name-calling. The two main vehicles are Janifa (Jennifer) who opens and closes the novel and Marita who sustains it. Through the eyes of these two characters we see the opposing forces ranged against each other; the freedom fighters, their patriotism, unequal encounters with superior forces, their atrocities, the seeming hoplessness of their struggle and the hope which sustains them; we see the might of the invaders – the mere word of Manyepo, the white farmer, exonerates his cook, Chisaga, from the brutal rape of Janifa; we see the paratroopers descending on the freedom fighters and the unequal struggle that ensues. Traitors, collaborators, maimed victims, sweating labourers with cracked feet, blistered palms and aching bones, victims of rape, exploitation and betrayal, are all paraded before our eyes without authorial comment. Behind all this is the spirit of the people which occasionally breaks out and spreads out the vision before them of their plight – of disease, famine, death and oppression – but also asserts the hope of triumph through suffering, a hope which is only realized with bitter irony. The Spirit speaks:

> my bones will rise in the spirit of war. They will
> sing war-songs
> with the fire of battle. They will compose new war-
> songs
> and fight on
> until the shrines of the land of their birth
> are respected once more. My bones will rise
> with such power
> the graves will be too small
> to contain them.
> The ribs of the graves
> will break when my bones rise,
> and you stare in disbelief,
> not knowing if your hunger for war
> can stand up to it. Then the locusts will not be seen
> again
> and strangers will not think that
> he who accepts them is full of foolishness ... (p. 60)

Here the language rises to the level of poetry.

The 'story' is centred on Marita whose son has left to join the freedom fighters and whom she determines to find in the city, leaving behind her young friend and confidante, Janifa, whom she had hoped would be her son's wife. But she dies anonymously in the city; Janifa is brutally raped and ends up in chains in a mad house. Now the lost son returns and seeks her out but she rejects the freedom that he offers and opts for the freedom of her dreams – the dreams inspired by the dead Marita – the freedom of chains. The irony here is bitter:

> ... I will stand here to watch the rising sun, to see the little animals jumping up and down with the power of the early sun with a new fire to cleanse the infected soil. I will stand here all the time, then walk so that these chains on my legs will have no purpose. Then the keepers of this place will come and say ...

> We will remove the chains soon when we know you are well
> ... But I will take the broken chains with my own hands and
> say ... Do not worry yourselves, I have already removed them
> by myself. I have been removing them from my heart for many
> years, now my legs and hands are free because the mountains
> and the rivers I saw with my own eyes could not fail to remove
> all the chains of this place ... Then I will go without waiting
> for them to say go. (pp. 134–5)

To everyone else, this is madness but this merely illustrates a
feature of the novel, that of opposed, seemingly irreconcilably
opposed, points of view – the white invader versus the indigenous
folk, the country contrasted with the city, the natural environment under the violation of the exploiters – except that the wise
Marita, in the middle of her sufferings can see possibilities of
reconciliation:

> The white man thinks we are children, that is why his tongue
> is loose. The day he learns that we are also grown-ups, he will
> learn to tighten his tongue.... One day we will also learn that
> the white man is like us, if you prick him with a thorn in his
> buttocks, he will cry for his mother like anybody else. (p. 75)

This is a powerful novel written with exceptional linguistic control, plumbing the depths of human suffering but having the
wisdom to hope.

The liberation war is also central to the collection of short
stories *Effortless Tears* by Alexander Kanengoni. Even a straight
narration of the causes, the course and the result of the war would
yield some irony, but through a deliberate use of this device,
Kanengoni exposes the discrepancies between intention and
result, high hopes and disillusionment.

Although the war was fought principally over the expropriation
of land yet much of the fighting on the ground was between
Africans on both sides of the conflict, the white invader being
off-centre, directing affairs, emerging at the end still in possession
of the bulk of the land. In 'The Black Christ of Musami', this situation is powerfully presented in the confrontation between
the narrator and Godfrey Munetsi, the 'Christ' of the title. With
his disembowelled comrade bleeding and dying on his back the
narrator suddenly comes upon Godfrey Munetsi in his Rhodesian
Army uniform, the only thing that distinguishes him from his
'freedom fighter' opponent. Even the narrator's rifle drops at
the suddenness of the encounter, and, powerless and burdened
he looks down the barrel of the 'enemy's' gun. The outcome is
totally unexpected:

'Pick it up,' he said calmly, as if he was a disinterested observer. I bent to pick up my gun staring all the while into the cold muzzle of his gun. Tichatonga groaned in pain.

'Now pass on,' he said but I kept standing as if rooted to the ground. 'I said pass on,' he exclaimed angrily, as if his patience was exhausted. 'There is no time to waste.'

In a bewildered daze I shuffled on.

'Not that way,' he called after me. 'There are some of us there. Go to your right.'

I did as he had instructed. (pp. 44–5)

Without obvious authorial intervention one of the glaring ironies of the war is exposed; its accidental oppositions, uncertain allegiances and something of its senseless waste.

The Christ figure returns at the end of the war and again offers assistance to the narrator with a gratuitous kindness that leaves him almost as bewildered as that of the first encounter. But even more startling is the later revelation that Godfrey Munetsi had been dead 10 years before this second encounter, the circumstances of his death further underlining the senselessness as well as the cruelty of the war. The 'Christ' had returned to his village just before the end of the war and had found himself an enemy to his own people:

Poor fellow. The war was almost over, when he came home for the weekend, just a few months before the cease-fire.... The guerrillas got wind of his presence from the local *mujibhas* and they shot him. He was left in the sun in the middle of the village for nearly a week. The whole village stank of his decomposing corpse. (pp. 49–50)

The undeserved ignominy of the death, at the hands of his own people, of one whose only acts had been of spontaneous kindness, clinches the Christ association but the survival of the spirit of kindness after death – one of the multiple ironies of the story – also holds a faint hope of salvation.

The war left its debris in the form of physically and mentally broken human beings and heroes who must have wondered what their sacrifice had brought either for themselves or their country. Comrade Zvenyika, one of the returning heroes, was a physical wreck with 'his crutches, his amputated leg, his broad-brimmed hat festooned with a leopard skin and the canvas travelling bag slung on his shoulder like a gun' (p. 37). Indeed a pathetic and rather ridiculous figure whose self-respect hangs on his war stories and the respect this earned him from his little nephew and kindly sister-in-law. His brother however, could hardly bear the sight of him and his contempt comes pouring out in an assault on his elder brother's only source of self-respect: 'Why do you always force everyone to endure your boring stories about a war that ended almost a generation ago?' (p. 40). To him, this 'stupid war' had left them worse than before. So what was it all about? Bewildered, the older man has to come to terms with the fact that the war had ended and he had to forget about his stories and be content with his stump, his crutches, his ridiculous hat and his miserable pension. With a deft touch Kanengoni gives us a glimpse of 'Heroes Acre' the monument to those who, like Comrade Zvenyika, had liberated the country! It is not only the little boy who is puzzled by this ironic juxtaposition of the wrecked hero and the glow of lights from Heroes Acre: 'He looked past them, at the lonely flickering red light of Heroes Acre and failed to understand something' (p. 42). It is not just the boy who is puzzled. In these war stories, by such ironic juxtapositions of the dream and the reality, Kanengoni points up the ironies of the 'liberation'.

At the end of 'Things We'd Rather Not Talk About' through the thoughts of the forlorn woman as she starts on a 60 km walk with her son's bottle of medicine, without which he had had a recurrence of his fit during which he had re-lived the horror of having been forced to take part in the killing of his father by freedom fighters, her plight illustrates with clinching irony the frustrated dreams of the people for whose land the war had been fought:

> Back at home in Mhondoro, when Paul's mother discovered that her son had forgotten his bottle of medicine and knew that even if the last bus to Harare had not gone she did not have the money to use it, she remembered to put on her torn black tennis shoes and began the long walk to Harare, more than sixty kilometres away, whispering to herself, pleading with God and all those gone, especially her husband, to help keep her only child safe and alive as the other one had not returned from the guerilla war that had freed the country. (pp. 63–4)

The telling irony of that almost throw-away last line compared with the more laboured reflection of Musiiwa on this theme in *Goatsmell* quoted earlier illustrates the difference in technique of the two authors. The land and the lingering links with the departed ancestors remain, and it is to these that like the woman just referred to, men must turn for help and reassurance. Kanengoni writes about the land and the natural environment consciously emphasizing this living element which makes it capable along with the spirits of the ancestors of giving such hope however faint:

There was a huge old *mukamba* tree watching silently over our home from a small hill in the east which never seemed to shed any of its brittle, evergreen leaves. It was a towering giant that marked our home from miles around. Each time I came home from the city, I went up the hill and crouched under the tree, talking to it, talking to my deceased grandfather, asking him to allow the man from Musami to come and rest in the old man's silent, protective gaze. Each time I asked, the wind would blow, slowly stirring the massive tangled branches, as if gently agreeing to my strange request. (p. 50)

The stories in the collection are told with a sureness of touch, a deft economy of language, a wealth of suggestive imagery and the most economical use of characters. With only two, three or four characters Kanengoni can open up a whole world depicting the horror of war ('The Black Christ of Musami'), the individual loneliness which separates three people forced together in a shebeen ('Burdens'), and the contrasting views of two generations, father and son ('The Rift'). Over most of these stories looms the bloody horror of the war of liberation leaving scars of madness, heartbreaking loneliness and despair.

For these Zimbabwean writers victory and liberation have a hollow ring. The war has not solved even the problem of land; it remains to be divided up, fought over, worked and suffered with, all over again. Their focus is mainly on the performance of those who now hold political power and on whose integrity or otherwise, depend the plight of the ordinary people whose lives are the central preoccupation of these works. The white occupiers of the land are not the central figures in this part of the history; the black people now in political control have to muster the necessary wisdom and honesty if the forebodings of these writings are not to be fulfilled. While they can highlight their people's plight as these writers have sought to do there is hope for the future of Zimbabwe.

WORKS CITED

Hove, Chenjerai. *Bones*. Harare: Baobab Books, 1988.
Kanengoni, Alexander. *Effortless Tears*. Harare: Baobab Books, 1993.
Madanhire, Nevanji. *Goatsmell*. Harare: Anvil Press, 1992.
Vera, Yvonne. *Nehanda*. Harare: Baobab Books, 1993.

Poetry & Repression in Contemporary Nigeria: Tanure Ojaide's *Labyrinths of the Delta*

Ode S. Ogede

For a variety of reasons, poetic activity is witnessing an upsurge in a manner unprecedented in Nigerian literary history. In the last few years only dramatic production has come close to standing in comparison with the pace of action that is currently going on in the terrain of poetry. It might well be that the impetus leading to this outburst of literary activity could be traced to the founding by Chinua Achebe in 1971 of the Nsukka-based literary journal *Okike*, which has done so much to inspire younger writers all over Africa to expose their work. The upsurge, however, has its culminating point in the ferment of the economic turmoil of the Babangida regime. No other journal except *Okike* has given as much support to literary activity in Nigeria as the Lagos-based newspaper, *The Guardian*, whose poetry contributions have already been gathered in *Voices from the Fringe* edited by Harry Garuba.[1] This spurt of poetic creativity has also borne fruit in many verse volumes published by individual poets.[2]

Because of the very nature of poetry as an art form which gains its effects largely by indirect means, it would have seemed, ordinarily, surprising that poetry should stand first among the artistic genres found convenient by many Nigerian writers to their purpose of voicing social discontent. But one would need to know the changes and innovations which modern Nigerian poets brought to the form in order to make it a handy idiom for carrying the burden of social commentary. As the economic difficulties aggravated by the introduction of the IMF-directed Structural Adjustment Programmes in the country began to show their sorrowful effects on the lives of the ordinary citizens, Nigerian writers have turned increasingly to poetry as a platform for expressing their grievances.

In large measure the writers dispense with the subdued ornamentation which were refined elements in the compositions of the earlier groups of poets like the late Christopher Okigbo, J.P. Clark-Bekederemo, Wole Soyinka, Gabriel Okara, and M.J.C. Echeruo. Outrage became such a key mood because the poets needed to speak with passionate, angry tones, defying all the previous conventions of restrained art. These younger poets learned that they must not only make powerful indictments protesting against the dismal state of affairs, but suggest clear measures to remedy it because the military rogues who preside over the maladministration of their country are hard of hearing and can only be moved with insults, full-throated and clamorous, not by beautiful images. Consequently, compelled by the need to sound factual and down-to-earth in re-creating the real mood of the down-trodden peoples born of their deprived status, the majority of the poets have been unable to resist the temptation of making a recourse to the use of plain prosaic language as a natural discourse of poetic composition.

In his article 'Post-War Nigeria and the Poetry of Anger', J.O.J. Nwachukwu-Agbada, scholar, critic and member of the younger generation of Nigerian writers, summarizes the situation of his colleagues in the following terms:

> The anger of the post-war Nigerian poet stems not only from the failure of the elite culture but also from the negative correlates of the Civil War, the oil wealth euphoria, the ideology of capitalistic economic formations, unambiguously adumbrated in the nation's constitution as 'mixed economy', and the culture of successive militaristic totalitarian dictatorships. These are issues which the pre-war poet may have perceived poorly or in themselves were yet to 'percolate' for intimate consideration or possibly still were regarded as too commonplace to require his attention: tyranny and oppression, corruption, suffering and persecution, ineffective public utility network, military intervention and military leadership, the new but crude cut-throat values of excessive materialism, pagan opulence and competition, armed robbery, ignorance, and what Obiechina describes as 'Mammon worship'.[3]

Since a general overview of the political temper of the younger Nigerian poets has been adequately provided by Nwachukwu-Agbada, my concern is with an in-depth exploration of one text produced in this period, Tanure Ojaide's *The Labyrinths of the Delta*,[4] which seems to me most representative of the two antithetical negative and positive strands at war with each other in this new tradition of Nigerian writing. This text merits such a consideration not only because of the author's growing reputation as one of the better new-generation Nigerian poets but also for the range of the technical experimentation it promises. *Labyrinths of the Delta* is the book with which the author won the 1987 African Regional Prize of the prestigious Commonwealth Poetry Competition. The collection therefore provides a good rod for measuring not only Ojaide's poetic skills but also the general state of the art of his contemporaries.

It is evident from Nwachukwu-Agbada's survey article that some of the formalistic traits which give the third generation Nigerian poets their separate identity have eluded him. Certainly, despite the many merits of his approach, a purely thematic study such as his can be expected to do little justice to the complex linguistic issues involved in such a substantial body of poetry as he covers. Although he thoroughly understands the general social, economic and political context of their work, Nwachukwu-Agbada believes that the dominant element in the poets is anger, and 'the recent Nigerian poet, it seems to me, sees only ugliness, boredom and horror and would not pretend to have yet beheld a beautiful world ...' (p. 3). The error here is to gloss over the evocative power which the more striking of these poets like Tanure Ojaide, Niyi Osundare, Okinba Launko (Femi Osofisan) and others do exhibit in their image-making discourse. In their best works, these poets are capable of counterposing to their present troubled existence a dream world which helps reveal the strong imaginative resources with which they approach poetry.

There is no doubt that since 1986 an undeclared state of emergency has existed in Nigeria, different only in degree from the predicament of the Civil War era. As the majority population wages a daily battle for survival against the hunger, disease, malnutrition and squalor that have been their experience in the midst of the insulting wealth and opulence of the minority élite, indeed each of the poets of the period would find his/her sentiments expressed in the following manifesto articulated by Ojaide:

> I breathe fire from my heart, not to burn any house but to drive vermin from our midst. I have the heart to scare the owl from sorcery and outsmart the tortoise in its cheating game. I have a desire to wipe out the people's plague with my own blood. (*Labyrinths*, p. 5)

The dominant mood of this poem is one of saturated indignation at the injustice, oppression and inhumanity of the oppressor. The

above excerpt registers the tone of much of the poetry of this
period. But it lacks the sense of the paced cadence, musical
rhythm, and profound structural and technical terseness of
much of an Osundare or an Osofisan. Then too, the imagery is
disappointingly predictable. Although Ojaide manages toward the
end of the poem to envision the birth of a future Nigeria where
'only love/can give peace a chance' (p. 5), he fails to elaborate
vividly on the dream content in such a manner as to create the
impact of a classic vision akin to that which places the work of
one of his own contemporaries, Femi Osofisan's *Minted Coins*,[5] in
the tested tradition of Wole Soyinka and Christopher Okigbo.

A major factor in the determination of organically vibrant
poetry such as that produced by Okigbo, Soyinka and their able
successors like Osofisan is the interplay of adequate language in
the exploration of the writer's dream. The corollary to this, as
Donatus Nwoga has put it so aptly, is a poetry of 'mental
cleverness and flights of imaginative fancy which are decorative
and do not work so well towards generating in the reader a
response akin to the poet's initial reactions'.[6] The tradition by
which poets express their symphonic dreams in a vibrant manner
certainly has much universal appeal. It preceded modern African
poets like Okigbo and Soyinka, though they were the first Nigerian
poets to develop dream into full blown ritualistic genres and
give it extended treatment, respectively, in *Labyrinths*[7] and
Idanre and Other Poems.[8] In such isolated poems like J.P. Clark-
Bekederemo's 'Olokun' and Okara's 'The Call of the River Nun'[9]
there is expressed also a similar longingness in lyrical language
which gives the works a compelling quality. The artist seeks to
free himself from the restrictions of the world of daily strife, the
routine world of hate and frustration and the result is a
luminously platonic reality to which the quester aspires. What
gives Osofisan's verse in *Minted Coins* a quality that Ojaide's
doesn't have in any meaningful way, is the poetic intensity of the
narrative. The whole idea coalesces around the object which
provides the text its title. The author looks closely at the figure
of coins. The drama of the event is enacted, and the spectacle
offers Osofisan's poetic faculty an opportunity to make wide-
ranging comments on the nature of existence in general and living
in contemporary Nigeria in particular:

> Love's always the starting point
> Till the season insists on corpses
> On memories of the dead ...
> But life re-affirms itself in new beginnings;
> And suddenly, it is morning again. (p. vii)

Here we find an interplay of philosophy, irony, quizzical humour, and controlled rhythm. Throughout the poem, the poet elaborates on the various ways in which love's changing faces occur. That is how the movement of life's propeller is mapped out. He suggests that the image of coins provides a striking angle from which one can examine the nature of existence, politics, government, ambition, corruption, animosity, hatred, love, poverty, and wealth, all of which motivate living in contemporary society.

Furthermore, technical diversity is the hallmark of Osofisan's verse. In such pieces like 'When the Drums Beat', 'Love's Discotheque', 'Olokun I', 'Olokun II' and others, he approaches his material not through the oppressive first person voice but through other external objects. In the 'Olokun' poems, for example, the speaking voice is that of a landmass, the Gambia. The West African country addresses its major river, the River Gambia and the goddess of that river, as man would his lover, a woman. Symbolically, the relationship between the poet and his imaginative creation thus finds an analogy in the experience of man and nature. Throughout the collection, Osofisan's poignant imagery, casual humour, dramatic vigour and distinctively musical complexity are what add pep to the incisive polemical thrust of his ideas.

In *Labyrinths of the Delta*, on the other hand, Ojaide's intent may have been to address the experience of living in Nigeria in the eighties, a moment of much emotional trauma, psychological distress and socio-economic adversity for the underprivileged people but he never fully progresses beyond strident negativisms – rantings and laments about exploitation of man by man. His poetry may be aimed at being an expression of the people's bitter experiences of deprivation but it lacks any comprehensive vision of the alternative humane society to replace the current depraved one. Though divided into two parts ('The Sentence' and 'The Struggle to Be Free'), the movements from one to the other are neither coherently explored nor organically integrated beyond the self-conscious speaking voice of the artist whose sense of (Ojaide's) self-importance as society's saviour is even over-dramatized.

Even in the more interesting poems of *Labyrinths of the Delta*, Ojaide's ceaseless struggle to inscribe the personality of the artist has the unintended effect of flippancy, driving not only the portraiture of the redeemer figure to ridiculous proportions but also the experience of the common people into oblivion – common people whose redemption the artist ostensibly seeks to achieve. In such poems as 'Exile' (a piece that uses the fates of artists from

Russia, South Africa and other places to lash out bitterly at inhumanism everywhere), 'When we have to fly' (a poem that advocates a trickster role for all artists engaged in the freedom struggle) and 'My share for Anne' (which employs word play and phallic imagery to pay tribute to the sources of the poet's creative inspiration, his wife!), the intended effects of pathos, sympathy, admiration and respect for the character of the artist who embodies strong will and martyrdom are diminished, in fact so thoroughly, that the reader instead despises the angelic figures created.

The suspicion raised in the reader by other pieces like 'Granny's Blessing', where Ojaide uses smooth lyrical devices to celebrate the hidden powers of an artist, and 'The New Warriors', which makes a brutal attack on the new wave of the negative destructive influences like opportunism, patronage, reckless status striving, graft, inordinate political ambition and corruption afflicting society, arises from the fact that everyone except the artist appears to be inadequate.

As indeed the limited success achieved by such few poems in the collection, as 'Africa Now', 'Message of Lust', 'Indirect Song', and 'We Are Many' make clear, Ojaide may be capable of creating some great and stunning, even if not always perfect, poetry but he would have to banish entirely his hubris – the tendency for self glorification – in order to be able to do so. The clinical realism that proves, for example, to be the source of animation in 'Africa Now', can offer a fruitful path along which Ojaide can develop his poetry in the future. Within this context, the acute sense of accuracy with which the poet dissects Africa's awful dilemmas reveals admirable commitment.

'Africa Now' is an important poem whose theme is the general political and socio-economic degeneracy of the African continent, a place where 'we barricade ourselves from outer gates/and blind our fate to unrooted pillars beneath swirling clouds' (p. 32). As the poet implicates all segments of society in the continent's unending predicament, damning everyone for paying lip service to the universal brotherhood of blacks, for example, an inspired vision of a reformed society emerges: 'For all the make-believe love and flair/for a surrogate identity, black brothers and sisters,/We stab ourselves with imported swords' (p. 33). 'Imported swords' is a polite way for the poet to call attention to the accomplished western war machines with which many of Africa's inter-tribal and international wars are fought, and irony is the hallmark of this poem, as traditional rulers, religious leaders of all denominations as well as the modern dictators all come in for their fair share of blame from the poet:

Where there's been no hyena, a cobra thrives;
a ghost-face unearths bones from quiet corners –
there's always a nuisance in every yard to cause
shame, and from coast to coast dung-painted floors.
And we await the rainmakers to trigger a downpour
to wash off the stains that mar our common face. (p. 32)

'Hyena', 'Cobra' and 'ghost-face' are deft metaphors to effectively portray the image of Africa's rapacious leaders, while 'nuisance', 'shame' and 'dung-painted floors' are terms that clearly describe the mess their policies create. Ojaide concludes the poem with a clear idea of the Africa he dreams – an independent and self-reliant continent where charity reigns supreme.

In 'Message of Lust', where Ojaide uses other animal images to reinforce his picture of African leaders as gluttons, 'Tigers', 'Vulture', 'armed robbers', 'fowl' are terms that connote the barbarity of those who should direct the affairs of their nation with humane feelings but have turned out to be the gravest threat to peace in the land. Referring specifically to Nigeria, he characterizes a situation where 'soldiers are firing bullets into the crowd':

They will boast of those they have killed;
The Pay and Records boys are riding Yamaha,
They are paying and wrecking Nigeria. (p. 36)

These lines serve a useful political purpose to force the attention of all civilized people to the inherent blood baths that follow successive military establishments in Nigeria. The fact that even those in the lowest cadre of the administration of the army are living in great affluence ('The Pay and Records boys ... riding Yamaha') highlights the degree of the corruption of the military. The paradox implicit in the image of the 'Yamaha' – the symbol of affluence among the soldiers – is that it is an imported product which is actually the source of impoverishment of the nation's wealth. The poem is a trenchant indictment of Africa's new military messiahs whose anti-social habits their Nigerian representatives exemplify.

'We Are Many', although in many ways an imperfect poem, may still be regarded as the best piece in *Labyrinths of the Delta*. It indicates many directions in which the poet can take his art to improve it. By employing the speaking voice in 'We Are Many' as being not just a speaker for the underprivileged and exploited Nigerians but an embodiment of their suffering, Ojaide succeeds in invoking the full horrors of their situation:

From birth I have been in the custody
of three overlords ...

They extract oil from my wet soil,
prospect for iron in my bones,
and level my forest for timber. (p. 72)

This refers specifically to the exploitation of the Delta tribes,
Ojaide's home area, by the Nigerian majority tribes, but it incar-
nates the essence of oppression in general, a situation in which
the exploiters 'heap barrels on my back', 'strap billets on my
shoulders and/tie hardwood to my sides':

And they take turns to ride me:
one, two, three. One mounts me
as another descends – my bane has
always been the incubus of powers;
the third busies himself
knocking out whoever is on top to
secure for himself
the comfort they find from my back.
They plot and assassinate
to benefit from my doom.
And when the lords arrive at their homes,
I am the shadow without its body ... (p. 72)

This gives a vivid image of the oppressors as callous, violent and
powerful, though a disunited group; and the masses are helpless
victims of their situation. So, Ojaide closes the poem by registering
his hope that the universal brotherhood of all oppressed peoples
will be realized, so that together they can 'summon our will/to
shatter the burden and the jinx' (p. 72).

For all that, the fact that Ojaide's verses only occasionally
manage to rise above the level of prosaic banality merely goes to
prove that he has not yet fully matured as a poet. It is not difficult
to see why, within this context, Ojaide is himself his own enemy.
Poetic practice is a matter of aesthetic perspective, depending on
where each writer stands in the theory of African poetry. It is not
simply the question regarding the use of masks and images of symbolic significance but the understanding that the poetry which
works depends on use of language with reticence or concision.
Poetic succinctness is simply the effective employment of syntax,
such that as each poetic line is penned it is loaded in a way which
is not stilted but free enough for music, rhythm, verbal echo and
heightened imagery to unite harmoniously. Donatus Nwoga has
said that:

There is a simplicity of language which is a result not of artistic
control but of failure of knowledge; a simplicity of perception resulting from an inability to reach out to any subtle

connotations from a setting, event, or situation; a naivety of thought which sees none of the varied implications, the subtleties and deeper reflections, attaching to a projected notion.[10]

A crucial undoing element in Ojaide's verse is that, against his own better judgement, he adopted the school of modern African poetry which Nwoga describes above – again in Nwoga's words – a practice of 'versified intelligibilities' which cannot 'make exciting poetry'.

In his 'Aesthetic Illusions: Prescriptions for the Suicide of Poetry', his rejoinder to the diatribes launched against him by the trio of Chinweizu, Jemie and Madubuike in their book *Towards the Decolonization of African Literature*, Wole Soyinka has termed the same sort of poetry 'the poetics of limited sensibilities'.[11] It is important to note that when Ojaide himself attempts to formulate a justification for the principle of poetry which figures in his poems, he reveals confusion and contradictions. Thus, in the poem entitled 'A Bottle in the Pit', where Ojaide proclaims an intent to avoid in his poetry the sort of obscurantism that has been associated with Wole Soyinka and his followers, he begins by describing Soyinkan writing as 'a corked bottle in a pit' – an item that has 'no label' (p. 19). 'A Bottle in the Pit' is, in general, an exceedingly delightful poem, and its terms sum up the great respect Ojaide has for Africa's first literary Nobel laureate. The poem, however, reveals much conflict, as it portrays the younger poet fighting to free himself with difficulty from what may be termed 'the seductive sweep'[12] of Soyinkan writing. Ojaide cannot resist the urge toward a sarcastic treatment of Soyinka's difficulty, though:

> Nobody knew what brew,
> Dung, or hoax –
> It defied telescopic eyes;
> Pilots were blind before it,
> *Shouldn't a bottle, needed*
> *As it might be,*
> *Show its content in a general way?*
> No luminance will violate it
> That is not lit
> In a cult, subhumed. (original emphasis, p. 18)

As the rhetorical question in the above-quoted excerpt divulges, the degree of Ojaide's exasperation with Soyinka's obscurity is enormous. Ojaide nails obscurity down to a shallowness on the part of an artist and says it asserts the lack of matter in whatever message a writer who is guilty of it wishes to impart. But even though he roundly condemns poetic isolationism and specifically attributes Soyinka's difficulty to his distance from the real situation of the ordinary citizens, he ends the poem with a sympathy for the sources of Soyinka's inspiration. Ojaide – who dubs Soyinka's writing as being the product of some 'divine gifts' (p. 29) – still urges his readers to wade through Soyinkan mystifications with patience and understanding:

> Whatever was in the bottle
> Was brewed when Soyinka
> Was alone with God (p. 18)
> ....
> But let no one
> Spite divine gifts,
> Let no one laugh
> At the tears of prophets. (p. 20)

These lines may express Ojaide's deeply liberal sensibilities – for despite the avowed radical posture he manifests in his poems Ojaide is a good sympathizer whose aspiration like that of all liberals is to see the walls of unfairness pulled down everywhere and to secure the freedom of the individual spirit to pursue its own interests – but the sympathy it extends toward Soyinka's work in theory is not matched with practice in Ojaide's own poetic compositions.

Since the appearance of *Labyrinths of the Delta* – his second book of verse – Ojaide has published four other collections: *The Eagle's Vision* (1987) with which he won the All-Africa Okigbo Prize for Poetry in 1988, *The Endless Song* (1989), *The Fate of Vultures* (1990), and *The Blood of Peace* (Heinemann, 1991),[13] bringing his total poetic output to date to six full-length books. By all accounts this is a prolific achievement given that the literary life span of writers is unusually brief in Africa. If the authority of literary awards is any reliable indicator of standards, Ojaide's brand of poetry can be said to have won much approval of late in the Commonwealth. *Labyrinths of the Delta* can thus be regarded as being his best book yet. But, as Stewart Brown, a very knowledgeable critic of Commonwealth poetry, has commented:

> With a few exceptions ... Ojaide's poems are mostly blunt 'messages from the front', imagistically flat but loud with rhetorical outrage. While there can be no doubting the poet's sincerity or the depth of his anguish, the unending self-righteousness of the narrative voice, the artless predictability of the sentiments and the cliched language of protest undermine the force of these poems.[14]

I concur with this judgement. Such blemishes in Ojaide as those outlined both by this essay and by Stewart Brown can, however, by no means be legitimately held up as being all that the new-generation Nigerian writing amounts to, for in the best of this tradition there is a directness of style which speaks of genuine talent in that it employs precious and startling imagery which is poignant in giving charming expression to the experience of living in Nigeria at a repressive moment.

NOTES

1. Harry Garuba, ed., *Voices from the Fringe: An ANA Anthology of New Nigerian Poetry* (Lagos: Malthouse Press, 1988).
2. I refer specifically to texts like Niyi Osundare's *The Eye of the Earth* (Ibadan: Heinemann, 1986); *Waiting Laughters* (Lagos: Malthouse Press, 1990); Odia Ofeimun's *A Handle for the Flutist* (Lagos: Update Communications, 1986); Ezenwa-Ohaeto's *Songs of a Traveller* (Awka: Towncrier Publications, 1986); Esiabi Irobi, *Cotyledons* (Lagos: Update Communications, 1988); Funso Aiyejina's *A Letter to Lynda and Other Poems* (Port Harcourt: Saros International Publishers, 1988); Afam Akeh, *Stolen Moments* (Lagos: Update Communications, 1988); Kemi Ataada-Ilorin, *Amnesty* (Lagos: Update Communications, 1988); Molara Ogundipe-Leslie, *Sew the Old Days and other Poems* (Ibadan: Evans Brothers, 1985), and many others.
3. J.O.J. Nwachukwu-Agbada, 'Post-War Nigeria and the Poetry of Anger', *Wasafiri* 12 (Autumn, 1990): 3.
4. Tanure Ojaide, *Labyrinths of the Delta* (New York: The Greenfield Review Press, 1986). All page references in the essay are to this text.
5. Okinba Launko is the pen-name for Femi Osofisan; see his *Minted Coins* (Ibadan: Heinemann, 1987).
6. Donatus Nwoga, ed., *Rhythms of Creation: A Decade of Okike Poetry Selected and Introduced by D.I. Nwoga* (Enugu: Fourth Dimension Publishers, 1985): *xxxv*.
7. Christopher Okigbo, *Labyrinths* (London: Heinemann, 1971).
8. Wole Soyinka, *Idanre and Other Poems* (London: Methuen, 1967).
9. See Wole Soyinka, ed., *Poems of Black Africa* (London: Heinemann, 1975): 43–4 for Clark's heavily anthologized piece and Gabriel Okara, *The Fisherman's Invocation* (Benin: Ethiope Publishing Corporation, 1978): 16–17.
10. Donatus I. Nwoga, 'Obscurity and Commitment in Modern African Poetry', *African Literature Today* 6 (1973): 29.
11. Wole Soyinka, *Art, Dialogue and Outrage: (Essays on Literature and Culture)* (Ibadan: New Horn Press, 1988): 87.
12. I borrow this phrase from *Art, Dialogue and Outrage*: 87.
13. All but the last of Ojaide's books of poetry are available from Malthouse Press, Lagos.
14. See Stewart Brown's review in *Wasafiri* 14 (Autumn, 1991): 43.

Lore & Other in Niyi Osundare's Poetry

J.O.J. Nwachukwu-Agbada

For a writer to merit a mention in literary history there are a number of criteria he/she must meet. One is his/her position in the tradition; another is the uniqueness of his/her artistic virtues; and yet another is the configuration of emphases to which his/her *oeuvre* is regularly returning. Niyi Osundare seemed to have been aware of these literary dictates before he set to work. To be sure, in each of his poems so far, his artistic anchor seems to be a recourse to lore, particularly the lore of his Yoruba people and a diagnosis of the social conditions of the ordinary person in society. Before his generation, poetry in Nigeria was essentially privatist; even though much of it recorded public issues, it was rendered in personalist terms with the aim of excluding the majority of its potential audience and cultivating a small coterie of connoisseurs (Chinweizu *et al.*; Osundare, 'A Distant Call'; Aiye-jina, 'Recent Nigerian Poetry'; Nwachukwu-Agbada, 'Matter and Form'). Niyi Osundare is not just a pioneer of the age who has sought to counter the trend in Nigerian poetry, he is probably the most prolific and consistent in his use of folk resources and the examination of the lives of ordinary people.

A proof of his awareness of his direction from the outset is to be found in two of his poems, 'The Poet' and 'Poetry Is'. As artistic manifestos, they are a deliberate contradiction of the school of poetry which insists that 'a poem must be "pure" and never "soiled" with "thought" (Knickerbocker and Reninger, p. 224). An examination of the poetry of the major Nigerian poets before Osundare shows that they were not averse to the thinking of this school. The dogmatic position of this poetic movement in Europe is encapsulated in Laurence Lerner's famous poem entitled, 'This Poem' in which poetry is said to be a 'mask' meant to conceal the poet's thought. A poem in Lerner's consideration is not supposed to reflect reality because it is essentially a 'fiction' which 'disfigures' and 'distorts' (pp. 105–6). In other words, poetry is neither a cognitive object nor a didactic medium outside of itself. According to Wilbur Scott, poets and critics of this persuasion 'shun all material such as the personal or social conditions behind the composition, the moral implications ... so long as these are "extrinsic" – that is tangential to an understanding of the poem' (p. 181). Lerner was of course articulating in verse the view of a poetic stance pioneered by Wordsworth, Coleridge, Keats, Shelley, Mill etc. and brought to its peak by such modernist poets as Hopkins, Lorca, Mallarmé, Cowley, Tagore, Pound, Eliot and Thomas.

In Osundare's 'The Poet' (*A Nib*, pp. 9–10), poetry must be infused with social consciousness. Here the poet 'is not a gadfly' who can afford urbane disinterestedness when 'urgent' social issues need to be commented upon. In other words, the poet cannot remain aloof, 'refine himself out of existence, paring his finger-nails' like a Joycean god when all over the place there are 'soiled streets' calling for 'collective action'. This position locates Osundare's poetry in the socialist realm. The socialist artist by orientation does not believe in 'the "magic" qualities of art works and the unique features of the artist's mind' (Caudwell, p. 127). Rather he believes that an artist must proffer a specific social and cultural philosophy 'towards the field of action'. The poet ought not be a 'prophet' or 'God's hollow ventriloquist' who remains superior to others on account of his possession of the so-called special innate traits. Osundare's 'The Poet' argues that since 'the poet's eyes are washed in the common spring' he must therefore serve as a social activist and salvage society from its own decadence. The belief is that,

> Literature is a social institution, using as its medium language, a social creation. Such traditional literary devices as symbolism and metre are social in their very nature.... The poet himself is a member of society, possessed of a specific social status: he receives some degree of social recognition and reward; he addresses an audience, however hypothetical ... (Wellek and Warren, p. 94)

Anybody reading Osundare's 'The Poet' or his 'Poetry Is' against Laurence Lerner's articulation of the 'purist' school in 'This Poem' may conclude that the former is not bothered by form. But in an interview with Sanya Oni, Osundare dismisses any misconceptions as to his notion of art: 'One is not asking for a simplistic kind of art, but for art that is accessible, relevant and beautiful' (p. 7). The truth is that in spite of the ideological intent of socialist art, an attention to form is equally important. Leon Trotsky, one of the Leninist faithfuls in socialist Russia in the 1920s, is known to have taken Mayakovsky to task over his *oeuvre* which the former says have 'no peaks, they are not disciplined internally. The parts refuse to obey the whole. Each part tries to be separate' (p. 152). However, in articulating the social conditions of the underprivileged in the historical development of the Nigerian society, Osundare has chosen to work within the oral tradition to which poetry is no stranger. He achieves two things by this choice: he convinces us that he is a cultural nationalist, what with his employment of the oral technique which is in fact an enduring African contribution to literary stylistics; secondly, he symbolizes his declared empathy for the condition of the ordinary man in the street by returning to a thought and speech pattern to which this class may easily respond.

I It was William Bascom who had sought to distinguish between verbal art and literature by his observation that 'verbal art is composed and transmitted verbally, while literature is composed in writing and transmitted in writing.' However, he never failed to have the two linked up when he said:

> Yet it is obvious that these two traditions have not followed independent courses, but have intermingled and influenced one another. One result has been reworked tales, proverbs or other forms of verbal art which have reworked and adapted to literary standards of style and propriety, and thereafter transmitted by writing or printing. (p. 249)

Niyi Osundare is one such writer who has not only reworked folklore but has also deployed folk items[1] for the purposes of enhancing his writing and projecting his ideological predisposition. It is clear from his revelatory preface to *The Eye of the Earth* (1986) that he is able to unite orality and writing because of his rich cultural background, he being 'farmer-born, peasant-bred', and having 'encountered dawn in the enchanted corridors of the forest, suckled on the delicate aroma of healing herbs, and the pearly drops of generous moons' (p. ix). Any wonder then that the titles of his collections either bear out his love for lore (*Songs of the Marketplace, Village Voices* and *Moonsongs*) or indicate at once that advocacy would be an essential element in his verse (*A Nib in the Pond, The Eye of the Earth, Waiting Laughters* and *Songs of the Season*).

In his 'Poetry Is', a poem we have described as one of his artistic manifestos, the very first line takes us to the associativeness of a folkloristic heritage, particularly when it objects to 'esoteric whisper/of an excluding tongue'. For him, poetry is not 'a learned quiz/entombed in Grecoroman lore'; instead it is the 'eloquence of the gong/the lyric of the marketplace' (*Marketplace*, p. 3). The 'lyric of the marketplace' subsumes musicality and collectivity because a marketplace in folk history is a gathering point, the heart of the village; the spirits of selling and buying come together here. In his important poems, lore and one human predicament or the other are brought together with an artistry that makes his work very memorable. In 'Excursions' (*Marketplace*, p. 7), the sundry commentator is either a folk or a folk sympathizer because of the manner in which he cultivates our emotion in favour of the ordinary person:

> in city fringes pregnant women
> rummage garbage heaps for
> the rotting remnants of city tables
> above, hawks and cultures hovering
> for their turn (p. 8)

His most touching line in 'Excursions' is where he calls attention to 'the family head' who 'roams the bush/trapping rats and insects'. This is a picture of poverty and underutilization of one's energy. The trapping of rats and insects is a folk chore meant for children in the villages, but when an adult engages in such an activity he is either mentally underdeveloped or abjectly improvident. Because the folks constitute the 'other' in his poetic vintage, Osundare is always reflecting their sordid lives in terms which either bespeak of their wretchedness and helplessness or their ignorance.

In 'Reflections' (p. 37), he objects to the way the world is socially structured and likens it to 'the Solel Boneh's steam-shovel' because 'it scoops earth from one place/To fill up the hole in another' (p. 38). What the rich gain is the loss of the poor; poverty is the aftermath of someone else's affluence. Often Osundare's metaphor for the poor is sheep, while wolf is his idea of the rich who savour the helpless in order to survive doubly. In 'Ignorance' (p. 33), he asks, 'how could sheep all agree/to give their crown to a wolf?' (p. 34). This is a side-step to the 'animal' story in which the wolf seeks the cooperation of the very creatures it regularly feeds upon. In 'To the Dinosaur' (p. 41), a folkloric, prehistorical animal is employed as a metaphor for the African tyrant's emptiness; the metaphor is a sarcastic reference to African rulers who adopt ancient, undemocratic postures in order to retain their places for life. One of their strategies is to dispose 'two million/ skeletons to purchase a gilded skull' (p. 41). This issue of sheep ignorantly ministering unto the wolf is re-echoed here

> . . .
> Knowing neither
> You have torn down the gate
> and asked wolves to tend your sheep (p. 41)

The 'leopards', the whites, take over the places of wolves in 'Namibia Talks' (p. 49) but the sheep remain Africa and Africans. The poet-persona chides fellow Africans:

> For so long we mistrusted our sheep
> to the care of leopards
> we have woken to the whitened skeleton
> of talkative folly (p. 50)

Osundare, a folk commentator, utilizes diachronic terms and divests them of their archaic denotation. Words and clichés which ordinarily would have been regarded as worn-out are refurbished for the sole purpose of creating original humour. Name-calling and term-twisting as we know are very common in folk life. The *oriki* singers in Yoruba culture invest beauty on their composition through action-imagery, alliteration, pitching and morphological innovations. A few examples of his neologism will suffice.

Let us begin with what he has done with the word 'archaic'. In more poems than one he has shown his aversion for stilted academicism because it is pretentious. Those who are guilty of this belong to the 'archaidemia' (*Marketplace*, p. 27). Other nonce words of his include, 'kwashiorkored children' (*Marketplace*, p. 3) for malnourished children; 'mercedesed Pharoahs' (*A Nib*, p. 15) for important people in Mercedes cars; 'kiwi-ed boot' (*Moonsongs*, p. 32) for boots polished with kiwi polish; 'darkdom' for kingdom (*The Eye*, p. 25); 'executhieves' (*The Eye*, p. 46) for people in executive positions who steal from government coffers; and 'kolatera' (*Village Voices*, p. 50) for collateral (but the poet here plays on 'kola', the Nigerian euphemism for bribe). Others are word distortion and inversion. These are copious in *A Nib*: 'comrades or comeraids/trail-blazers or blaze-trailers' (p. 21); 'from democracy to demoncrazy/from conscience to con-science' (p. 21); 'allies or all lies/adultery or adult tree/message or mess age' (p. 21); 'suffrage or suffer age' (p. 22); 'of statesmen and statemen'.

Osundare copiously uses metaphors and images that point to the past for purposes of making a contemporary statement on various issues which affect the lives of the ordinary person. In

'The Horseman Cometh' (*Marketplace*, p. 45), the horseman is the military tyrant who 'will build arsenals/in place of barns/and prod the poor/to gorge on bullets'. Apart from 'horseman', a term which takes our minds to antiquity, the word 'cometh' is on its own an archaic item. However, in the employment of these words, the poet is playing with the synecdoche of modern African anachronism when unelected individuals snatch power by force:

> A horseman gallops to power
> and tyrants of all the world rejoice
> torture chambers multiply apace
> and the noose thickens, descending (p. 45)

His references to sword in 'Killing without a Sword' (*Village Voices*, p. 13), 'The Land of Unease' (*Village Voices*, p. 45), 'The Rocks Rose to Meet Me' (*The Eye*, p. 14) or the words closely associated with the sword such as 'scalpel', 'knife', 'matchet', 'mattock' etc. are his metaphors for mindless eating. It is 'mindless eating' which leads to the request for 'a fruit deliciously beyond our reach' in 'Killing without a Sword'. In 'The Land of Unease', the persona castigates men that 'forge unequal knives/... with machetes greedier/than Esimuda's sword'. These are men who want to have everything to themselves. They are the prodigal in 'Eating Tomorrow's Yam' (Village Voices, p. 16) who 'calls for a knife' when 'there is only one yam left/in the village barn'. The point here is that the word 'sword' and associated words take us to the time of gladiators who amused by being reckless.

The aura of lore which suffuses Osundare's poetry is justified by his decision from the outset to explore the pool of communal memories. His stance as the conscience of the folk after all accords well with the role of the artist of old whose bounden duty it was to 'wear courage like a shield/telling kings their fart/chokes the village nose' (*Village Voices*, p. 1). The 'other' in whose favour he has chosen to resolve his art is the folk whose concept of the earth is gradually being distorted by 'executhieves'. In *The Eye of the Earth*, for instance, the autobiography is collective rather than private. According to Funso Aiyejina, 'the animistic energy with which the volume is charged does not originate from the poet as an individual but rather as the sensitive heir to, and interpreter of a complex tradition and a collective philosophy' ('To Plough', p. 2106).

In performing this role, Osundare chooses to be a griot, but a modern one. Unlike the griots of old who

> ... conserved the constitutions of kingdoms by memory work alone; each princely family had its griots appointed to preserve tradition. (Niane, p. *vii*)

Osundare would like that which is worthy such as the earth's ecology to be conserved and our capitalist tradition which is retrogressive to be done away with. In 'Forest Echoes', the persona recalls the time when,

Bouncing boughs interlock overhead
like wristwrestlers straining muscularly
on a canvas of leaves wounded
by the fists of time (*The Eye*, p. 3)

The poet chooses a journey motif very common in folktales. The trip is towards the forest comparable to that undertaken by D.O. Fagunwa's hero in *The Forest of a Thousand Daemons* or Amos Tutuola's *Palm-wine Drinkard*. The poet's allusion to Fagunwa's protagonist's journey in,

Here they are
midget and monster still
. . .
A forest of a million trees, this,
a forest of milling trees (p. 5)

is revealing. In 'The Rocks Rose to Meet Me', the Romantic picture of a communion with the elements is complete. Here the Rocks – Olosunta and Oroole – are personified: 'Olosunta spoke first/the riddling one whose belly is wrestling ground/for god and gold' (p. 13). After Olosunta, spoke Oroole: 'Oroole came next/his ancient voice tremulous in the morning air' (p. 15). We may interpret this interlocution between man and the rocks at the metaphorical level to mean a reading of their history and the process of disintegration they might have experienced as a result of the 'plundering' to which they had been exposed over the years, yet in folklore, animate/inanimate communication is realistic. The desolation which has visited the forest in recent times is due to the impact of capitalistic exploitation of resources and the nuclear experimentation which have tended to undermine the original status of the earth:

a lake is killed by the arsenic urine
from the bladder of profit factories
a poisoned stream staggers down the hills
coughing chaos in the sickly sea
the wailing whale, belly up like a frying fish
crests the chilling swansong of parting waters. (p. 50)

Like a typical traditional bard, Osundare employs forms of folklore in varying proportions. Apart from the songs (*orin*) which still retain part of their original Yoruba structure, proverbs (*owe*), curses (*epe*), incantations (*ofo*), riddles (*alo apamo*) and myths (*itan*) are largely reworked, and in most cases built in snippets into the lines. In Segment IV of *Moonsongs* he instructs that the poem be read 'to the accompaniment of the song: *Osupa oi yuwa mi o, osupa o, i yeyin mi . . .*' (p. 8). He does not supply the Yoruba song, not even in a glossary. In most of the poems the musical instruments to be used are suggested: omele, gbedu, ibembe, bata, adan, agba, ogbele, woro, reso, gangan (all types of drums), gong, shekere, the flute etc. are recommended for various poems. Outside the songs, these other folkloric forms are integrated into the poems so that it becomes difficult to draw lines in their usage. For example, *Moonsongs* which flows like an *ijala* verse (Yoruba hunter's incantation) has several stanzas in which bits of these oral forms are incorporated in varying proportions:

> How many hours will make a minute
> How many oceans total one drop
> Of elusive water
> How many forests will make one tree
> In regions of meticulous showers
> How many . . .? (*Moonsongs*, p. 17)

In 'Under the Mango Tree' (*Moonsongs*, pp. 49–50) alliteration, tongue-twisters, punning and word reformulation are easily noticeable in a passage such as this:

> the mortal murmurs of musing mangoes,
> of crude climbers and missiles
> from starving quivers;
> and suddenly, each fruit a toll
> of expiring winds
> each toll a tale
> each tale a tail of coiling snakes
> ah! mangoes man goes. Man (p. 50)

Direct Yoruba terms and expressions in his lines show his fidelity to lore and orality. In all his collections so far Yoruba interjections are quite numerous. Many of these are glossed but there are indications that they might be direct borrowings from local songsters who use them in their various compositions: Expressions such as '*Iya jajeji l'Egbe/Ile eni I'eso ye'ni*' (suffering afflicts the stranger in a strange land/One is most important in one's own home) in *Songs of the Marketplace* (p. 40); '*Ogeere amokoyeri*' (the one that shaves his head with the hoe) in *The Eye of the Earth* (p. 1); '*Ise losupa nse lalede orun, lalede orun/Is losupa nse . . .*

(Busy is the moon in the compound of the sky/busy is the moon) in *Moonsongs* (p. 21). However, some of the words and expressions are apparently used for their musical effect since they are not explained. In *Moonsongs*, there are 'agbamurere' (p. 1), 'kiriji kiriji kiriji pepelupe' (p. 1) and 'Teregungu maja gungun' which the poet in fact says is only a 'rhythmic refrain, it has no meaning' (p. 44).

II The other major prong of his poetry is the 'other', referring to the social condition of the African and Nigerian citizenry. In his assessment of Osundare, Biodun Jeyifo has remarked that,

> In all of modern African poetry, all, I repeat, only in the poetry of Agostinho Neto and David Diop will you find the same depth and passion and lyricism in solidarity with the oppressed, the down-trodden, the dispossessed, and a corresponding faith in their aspiration and will to revolutionary change as we confront in Osundare's poetry. The dispossession of the majority of our people, and more specifically of the rural producers, may, in fact, be said to be the grand theme of Osundare's poetry. (pp. 317–18)

The tendency on his part to let the burdens of the ordinary man take over the prop of his poetic vintage is justified in 'The Poet' in which he projects the view that,

> The poet's pen is
> the cactus by the stream
> (shorn of its forbidding thorns)
> each stem a rib
> towards the field of action
> its sap the ink of succour
> when doubt's drought
> assaults the wall (*A Nib*, p. 10)

The implication of the above poetic programme of action is that the poet believes in a poetic mediation whose content is ideological, whose resolution favours civic causes.

To be able to perform this crucial function for the ordinary citizen, Osundare's poetic stance is modelled on the town-crier. Fortunately this stance is not far from a griot's with which we have also associated him. In the words of Griot Mamadou Kouyate, griots 'are vessels of speech ... the memory of mankind' (Niane, I). But Osundare's town-crier is in addition the consciename. This is perhaps one obvious example of his debt to the late Christopher Okigbo who called himself 'town-crier with my iron bell'. In 'I Wake Up This Morning', Osundare's persona says:

I have borrowed the earful clamour
of the towncrier
gained the unkillable clarion
of the gong
. . .
when I sing ears shall bend my way (*Village Voices*, I)

Having adopted this posture, the poet-protagonist is then able to call attention to the contradictions in society to which the common man is easily a victim. One of these contradictions is the disadvantage which the ordinary person suffers as a result of his position in the social and economic relations network. Often his means of existence is threatened as the poet observes in 'Eating with all the Fingers' because whereas members of the privileged class in society can afford to 'eat with all the fingers', the poor are not usually so lucky. The poet-persona, having deployed himself as the spokesman of the people, intones:

we will raise our voices
and tell the world
we will not be watchers
of others eating (*Village Voices*, p. 15)

This position is restated in 'Unequal Fingers' in which the speaker says,

Let no-one tell us again
that fingers are not equal
for we know
how the thumb grew fatter
than all the others (*Village Voices*, p. 60)

Poems such as 'The New Farmer's Bank', 'A Farmer on Seeing Cocoa House, Ibadan', 'The Eunuch's Child', 'A Villager's Protest', 'The Politician's Two Mouths', 'Akintunde, Come Home', 'Chicken Story' are the voicing of these issues which daily agitate the minds of peasants. 'The New Farmer's Bank' (*Village Voices*, p. 50) is a satirical thrust at the contradiction in establishing agricultural credit banks all over the country to which the grassroots farmers have little or no access:

Then go till your land
with closed fists
how can you borrow government money
without *Kolatera*

'A Villager's Protest' and 'The Politician's Two Mouths' are swipes at the politician who would make promises upon promises

before election time only to fool the villagers who voted him into
office. The truth is that if,

> A politician tells you to wait
> and you heed his words
> ah! friend
> your sole will tell you
> the biting pains of folly (*Village Voices*, p. 57)

Rather than fulfil his promises, the politician will seek his own
pleasure. Listen to 'A Villager's Protest':

> Now in
> and promises forgotten
> fat cars, juicy damsels
> and the best there is (*Village Voices*, p. 48)

'Excursions' (*Marketplace*, pp. 7–15) is a searing indictment of
society for structures which ensure that the poor are perpetually
held to their miserable places. All over the land, poverty,
ignorance, want and disguised slavery are evident:

> halfnude, toughbiceped labourers
> troop in tipperfuls from sweatfields
> drilled by foremen soulless like
> a slavemaster, a few kobo greet
> the miserly homecoming
> of a pilgrimage of misery (p. 8)

Even in the churches, the oppression of the poor goes on through
deceit and cant:

> between belches the plump preacher
> extols the virtue of want,
> the only ticket to the wealth beyond (p. 9)

And in the markets, greedy businessmen, now overnight million-
aires, are making their money simply by being

> exporters
> importers
> emergency contractors
> manufacturers' representatives
> buying cheap
> selling dear (p. 15)

'Sule Chase' (*Marketplace*, pp. 16–18) equally indicts society
for its tendency to react to social symptoms rather than cast
a lingering look at their causes. Sule who is chased even by

dishonest and unpatriotic members of the various strata of society on account of his pilferage of a piece of bread is no more than a victim of a heartless capitalist orientation. Yet, unlike Sule, his chasers are guilty of even more heinous crimes against society:

> The race gathers more legs
> In every lane
> Tailors with giant scissors
> Permsecs with PENDING files
> Barristers with fused bulbs
> Telephonists in dead head-sets
> The doctor with his chair aloft ... (p. 16)

Even those who merely hear Sule has stolen join in the chase without actually knowing what he stole until they stone him to death and behold 'they arrest Sule's corpse/His left hand clutching/ A rumpled three kobo loaf' (p. 18).

Osundare's town-crier model is further advanced in *The Eye* and *Moonsongs*. To begin with the social issues in each are fused and continuous, story-like in fact. And secondly in each case one voice is heard throughout. In *The Eye*, the poet is still concerned with the plight of the people, but this time his concept of people is global. Here he is no longer addressing the local chieftains running their country like a personal estate, but all those in influential places world-wide whose duty it is to ensure that 'our earth ... neither wastes nor wants'. The earth is described as the 'breadbasket/and compost bed/rocks and rivers/muds and mountains'. The entire collection calls attention to the dwindling state of forests, rocks and rain resulting from the bizarre approach of the earth's inhabitants to the survival of plant and animal life. The volume is also a surreptitious ideological banter on capitalists and multinationals, scattered in different parts of the world, busy plundering rather than ploughing the earth. In 'Ours to Plough, Not to Plunder', the poet beckons the inmates of the earth to 'let gold rush from her deep unseeable mines/hitch up a ladder to the dodging sky/let's put a sun in every night' (p. 48).

The central symbol in *Moonsongs* is the moon; like 'the eye' in *The Eye* the moon is here a watchman, an observer, the one who oversees the earth. The moon is 'the eye of the sky', the 'hourglass', the 'serenade of the storm', the 'lymph of the lore', the 'historian's if' (pp. 24–5). It is the harbinger of new seasons and the signal of the passage of years. It is also a mask through which the poet is able to make sundry statements about the joys and chaos of the seasons, about night and day, sea and sky, the poor and the prosperous. The intention of the poet is civic since all these things affect the ordinary person. The most transparent and

graphic of the poems in *Moonsongs* are those addressing the fate
of the other person, the underprivileged. An example will suffice.
In Segment XXII, the poet contrasts the experience of the moon
in Ikoyi with what is observed in Ajegunle, both parts of Nigeria's
Lagos now metaphors for affluence and squalor respectively.
In Ikoyi, 'the moon . . . is a laundered lawn/its grass the softness
of infant fluff' whereas in Ajegunle 'the moon/is a jungle/sad
like a forgotten beard/with tensioned climbers' (p. 42). By this
comparison, the poet is able to strike our ire and win our sympathy
for the misery of a large section of the world's populace.

III Niyi Osundare is not only the most prolific of Nigeria's
post-Civil War poets, he is the most consistent in the
manner in which he employs folkways to advance public advocacy. Often the pose of his persona is folkloric, rather quixotic
and prattling, relying so much on the oral stylistic technique and
morphological inventiveness, two crucial elements in folk speech
and drama. Since his first collection of poems was published in
1983, the quality of poetic mediation in his *oeuvre* has continued
to improve. *The Eye of the Earth*, his fourth volume, epitomizes
the success of his poetic career because here content and form
are conjoint; here too he shows that accessible language need
not lead to doggerel. However, in *Moonsongs* the symmetry of
scope of concern and artistic language is awfully absent;[2] the
poet who had in his various pronouncements denounced the
recondite language of pre-Civil War Nigerian poetry here allows
his language to tilt upwards with the result that whereas he
employs various dimensions of lore and discusses the fate of the
people as in the other collections, his linguistic medium is more
complex, more obscure as he piles images, metaphors and symbols
which ordinarily have little associations.[3] Be that as it may,
Osundare will remain an unforgettable member of the post-war
Nigerian revolutionary poetic vanguard who daily carve anguish
out of the simple words our elders taught us.

NOTES

1. Alan Dundes considers as folklore all the activities of the folk, written
   and unwritten. See his 'What is Folklore?' in *The Study of Folklore*,
   ed. Alan Dundes (New Jersey: Prentice-Hall, 1965): 1–3.
2. Chinyere Nwahunanya has said so too. In a paper he presented at the
   1989 Modern Language Association of Nigeria Conference held at the
   University of Nigeria Nsukka entitled, 'Osundare's New Esotericism:
   The Genesis of Poetic Disintegration', Nwahunanya warned that if the
   new trend of obscurity continued in his poetry, 'Osundare would be

cultivating the same problems which made the troika (Chinweizu *et al.*) scream at the Okigbos, the Soyinkas and their ilk. Most importantly, instead of leading to poetic growth, it would result in an obscurantism that would mark the beginning of his distintegration as a poet.' (p. 12).

3. During a chat with Niyi Osundare in his office on 29 January 1990 he freely accepted that *Moonsongs* was largely obscure, but attributed it to the pains he suffered from the multiple head injuries he received in 1986 from a robbery attack which took place right on the University of Ibadan campus. According to him, the poems were written on the hospital bed against the advice of his doctor. Luckily, his post *Moonsongs* collections – *Songs of the Season* (Ibadan: Heinemann, 1990) and *Waiting Laughters* (Lagos: Malthouse, 1991) – belong to the mainstream of the Osundare tenor.

WORKS CITED

Aiyejina, F. 'Recent Nigerian Poetry in English: An Alternative Tradition.' In *Perspectives on Nigerian Literature: 1700 to the Present*, Vol. I. Ed. Yemi Ogunbiyi. Lagos: Guardian Books, 1988.

—. 'To Plough, not to Plunder.' A review of *The Eye of the Earth* in *West Africa* (London) 6 October 1986.

Bascom, W.R. 'Verbal Art.' *Journal of American Folklore* 68 (1955).

Caudwell, C. *Illusion and Reality*. London: Lawrence and Wishart, 1977 (1937).

Chinweizu, Onwuchekwa Jemie and Ihechukwu Madubuike. *Toward the Decolonization of African Literature*. Enugu: Fourth Dimension Publishers, 1980.

Jeyifo, B. 'Niyi Osundare.' In *Perspectives on Nigerian Literature: 1700 to the Present* Vol. 2. Ed. Yemi Ogunbiyi. Lagos: Guardian Books, 1988.

Knickerbocker, K.I. and Reninger, H.W. *Interpreting Literature: Preliminaries to Literary Judgement*. New York: Holt, Rinehart and Winston, 1979 (1955).

Lerner, L. 'This Poem.' In *New Lines II: An Anthology*. Ed. Robert Conquest. London: Macmillan, 1963.

Niane, D.T. *Sundiata: An Epic of Old Mali*. Trans. G.D. Pickett. London: Longman, 1965 (1960).

Nwachukwu-Agbada, J.O.J. 'Matter and Form in Post-War Nigerian Poetry (1970–1985).' MA Dissertation, University of Ibadan, 1986.

Oni, S. 'Osundare, Poet of the Marketplace.' *National Concord*, 24 June 1988.

Osundare, N. 'A Distant Call.' *West Africa* (London) 4 November 1985.

—. *A Nib in the Pond*. Ife: Ife Monograph Series, 1986.

—. *Moonsongs*. Ibadan: Spectrum, 1988.

—. *Songs of the Marketplace*. Ibadan: New Horn Press, 1983.

—. *The Eye of the Earth*. Ibadan: Heinemann, 1986.

—. *Village Voices*. Ibadan: Evans Brothers, 1984.

Scott, W. *Five Approaches to Literary Criticism*. New York: Collier Macmillan Publishers, 1962.

Trotsky, L.D. *Literature and Revolutions*. Ann Arbor: University of Michigan, 1960.

Wellek, R. and Warren, A. *Theory of Literature*. Harmondsworth: Penguin Books, 1973 (1949).

Conscious Craft: Verbal Irony in the Poetry of Jared Angira

Ezenwa-Ohaeto*

The achievement of Jared Angira, one of the most exciting poets in Africa, lies in his utilization of irony to explore the social realities of his country, Kenya. In his five collections of poetry: *Juices* (1970), *Silent Voices* (1972), *Soft Corals* (1973), *Cascades* (1979) and *The Years Go By* (1980), he uses verbal irony to deepen insight and make his poetry intellectually satisfying.

It is in the conscious use of irony that Angira is distinct from other East African poets. While Okot p'Bitek uses a single persona in each of his poetry collections, Angira uses varied ironic characters in his poems. Richard Ntiru also uses irony in some of his poems but not as pervasively or effectively as Angira. Compared with Okello Oculi, Angira's scope is wider and deeper.

Critics of Angira's poetry, Adrian Roscoe, Angus Calder and Yesufu, have stressed the fact that he successfully enlarges the reader's consciousness but have not examined his artistic use of irony. Adrian Roscoe agrees that 'good clear imagery, a gift for compression, lyrical delicacy' (Roscoe, p. 94) are among Angira's achievements while Calder calls him an 'alert, witty writer' (Calder, 1979, p. 37) and Abdul Yesufu sees his poetry as 'an acutely ideologized' body of works (Yesufu, 1984, p. 327). The purpose of this study is therefore to discuss the use of verbal irony as a conscious device in Angira's five collections and illustrate how he uses this device to highlight the deficiences in his society.

Verbal irony features as his artistic epitome for it contributes immensely towards the enhancement of his vision in the portrayal of social realities. The association of verbal irony with the presentation of these social realities requires a two-dimensional

*The author acknowledges the assistance of the Humbolt Foundation, Bonn, Germany.

approach from the reader, for verbal irony 'is a statement in which the implicit meaning intended by the speaker differs from that which he ostensibly asserts' (Abrams, p. 89). Abrams furthermore explains that 'such an ironic statement usually involves the explicit expression of one attitude or evaluation but with the implication of a very different attitude or evaluation' (p. 89). It is this implication of another level of evaluation which makes verbal irony require an intellectual response towards its appreciation. A poet like Angira who makes use of this kind of irony, is thus expected to place the written words of the poem in such a way as to eliminate doubts concerning the implicit meaning which differs from the asserted meaning, because printed words cannot easily exhibit the tone of voice which could make verbal irony conspicuous.

Despite this limitation, Angira fashions his poetry with utmost care through an adherence to social reality and a poetic analysis of that reality which is imbued with profundity of thought. Moreover, as a modern poet who is aware of the human differences between individuals and the consequences of those differences pertaining to opinions and issues, he functions as what Okechukwu Mezu regards as the 'neo-African poet', who 'sees people as living entities and not as helpless toys caught up in a tumultuous cultural swirl' (Killam, 1973, p. 105). This recognition of the individuality of man is an essential step towards the understanding of the peculiar tribulations, regrets, hopes and fears of each human being. It is equally possible for this understanding to aid the onerous task of identification and rectification of the deviances in norms and mores as the poet portrays in 'The Hero' (*Juices*, p. 14).

The poem is made not only profound but also relevant through the expression that incorporates the verbal irony which is – 'I am the trouncing hero.' This expression appears innocuous but when the nature of heroism is considered, the implication of that assertion in the context of the poem becomes significant. A hero is a person respected for bravery or noble qualities and a trouncing hero means that the person is respected for either beating, thrashing, defeating or reprimanding somebody or people. However, the poem does not portray a 'hero' who shows bravery in the elimination of vices, rectification of the social lapses or outstanding achievements that have changed the society positively. The falsity of the persona's insistence that he is the 'world's trouncing hero' is made pathetic through the adroit use of verbal irony in the subsequent stanzas. Thus when the 'hero' declares with glee:

I am the trouncing hero
Whose success at failures is unrivalled
Whose abortive attempts in life's span are
unsurpassed

he is revealed as quite unheroic. Heroism is generated by outstanding achievements which are usually allowed to pass through
the sieve of time, or repeatedly demonstrated as an enduring
trait. The 'hero' is neither distinguished through bravery for he
is noted for 'success at failures' nor is he identified through
noble qualities. The self proclaimed hero fails in almost all his
enterprises and what he regards as achievement is trivial and
irrelevant:

I have countless scores on my name
towards the goal of meaninglessness
and in the net of standstill. (*Juices*, p. 14)

The society emerges as confused and insincere, glorifying trivial-
ities. Thus the poet, by his use of irony, sensitizes the reader to
this insincerity and lack of awareness in order to reverse these
trends.

Similar social defects are treated in 'On Market Day at
Ugunja' where Angira's artistry justifies the view that 'verbal
irony implies an ironist, someone consciously and intentionally
employing a technique' (Muecke, 1969, p. 42). Angira employs
this technique in the juxtaposition of a market scene and the
paraphernalia of war under a fig tree. The irony suggested by
incompatibility of the juxtaposition of the implements of war
beside a bustling market is reinforced and clarified in the last
stanza:

It may be peacetime we know
but under the fig tree
are clubs and shields
ropes for our bulls
axes and jembes for our farms
and all for
nationbuilding. (*Juices*, p. 21)

The reference to peacetime may not betray the poet's real motive
but when he catalogues all the weapons under the fig tree, it
becomes clear that they are not items for nationbuilding. The
clubs and shields are obviously implements of war. The ropes
which could be used to tie the bulls have other uses, just as the
axes could be used on the farms and also for destroying homes.
The poet is not just listing these items unnecessarily for when he

insists that they are all for 'nationbuilding' irony implies that the people are interested in destruction. Angira is saying that weapons of war cannot be used to enforce peace and that patriots involved in nationbuilding should be devoted to the creation of a conducive environment that would enable the production of abundant agricultural products for sale in the market at Ugunja. The juxtaposition of the contradictory positive tendencies exhibited through the attractive goods in the market and the negative tendency in the devotion to irrelevant destructive wars is enhanced by the verbal irony which gives prominence to the poet's disapproval of all human acts that could lead to disaster.

In 'Fanfare at the Devil's Playground', the poet depicts his longing for a sane society in which the dynamics of organization are geared towards general improvement. However, this longing makes the undesirable reality abhorrent. The verbal irony is used to open the poem with the injunction:

> Sit in peace
> Sit in peace.

The demand that the people should sit in peace is negated by the itemization of factors which make peace impossible: 'the flies are my flies' and 'the mosquitoes are my mosquitoes'. The implication is that the filthy physical environment breeds numerous flies and mosquitoes which, however, are only minor irritants compared with those of the filthy social environment which would tax the capacity of even a saint to sit in peace:

> I am the city itself
>   where eyeballs roll
> Floating
>   On the muddy pool
> I am where swarms
>   of jobless flock
> The labour compound
>   where they compound
> Their labour unrest (*Cascades*, p. 80)

Joblessness, the result of an inequitable distribution of resources – and the jobless are in 'swarms' – may not by itself pose a danger to peace. It is the juxtaposition of the wretched poverty of the unemployed with the affluence of the opulent which amplifies the danger and makes the irony much more effective:

> We are rally drivers
>   Driving sleek Lancias,

Swift Ferraris
Durable Alpines (*Cascades*, p. 81)

These luxurious and expensive cars dramatize the fact that the poverty of the people is due to the endemic exploitation in the society. These realities of social life make it impossible for the individual to 'sit in peace' thereby illustrating that the poet is not really insisting on peace but insisting on social transformation that would rectify the economic discrepancies.

Jared Angira also shifts his focus to the people in their respective families in order to highlight how humanity is constantly disorganized and changed through the in-built mechanisms for creating confusion. The verbal irony in 'Your Homecoming' is not the fact that the individual has lived for a considerable time away from home but that the education he acquires is not constructively helpful. The persona thus laments: 'everytime you come/I see you less of us/and more of a guest', and also: 'this homecoming was odd/you still dream/of reading more books.' However, the persona is not against knowledge acquired from books. He is rather against the fact that this knowledge creates ignorance and it is that ignorance which is at the core of the verbal irony. This is why the poem conveys with sarcasm the ironic demand:

then read all the books of the world
one day you'll find
the length of the night
the fur of the sheep
one day you'll find
thunder's dwellings (*Juices*, p. 49)

The scholarship is a façade; the knowledge acquired, futile; all he has discovered is 'the length of the night'. Finding 'the fur of the sheep' – what he had wasted time searching for in books – had been common knowledge in traditional wisdom. However, the comment that 'one day you'll find/thunder's dwelling', projects the destructiveness of this kind of knowledge which is capable of destroying the searcher. In effect, Jared Angira shows through the irony here that knowledge must be directed towards a refinement of the society. The depth of the telescopic insight which he conveys within such a short space and with the use of few words further substantiates his awareness and perception of reality through irony.

Human behaviour equally provides Angira with copious material to examine and assess the attitudes of his characters to the realities of life. It is not surprising that the poet records instances of social deviations that arise from a negative application of knowledge in a society where such an attitude to knowledge is prevalent. These recordings of social misdemeanours are created in such a manner as to justify the observation of a fellow East African poet Okello Oculi who notes that 'a writer from Kenya who does not know the geography, the history, the commercial and general economic conditions (and potential) of Kenya cannot be expected to make a statement about Kenya that is to be taken with seriousness' (Gurr and Calder, 1974, p. 31). Such awareness is seen in 'The Song of the Ugly Woman', where the persona is apparently lamenting her ugliness: 'they say I am ugly as an owl/yet it is my body', '... only yesterday I brought wood for fire/.../only yesterday I brought food' (*Juices*, p. 51). The verbal irony arises from the observation that ugliness is equated with uselessness and the poet shows through the contributions of this woman that the beauty of the skin is superficial and cannot be equated with the beauty or goodness of the soul. Angira is also indicating through this irony that a society which attaches value to the superficial aspects of the person is obviously warped. His stimulation of emotional and intellectual responses in this poem is a way of making graphic his awareness of human feelings.

The exploration of the foibles of man and the degeneration of human feelings further provide material for the examination of human relationships. The poet is clearly troubled that a lack of refinement in human nature could take strange forms all geared towards a debasement of human feelings. In 'Armanda' this debasement is shown through the relationship between her and Ray, a cripple. 'Armanda is a well-meaning lass', which prefaces each stanza, is ironic. The word 'lass' connotes 'sweetheart' which is further sharpened by the adjective 'well-meaning'. But Armanda's actions contradict this idea of true love. She:

> danced the tango quite a lot
> Drank the whisky on the rocks
> smoked Dunhill to the hills
> And drove men off their head
> By her beauty, the beauty of a peahen (*Cascades*, p. 133).

'Peahen' suggests exhibitionism and a hint that Armanda's beauty may be artificial. Her surprising decision to marry the cripple – she 'hated the kitchen' – is revealed as a cynical move. Her explanation that the crutches were the part of Ray that sent her on heat and tickled her most! (*Cascades*, p. 133) is exposed by the cold calculation of her farewell note:

> Goodbye love, goodbye Ray
> I thought I could change it

But I have failed,
And I've flown home ... (*Cascades*, p. 135)

Her conduct is another illustration of the materialism of the society. Armanda's degenerate behaviour is used to recommend the cultivation of a positive way of life in order to create amity and erase rancour and false values in human affairs.

A similar attachment to false values is demonstrated in 'A Child of No World' where the persona who is a black man seeks acceptance in England and America but is rejected as different. The pathos emerges acutely when the persona is also rejected in Africa because he has 'lost much .../No longer one of their one-time son[s]'. The consequent confusion of the persona at this occurrence makes him declare:

I came to nowhere
with sprouting seedlings
And emerging buds
of neo-African culture
So
I stood in the expansive world
A child of no world. (*Juices*, p. 53)

The paradox in the use of 'world' notwithstanding, the irony is that the persona is a child of a world, the black world, which has assimilated the characteristics of the world of other races. The poet portrays through this persona the implication of social confusion; for the persona sought unity in a world that is structured on a foundation of racialism. The poet insists that the persona is the child of a world in which discrimination and social segregation have been built into its structure. Angira is clearly condemning racism here.

He is concerned that the issue of discrimination shown either locally through despising the 'ugly woman' for instance, or internationally through the 'child of no world' has to be eliminated in order to avoid social turmoil. What makes the anomalies in the East African society which Angira explores particularly unfortunate is that this is a society, according to R.N. Egudu 'where the socialist principles of social justice, equal distribution of social amenities and opportunities, and fellow-feeling have been most fervently preached' (Egudu, 1978, p. 142). The absence of fellow-feeling particularly makes it possible for such horrendous deceptions as the ill-treatment of the disabled Ray by the worldly-wise, materialistic Armanda to be practised.

Part of Angira's success in the use of verbal irony is the subtle difference he creates between the meaning and the actual words of the poem; the skillful presentation of the poem in a manner that enables the reader to register the clash between the words and the content. In some poems Angira does not present the verbal irony directly because this type of irony 'usually operates by exploiting deviations from syntactic or semantic norms, and the ability to recognize such irony depends upon an appreciation of the particular linguistic, or sometimes more general social or moral, context' (Fowler, p. 102). The poet makes oblique reference to the issue that informs the verbal irony in 'Decay'. This poem commences with the expression: 'Trees die from their heads', which appears to indicate through a literal interpretation that when the leaves of trees wither, they are dying. This expression is ironical for it is not the withering of the leaves that causes the death of trees but the withering of the roots. A tree in actuality sheds its leaves in a semblance of death during the harmattan season.

However, the attribution of death to the heads of trees becomes clearer when it is seen from the semantics of the poem that the tree is a metaphor for man. It then seems natural to expect men to die 'from their heads' through mental decay. What the poet is thus saying obliquely is that lack of mental exercises, inability to use the brain positively and laziness of the mind are forms of intellectual death. He clarifies this verbal irony when he says that mental decay occurs

> When we resign from thinking
> And resort to collective laziness
> When we cannot remember the present
> Nor conceive of the future
> Since the past is no more.

He is also saying that the mind that is incapable of reasoning is failing to exhibit one of the distinguishing features of the human being. Humanity is, without doubt, ennobled through the quality of thoughts that generate human actions:

> And that past which is gone forever
> Is all we can see
> When reason takes leave
> of our little heads
> What else can it be
> If not withering from the head? (*Soft Corals*, p. 94)

The complexity of this poem arises from its intricate structure because when the poet refers to the tree as dying from the head he is using a metaphor and when he refers to man as 'withering from the head' he is using verbal irony. It is not possible for a living human being to wither or dry up from the head and still remain alive for the head is not like the appendages of arms and legs. When the head withers, the body dies. The poet is therefore showing that the lack of mental activities devoted to a refinement of the society amounts to intellectual death and even incompetence which leads to degeneracy of life and humanity.

In as much as Angira could make complex references in his poems, he is not interested in rhetorical gymnastics and this is why his poems indicate his social commitment in clear terms. He is conscious of the ironic implications of life even after death. In 'Conversation of the Skeletons', he comments on a wider scale on the lack of reason associated with human affairs and highlights the fact that death is a great leveller. The idea is that when the flesh rots at death, the skeleton that is left is normally white and it does not reflect the racial group of its former human possessor. The question asked by the skeleton is significant: 'What is the colour of our existence here?' (*The Years Go By*, p. 71). This question is better appreciated when it is recollected that the skeletons had asked themselves penetrating questions like these:

Did you have a wife
And children
   dear friend?
A black wife
Four little things
   and you?
A blue-eyed brunette
Soft, tender skin, brown ...
What colour is brown
In this world of egret white bones?

The implication in the observation that these bones possess the same colour is that the frenetic action in real life where individuals struggle for wealth, fame and social superiority are peripheral to the actual worth of life. The monochromatic skeletons indicate that they are no longer capable of illustrating the prejudices of social realities. The poet thus uses the irony in the poem to highlight the error in the belief that selfish regulations are eternal. This irony forces the reader to reassess his views and it is this kind of use that makes Angira's vision unique.

In addition, Jared Angira focuses on a poetic cosmos that is saturated with the tribulations of life although the reality he perceives does not generate feelings of despair. In 'The Harp's

Friend', he uses the nostalgic feelings of music with verbal irony
to explore the issue of death:

> better to hear
> and let the word be
> like the maize grain
> that plants the farm
> than to see and leave
> like an uninterested cinemagoer
> people always recall rich men and beauty
> but not beggars
> death is a strategist
> striking at his convenience
> getting the enemy unmobilized
> death is a VIP
> never seen publicly save on special occasions
> (*Silent Voices*, p. 7)

The association of death with the term 'VIP' introduces an uncom-
fortable insight. If death like a 'Very Important Personality'
strikes at his convenience, gets the 'enemy unmobilized' and is
'never seen publicly save on special occasions', by implication
these VIPs themselves possess the destructive capabilities of
causing unnecessary deaths. The irony is in the line 'death is
a VIP'. Contrary to the positive associations with 'VIP' –
responsible, useful and valuable – death destroys 'when life is
sweetest'. Like death, the VIPs in the society are harbingers of
doom. Their inadequacy is thus demonstrated.

Peace, the poet suggests, can only be achieved by a conscious
effort to eliminate death, and social stability is based on harmony.
In 'Peace', although the persona intones: 'in peace have we
come/to this island', there is also the awareness that 'the axe
stands erect/to split the nut/before the hunt/for deer/in the jungle'
(*Silent Voices*, p. 14). The irony is that though peace is essential,
it has to be curtailed when it infringes on safety and freedom
in order to prevent death. This interpretation could even be
extended to illustrate the importance of curbing excesses in
beliefs and actions, and the need for an awareness of individual
limitations.

His ironic vision emerges in 'An evening Libretto':

> the irony of life
> That at times you believe
> that you know yourself best
> only to discover
> the great self-deception (*Cascades*, p. 29)

This awareness that there is an 'irony of life' captures effectively that subsumed quality of irony that dangles between what is asserted and what is intended. It also indicates that knowledge can be acquired by making a self appraisal and also by appraising the individual's position within the wider society. Self-deception leads to a failure in this appraisal and the poet is insisting that its consequences could be socially devastating, for the destruction of an individual could set in motion a chain reaction that may annihilate a society. It is thus not right, as Yesufu has done in his critical comparison, to regard a poet who is so aware of the irony of life as deficient. He writes: 'where Angira would recommend a purgative violence to rectify the pernicious human situation, Ntiru regards true salvation as a natural emanation from a sort of chaste "inner music"' (Yesufu, 1987, p. 41). Contrary to Yesufu's view that Angira's approach is violent his adept use of verbal irony indicates that his panacea also involves salvation that introduces moral and spiritual rejuvenation. Verbal irony depends on the expression of an attitude that is different from the implied one, so that even the 'purgative violence' indicated cannot be accepted superficially from a poet whose ironic vision is so pervasive.

In 'My Best Poem', the lines

This poem
It is most beautiful
the result of a life-long labour

suggest a poem that is either grand in content or dazzling in style, but through irony he deflates this expectation:

It is not a sonnet
It is not a lyric
It has no earthly description
It is the frustration of the critics

so that by the time it ends with the lines 'the poem exists/In the strong room of the mind (*Soft Corals*, p. 107), it is revealed as a reflection of the poet's life, imbibing his tribulations, his hopes and his despairs.

An analysis of the semantics of the poems shows his consciousness through verbal irony of the fact that reality could be disorganized due to the human capacity for self-deception.

The Christian religion is subjected to close scrutiny in 'He Will Come' which concludes: 'I have no sins worth forgiving/I came to buy beans, you sold me peas' (*Silent Voices*, p. 47). The irony here is that where an individual is denied self-actualization, that individual cannot be held accountable for his frailties. The refusal to submit to the judgement of God then ironically implies an indictment of the unrealistic nature of a religion which prides itself in justice and fairness. The fundamental aspect of the irony is that in the implementation of rules in the society, as illustrated by the doctrine of the Christian religion, one must consider the humanity of the members of that society.

It is this insistence on a reassessment of social activities and the rules guiding them that provide the motivation for 'A Dream'. Dreams must not be confused with reality. In the dream-garden – a metaphor for life – the persona encounters harmful animals but he is also aware that reality cannot be replaced with the depiction of a number of unrelated objects as seen in a dream. He reflects that 'piles of decisions/compose verses of life' and that

> My garden must make profit
> If it is to survive
> But the garden is misty
> the morning chilly. (*Silent Voices*, p. 86)

'Mist' and 'chill' suggest the extent to which reality intrudes becoming tangible and disconcerting thus alerting the reader to possible conflicts.

Although his later poems in *The Years Go By* seem much more radical, he has not discarded the artistic device of verbal irony for reality has remained reactionarily unchanged. In '3', (*The Years Go By*, pp. 3–4) he uses the famous retort of Jesus to create irony:

> Give to Caesar
> What is Caesar's.

Apparently there does not seem to be any controversy concerning what should be given to 'Caesar' or the ruler in real life but the verbal irony emerges when the poet lists the instances where this injunction is deliberately ignored:

> But when Caesar begets vices
> Vices unto the poor are given
> When Caesars of the land
> Bring forth poverty and decay
> Unto man are these passed. (*The Years Go By*, p. 3)

The nature of the society is presented as that in which the appropriation of the resources of the people by the Caesars is performed only when there is no risk of ruin. The poet explores this idea with the verbal irony that the 'Caesars' should not only be given the abundant harvest of wealth but also that they should bear the pestilences which they originate at the same time. The issue becomes distinct when the poet comments:

> What is good
> Is everyone's desire
>
> What is bad
> Belongs to nobody
>
> When misery sings
> Who dances the tango? (*The Years Go By*, p. 4)

The poet's sympathy lies with the ordinary people who are not involved in the formulation of policies that concern them. The poet's verbal irony is thus making clear the fact that the leaders must be prepared to confront the dangers before the rest of the people, for the role of a 'Caesar' is not just to consume the products of the country at the expense of the producers.

Furthermore, in 'Ode to the Beautiful Nyakiemo', Angira uses an ode woven in praise of a river which has provided life-sustaining water for a vast section of the society, to explore the issues of deprivation and exploitation associated with development. The river Nyakiemo could equally be perceived as a metaphor for man's failure to attach value to natural objects. However, this ode extends beyond the appreciation of the usefulness of a river to incorporate an insightful verbal irony. In the eighth section of the poem the poet states: 'all men are born equal' (p. 87). This assertion is contrary to the context of the poem for the poet portrays, a few lines earlier, those aspects of life that indicate the fact that all men are not equal:

> Hanging years
>   On a slab of existence ...
>   left ten million men
> Coiled bellies
>   Feeding on droplings
> Beneath
>   The giant Oak table
> Left million men
> Scratching a surface.

The sufferings of these millions feeding on 'droplings' from the giant Oak table of those obviously superior in status to them accentuates the social disparity. Moreover, the 'surface' they are 'scratching' indicates that they lack the energy to probe deeper and there is no indication that a persistent search would yield good results. The impossibility of equality of all men is shown further through the observation that:

Today,
  we must buy existence
At the going price
  of the stock exchange
Today,
  we must hide
In the drawers
  Skeletons of stone age
For to stay in daylight
  The price so high
Keeping to the lane
  from the Iron Heel. (*The Years Go By*, p. 89)

The poet's reference to those who 'must buy existence' emphasizes the reality of the social stratification in which all men are not born equal. If it is true that 'all men are born equal' then there would be no need to 'hide/In the drawers/Skeletons of stone age'. The image 'iron heel' suggests the power of the privileged to keep the lower orders in perpetual subjugation.

Angira's verbal irony is not obscured by the syntax for it depends on intellectual appeal. He chooses words that are accessible but not simplistic and as Wangusa has declared: 'in Angira simplicity is definitely a strength' (Wangusa, p. 52). Verbal irony raises his poetry beyond an ordinary collation of emotions and experiences and its artistic use enables him to range through the complexity of human nature, cast insight on the intricacies of life and use his vision to warn the reader, thereby fulfilling that poetic quality which Okeke-Ezigbo identified when he stated that 'only the mature poet, the true seer, can warn' (Okeke-Ezigbo, p. 62). But Angira does not stop at warning, for his poetry possesses the corollary of suggestions to correct social attitudes.

WORKS CITED

Abrams, M.H. *A Glossary of Literary Terms*. 4th ed. New York: Holt, Rinehart and Winston, 1981.

Angira, Jared. *Cascades*. London: Longman, 1979.

—. *Juices*. Nairobi: East African Publishing House, 1970.

—. *Silent Voices*. London: Heinemann, 1972.

—. *Soft Corals*. Nairobi: East African Publishing House, 1973.

—. *The Years Go By*. Nairobi: Bookwise, 1980.

Calder, Angus. 'Jared Angira: A Committed Experimental Poet.' In

Individual and Community in Commonwealth Literature. Ed. Daniel Massa. Malta: University of Malta Press, 1979: 36–44.

Dictionary of Modern Critical Terms, A. Ed. Roger Fowler. London: Routledge and Kegan Paul, 1973.

Egudu, R.N. *Modern African Poetry and the African Predicament.* London: Macmillan, 1978.

Fowler, Roger ed. *A Dictionary of Modern Critical Terms.* London: Routledge and Kegan Paul, 1973.

Gurr, Andrew and Angus Calder eds. *Writers in East Africa: Papers From a Colloquium held at the University of Nairobi, June 1971.* Nairobi: East African Publishing House, 1974.

Killam, G.D. ed. *African Writers on African Writing.* London: Heinemann, 1973.

Muecke, D.C. *The Compass of Irony.* London: Methuen, 1969.

Okeke-Ezigbo, F.E. 'Vampires of Bread and Blood in Mud: The Apocalyptic Vision of Pol Ndu.' *Okike* 25/26 (February 1984): 50–64.

Roscoe, A. *Uhuru's Fire: African Literature East to South* Cambridge: Cambridge University Press, 1977).

Wangusa, Timothy. 'East African Poetry.' *African Literature Today* 6 (1973): 46–53.

Yesufu, Abdul R. 'Darkness and Light: The Interplay of Pessimism and Hope in the Poetry of Richard Ntiru.' *Ariel* (18.3) (1987): 31–46.

—. 'Jared Angira and East African Poetry of Social Testimony.' *World Literature Written in English,* 23.2 (Spring 1984): 327–35.

Form & Technique in Femi Osofisan's Plays

Femi Osofisan occupies an eminent position among contemporary Nigerian playwrights because his plays are the most frequently performed within the country today though they are less well known outside. A post-Wole Soyinkan playwright, he barely qualifies as 'new'; but he has developed significantly in the last seventeen years.[1] He has written well over thirty plays with about sixteen of them published,[2] and has been experimenting with form and technique for almost two decades. Equally active in every aspect of the literary genres: poetry, fiction and drama, he is also a critic, scholar, play director and a columnist in two of Nigeria's leading national newspapers. He has twice won the annual literary prize of the Association of Nigerian Authors (ANA) in drama and poetry, and has been twice elected president of the association.[3] He is probably the most gifted and the most prolific of the second generation[4] of Nigerian playwrights.

Like other contemporary African dramatists – Ngũgĩ wa Thiong'o, Efua Sutherland, Wole Soyinka, Ama Ata Aidoo, J.P. Clark, Ola Rotimi – Osofisan is engaged in the quest for suitable forms with which the African experience can be transmuted into drama. In Nigeria, Soyinka has perfected the satiric art as a medium of interpreting human experience in the theatre. But Osofisan differs greatly from Wole Soyinka or any other African playwrights in his conception of form, stylistic innovations and manner of organizing his plays. The uniqueness of Osofisan as a dramatist lies in the enormous range of his theatrically viable forms and his ability to fuse social themes and ideological commitment with appropriate dramatic forms without sacrificing one for the other. It is a measure of the playwright's skill that this structure never appears boring or overdone.

This paper will not only attempt to identify the distinctive forms and techniques he employs in his published plays but will also examine the relative purpose which the structure of the plays is designed to serve.

Osofisan's greatest contribution to African theatre is his extraordinary theatrical fertility of forms. As part of his artistic revolution, he has been exploring new forms, searching for new ways of conveying his message, using the same stage: 'I am experimenting with form, I am discovering forms, some of which are already in use. Attention to form is really my concern. I pay great attention to form, to manner ... these have been my guiding principles in all my works. If people pay attention to form, manner, ways of expression, our society would be much better than this.'[5]

Osofisan's penchant for suitable artistic forms is manifested in the way he structures his plays to suit both his artistic goals and relating effectively to his audience. As D.S. Izevbaye observes, 'I think his stagecraft is very good. He has a talent for experimenting with form. He has this feel for keeping his audience both in terms of language, action and entertainment.'[6] The distinctive way he composes beautiful stage pictures and the adventurous manner he manipulates form are the important qualities that distinguish Osofisan's theatre from other Nigerian playwrights. According to Richard Southern, 'The essence of theatre really is not the vigour and wisdom of the script but the way things are handled on the stage and that alone.'[7] In this regard, Osofisan defends his adventurous experiments on African theatre forms and asserts that 'competence in form is what art is all about. There is nothing we are saying now that has not been said before. What survives is the way you say it. What distinguishes Brecht from Shakespeare is the way he says his things.'[8]

Repertory

For analytical convenience, Osofisan's work may be divided into three broad categories of plays in his repertory. The divisions are, however, not absolutely rigid as there are overlaps and some plays fall into more than one category. These are: realistic, experimental and African total theatre plays.

The realistic plays are based on real-life situations, the settings usually sitting-room, hotel lobby, beachside, etc., and the themes mostly domestic. They usually protest strongly against rampant materialism, widespread political corruption, injustice, oppression and brutality of the ruling class. In the realistic protest plays like *Birthdays Are Not For Dying, Altine's Wrath, The Inspector and the Hero, Fires Burn and Die Hard, A Restless Run of Locusts, No More the Wasted Breed, Midnight Hotel* and *Who's Afraid of Solarin?*, Osofisan presents ordinary, recognizable characters and convincing real-life situations to create an illusion of reality. Strongly pedagogical with entertainment as a secondary option, these plays rely more on words than on symbolic actions and their economy of means makes them especially suitable for production by schools, small theatre groups and also ideal for television on which many have been produced.

The experimental plays are usually stylized and conventionalized employing symbolic setting, suggestive rather than sequential storyline, improvisation, and characters that are not rounded or fully developed. They each involve only a single situation, set and location. In *The Chattering and the Song, Once Upon Four Robbers, Midnight Hotel, The Oriki of a Grasshopper* and *Another Raft* he experiments with space, form, language, acting, directing, setting, dance, songs and movement. For example he experiments with the flashback technique, the Orunmila motif (e.g. Iwori Otura Song) and the use of traditional magic and incantation in *The Chattering and the Song*; parabolic narrative form in *Once Upon Four Robbers*; stylized setting and traditional masque in *Another Raft*; music, songs and humour in *Midnight Hotel* and symbolic characterization and setting in *The Oriki of a Grasshopper*.

Most of Osofisan's plays are flexible enough to be done effectively either in the Grotowski tradition of poor theatre where means are scarce or more lavishly where resources are abundant.

The African total theatre plays are illustrative of an African concept of 'total theatre'[9] that use all the theatre resources by incorporating elements of music, song and dance into a spoken text; insist upon theatre as artifice through frequent multiple role-playing and story-telling techniques; use improvisational structures without set; conjoin spatial and temporal frames into a seamless experiential present; arrange linguistic localization through proverb, parable and riddle; and place high value on episodic and open-ended structures which challenge audiences to impose meaning upon the event. In this category are Osofisan's most entertaining and conceptually and stylistically complex plays: *The Chattering and the Song, Once Upon Four Robbers, Morountodun, Red is the Freedom Road, Farewell to a Cannibal Rage* and *Esu and the Vagabond Minstrels*.

Taken together, the contents of the three categories of plays are embedded in social and political issues which the playwright views not just as they exist, but as they can be changed. He registers in them the widespread political corruption, brutality, oppression, rampant materialism of the ruling classes, intellectual failure, coups and counter coups of post-independence Nigeria. Structurally, Osofisan's dramaturgy takes cognizance of the often limited theatre resources in Nigeria like lack of sophisticated theatre machinery, trained personnel and adequate infrastructures. The setting and decor are symbolic and representational, emphasizing the illusion of reality. This is in consonance with his stated aim: 'to write plays where we have limited financial means. Where there is no money to build elaborate sets, huge stage, buy elaborate costume or lighting ... which are the major problems with producing Soyinka's plays.'[10]

Forms & Techniques

Osofisan experiments with various styles of dramatic presentation to determine which forms are the most suitable vehicles to convey his messages, especially when the audience in view is the common man in the Nigerian society. These include orthodox comedy, realism, compressionism, epic theatre and traditional African theatre. He also employs the techniques of repetition and inversion, play-within-the-play, contrasts and flashbacks, cinema, as well as expert manipulations of language, theme, characterization, metaphor and symbolism, and dialectical confrontation between characters, to ensure audience participation in the dramatic experience.

In the realistic plays, Osofisan still experiments with other forms like tragi-comedy in *A Restless Run of Locusts*, farce in *Who's Afraid of Solarin?* and comic opera in *Midnight Hotel*. Similarly in the experimental plays, Osofisan's persistent and systematic renewal of the different methods of reaching his audience, leads him to employ the absurdist technique in *The Oriki of a Grasshopper*, compressionism in *Another Raft*, epic theatre in *Once Upon Four Robbers* and African theatre technique in *Morountodun* and *The Chattering and the Song* – an unorthodox and comprehensive range of forms suitable for all kinds of staging conventions.

Realistic Plays

A similar range of forms can be seen in the realistic plays. In *A Restless Run of Locusts*, the playwright starts with the conventional form of comedy. This comedy is realized through criticism, humour and ridicule of the Nigerian society. The play begins by being witty and comic but as the plot progresses, the humour becomes wry, the laughter dissolves and what results from the experimentation in form, is a realistic play with tragi-comic tone.

A Restless Run of Locusts treats political violence and takes a moral stand against the physical assaults that characterize political activities in Nigeria – a country known for the turbulence and violence of its politics. In the play, the families of Chief Kuti and Sanda Adeniyi are political opponents who engage in the use of thugs to assault each other as the first Elder observes: 'Your elections have divided our land. Broken families. Wrecked homes. ... Every day of your campaigns has brought fresh woes and new wounds, has brought another grief to another home. ... No place is safe again from your thugs.'[11] To win more votes, Sanda builds his political campaign on the feigned death of his brother who he alleged was killed during political violence caused by his opponent, Chief Kuti. As a result of the sympathy this story wins from the electorate, Chief Kuti commits suicide but Sanda too is murdered by the political thugs of his party.

Through the elders and Kabiyesi he reduces the traditional system to ridicule and laughter but the laughter is not sustained and by the deaths of Sanda and Chief Kuti he manipulates the comic incidents to achieve a tragi-comic effect. *Birthdays Are Not For Dying* and *Altine's Wrath* also fall into this category of realistic tragi-comedy.

In *Who's Afraid of Solarin?* – a loose adaptation of Nikolai Gogol's *The Inspector General* – Osofisan experiments with the realistic mode under the popular form of farce which relies on exaggeration of situation, character, and language to heighten the comic effect. (*The Engagement* is also an adaptation – of Anton Chekhov's *The Proposal*.)

In *Who's Afraid of Solarin?* Osofisan paints a scathing picture of municipal corruption in Nigeria. In the play, the insignificant rogue, Isola, who has jumped bail in Lagos, is mistaken for Solarin, a government appointed Public Complaints Commissioner whose arrival is anticipated with panic by the corrupt local council officials. Isola is bribed and fêted and finally betrothed to the daughter of a materialistic, corrupt Christian pastor who wears charms around his waist. After he has left with his pocket full of money, the mistake is discovered and the arrival of the real Public Complaints Commissioner is announced.

The dramatic irony created through the device of mistaken identity which persists in practically every scene performs the function of structural irony which helps to sustain the duplicity of meaning throughout. In addition to this device of mistaken identity the plot also depends on two elements of fantasy and absurd illogicality to produce grotesque humour.

The absence of a convincing motivation for action gives the impression from the onset that the playwright is not about to create a realistic world but a 'fabulously fantastic world where such a mundane fact as the demand for motivation for action must be dispensed with'.[12] The absence of motivation also shows that the world where an unfounded explanation such as given by the Price Control Officer (that they are going to be attacked by Vorster or Iron Smith, p. 13) can even be contemplated must be an illogical world where absurd logic prevails.

Although Osofisan is faithful to the artistic technique of Gogol in the use of irony, unmotivated surrealist plot, fantasy and absurd illogicality, to produce grotesque humour in *Who's Afraid of Solarin?*, he has, however, modified the Gogolian humour by introducing his own brand of like witticism, malapropism, characterization and apt turns of phrase such as 'armed seduction' (p. 35), 'engagement by cutlass' (p. 62), 'you all have enough crimes in your lives to justify your posts' (p. 20), 'I suspected something terrible would happen today, but I thought it was merely seeing your face' (p. 11). His adaptation is also certainly more comical for the numerous malapropisms of the Chairman exemplified by: 'women lips' for 'women's lib' (p. 17), 'you are fainted to perish' for 'you are fated to perish' (p. 40), 'suscemptible' for 'susceptible' (p. 42), 'physical apparition' for 'physical appearance' (p. 43), 'I'm quite flattened' for 'I'm quite flattered' (p. 45).

A distinctive Nigerian quality of humour is effected through the creation of dream-like characters that are grotesquely caricatured. He strips the characters of their Russian peculiarities and re-clothes them in Nigerian habits and costumes. Solarin is recognizably Dr Tai Solarin, a forthright social critic who was appointed a Public Complaints Commissioner because of his incorruptibility.

The dialogue reveals the moral universe of the characters. The first scene accurately depicts the usual bickering that goes on among irresponsible Nigerian officials when they are supposed to be discussing serious issues. The name-calling is also typically Nigerian: 'That's not the point of our complaint, you eunuch' (p. 6), or 'Look at this unnamed monster, who eats up Council contracts like a woodworm' (p. 7). Equally Nigerian is the boasting:

> What's all this about Baba Fawomi? Let me remind you that I, Abeni, second daughter of the late renowned organist and lay preacher, Reverend Durosimi, I am a staunch christian ... My Bible bought in London, was blessed ten years ago by no less a personality than Leader Ezekiel Ijonru himself ... I have a rosary from a special curio shop in Jerusalem, birthplace of the Saviour. I pay my dues every Sunday to the First C.M.S. Cathedral ... (p. 9)

Osofisan is perhaps best appreciated for combining local and universal thematic relevance with the zest of a restless researcher for the most appropriate stylistic medium to express the concern of every new play. He is thus constantly experimenting with styles. When he is not creating something new, he is imaginatively adapting the styles of accomplished masters. Experimentation with (playwright's) farce, therefore, indicates that the play-wright's style is at the fringe or transitional stage to a more revolutionary form which he realizes when he discovers the technique of comic opera in the *Midnight Hotel*.

Using the comic opera style in the *Midnight Hotel*, Osofisan grafts music to bedroom farce to produce a bitter-sweet realistic play which induces laughter while carrying an acerbic message; through the hilarious comedy gleams the harsh light of truth. The balanced nature of the festal energy of the songs and the corrosive satire of the message make the play a delightfully indicting theatrical experience. The use of music by a live band – the Petronaira Band – and songs constitute the Brechtian alienation elements in this adaptation of Georges Feydeau's *L'Hotel du Libre Echange* (*Hotel of Free Exchange*), which portrays ills like political corrup-tion, moral depravity and religious charlatanism that plague the Nigerian society. Awero, a female member of parliament, like other members believes in having sexual pleasure with would-be contrac-tors before awarding contracts to them. They call it 'sampling the goods'. Awero takes a contractor, Pastor Suuru who is a friend to her husband and who has a Swiss Bank account to the Midniqht Hotel to 'sample' him. At this hotel, which is a metaphor for corrup-tion, they meet Alatise, a family friend and a headmaster from the provinces, who has come to lodge at the hotel with his three daughters. Awero also meets her husband Asibong, who has come to the hotel that night as a housing agent to inspect some fault in the design of the hotel. The unexpected presence of both Alatise and Asibong at the hotel and the rude interruptions of the hotel atten-dants, prevent Awero from sampling Pastor Suuru. What a night!

In the play, Osofisan combines Brecht's anti-illusionary theatre with Feydeau's theatre of illusion to create a unique style, comic opera, that is quintessentially Osofisan. He achieves this by breaking the flow using the songs as comments on the main actions as well as on the state of the Nigerian society:

We'll draw up a Constitution
And put the real rogues in power
The people have no peace
The people have no rest
For the robbers have come to power
And the robbers are now in power.[13]

Through the lyrics of the songs, Osofisan indicates his ideological position as a playwright with commitment to materialist and socialist perspective.

If experimenting with realism indicates his style at the transitional stage, discovering experimental forms then perfected the change to a more revolutionary form.

Experimental Plays

The formal strategy of *The Oriki of a Grasshopper* uses the absurdist style of Samuel Beckett's *Waiting for Godot* as structural prop and accessory to portray the dilemma of Imaro, a revolutionary university lecturer who is waiting in vain for revolution that will sweep away corruption, oppression, injustice, and bring paradise in a truly new world order. Imaro, who, along with other colleagues, tries to initiate a revolution by indoctrinating students, now discovers that his life as a revolutionary intellectual is a waste, as nothing ever changes in the society. Not even the numerous students he has instructed could effect the desired change: 'I can see for myself that my life's in a shred. What have I achieved? I have talked and talked. Like the others. I've tried to teach my students that we can build a new world. That a brave new world is within our grasp. But to what purpose?'[14]

Nonetheless, Claudius, a capitalist millionaire friend of Imaro enlightens him about the realities of the society: that as it is presently constituted it is immoral, brutal, and that events in it work to stifle human potential especially the revolutionary intellectuals who are inadequately equipped to effect any meaningful change.

The cyclic plot keeps the situation static: waiting pervades the entire play as in Beckett's *Waiting for Godot* to which there are clear references. Osofisan uses the idea of futility of waiting as a mockery of the aspirations of frail humans like Imaro who entertains no doubt in his blind belief in an impending, all-cleansing revolution. Just as Godot never comes in Beckett's play so the revolution does not materialize in Osofisan's.

Through the structural technique of compressionism which Osofisan adapts in his experiment in *Another Raft*, long periods of dramatic time and a multiplicity of locations are reduced to 'two hours' traffic of the stage'. There is also restraint in the use of space, set, character and other dramatic components.

Another Raft, written nearly a quarter of a century after the Nigerian playwright J.P. Clark's *The Raft*[15] relates to the latter in both theme and structure. The plays have a lot in common; they are constructed upon a symbolic plane; their subject matter, the troubled state of the Nigerian nation and their dramatic setting, a floating raft. However they differ in their handling of the theme. While Clark fashions his play in classical style that bases contemporary woes on some original sins of the ancestors whereby punishment is handed down to the innocent offspring by the gods, in Osofisan's *Another Raft*, the thematic preoccupation is that the salvation of the society is in the hands of the people of that very society.

In *Another Raft*, Aiyedade, a riverine coastal community, is beset with terror of flood and other disasters. The people firmly believe that the cause of the disasters is the neglect of the worship of Yemosa, the sea goddess. Consequently, in order to calm the raging goddess, a cleansing mission is embarked upon in a raft on the sea to locate the shrine and propitiate her.

However, the raft is adrift not due to the whims and caprices of the gods, but owing to the intrigues and corruption of some members of the cleansing mission aboard the raft who have had their hands soiled by embezzling the drainage contracts. Ironically, it is this very lack of good drainage that caused the flood in the first place. In the end, the shrine cannot be located and six of the nine who set out on the ill-fated journey drown.

The compressionist technique of staging which employs symbolic sparsity of set where the raft is represented by mats, the sea by the stage, and the moon by a spotlight, also portrays, in symbolic representation, the ills that plague the Nigerian society: corruption, intrigue, deceit of 'priests' called religious leaders, reckless politicking that brought the military into dictatorial governance, and other woes that kept the nation perpetually underdeveloped since independence.

Apart from these ills, *Another Raft* expands its thematic concern to the overall fate of the black race presumed adrift in the sea of history:

> Gbebe: ... It's our destiny.
> We of this continent, we're like a raft lost in the stream of history, bound for an Island of pain. We can scream all we want, sing our complaints to the air, but we cannot leave the raft. We're doomed forever to be the slaves of conquerors.[16]

The desire for a new dramatic structure that will involve and relate to the audience leads Osofisan to experiment with, and radically revise the technique of epic theatre in *Once Upon Four Robbers*. The epic theatre is oriented towards episodic plotting, unsequential events, role-playing, story-telling, metaphor and song, reason and argument, is anti-illusionistic and anti-cathartic. The result of the use of these techniques is the alienation effect which, according to Brecht, enables the audience to detach itself so that it may see familiar objects in a new light.

It is important to point out here quickly the relationship between Epic Theatre and Traditional African Theatre. The prominent features which animate Brecht's fundamental theory of alienation effect already existed in traditional African theatre. The similarity in form and technique of both genres means that they share strikingly similar features but this fact need not concede primacy of ingenuity to Brecht because 'the features which define epic theatre are not singularly of Brecht's genius, as they are being glibly made to appear in the African world. Rather, it is clear that those features had existed in our African theatre tradition long before Brecht was born in 1898.'[17]

Epic theatre technique constitutes the vehicle of plot and dramatic action in *Once Upon Four Robbers, Morountodun, Farewell to a Cannibal Rage* and *The Chattering and the Song.* Only *Once Upon Four Robbers* will be discussed here.

The four robbers who, in *Once Upon Four Robbers,* are bred by the society through hunger and unemployment are faced with the problem of how to rob without being captured and executed. Later on they meet an Aafa, a Muslim priest-cum-Ifa practitioner, who gives them just such magical powers.

However, the greed of one of the robbers who is so avaricious as to steal from his colleagues, leads to their arrest by the soldiers who are as much thieves as the robbers they are out to catch. The soldiers, backed by the might of state guns, brazenly steal from the armed robbers. Ironically, it is this same set of soldiers who are to execute the armed robbers from whom they have stolen.

The play then poses a question: whether a corrupt, immoral, materialist state has the right to take the life of a citizen who carries the ethics of corrupt, immoral materialism to the logical conclusion of armed robbery? The playwright does not answer the question. Rather, he lays the story bare in front of his audience and asks them to decide.

The story-telling technique is used by Osofisan to achieve what Brecht called the alienation effect (*Versfrumdungs Effekt*) in epic theatre. This device enables the characters on stage to elicit audience participation in both plot and the dramatic action. For example in *Once Upon Four Robbers,* the story-teller introduces the play by soliciting the audience to participate by answering 'Aalo'. Then he continues with the story-telling technique: 'Once upon a time. An ancient tale I will tell you. Tale ancient and modern. A tale of four robbers.'[18] The fact that the story is 'ancient' but familiar creates the effect of historical distancing in terms of time. This is to remind the audience that the story is familiar to them and therefore the purpose of their gathering is to give 'a second thought' to the tale as Osofisan says in the programme notes.

With the use of role-playing or role-changing technique, the alienation effect is also created. Occasionally too, the audience cease to be spectators and are mobilized by the playwright to become 'characters' and participants in the play they are supposed to be watching. In *Once Upon Four Robbers*, the story-teller plays the role of both Aafa and narrator.[19] Characters who perform as cast in the play are invited from the audience and they visibly pick up their roles and costumes on the stage.[20] The audience perform the role of judges when the play ends in stalemate and decide whether the robbers should be shot or spared.[21]

Reason and argument are devices employed in the epic theatre to reduce empathy, emotional identification with action and characters on stage, in order to achieve distancing or the alienation effect. The audience is thus challenged to 'think' rather than passively to find amusement.

In *Once Upon Four Robbers*, the reason and argument concern the 'callous contradictions' of an 'unjust society' in a state of 'rapid modernization' – cars, boutiques, supermarkets and amusement parks side by side with congested hospitals, crowded schools and 'sprawling slums and ghettoes' – which lead to armed robbery. This juxtaposition of extreme wealth and extreme poverty leads to the 'manufacture' of 'potential assassins'. Osofisan argues that if armed robbery is a disgrace and a death-affirming reality, so are hunger and unemployment. Indeed, his ultimate intention in writing the play is to 'shock' the public into a 'new awareness' so that its attitude of 'passive acceptance or sterile indignation' may be channelled towards a 'more dynamic, more enraged determination' to confront itself.[22]

The alienation effect is also achieved by the use of metaphor. Angola, in *Once Upon Four Robbers*, uses the metaphor of slum and corpse to highlight the sordid social conditions of the poor.[23] Major also uses the metaphor of the rich and the servants to portray the stratification of the society which perpetually condemns the poor to be victims of the rich.[24]

Song is used to 'interrupt' the play in order to reduce audience emotional involvement in the characters so as to highlight the theatrical debate.[25]

Traditional African Theatre

While the formalistic strategy of *Morountodun, Farewell to a Cannibal Rage, The Chattering and the Song* and *Once Upon Four Robbers* derives from the epic theatre, Osofisan exploits the technical resources of traditional African theatre[26] in *Esu and the Vagabond Minstrels, Another Raft, Farewell to a Cannibal Rage, Morountodun, Once Upon Four Robbers* and *The Chattering and the Song.* All the plays unmistakably convey an African atmosphere where very skilful use is made of singing, dancing, drumming and miming and this helps to reinforce the ritualistic and festival aura. Indeed, *Another Raft* thrives on the re-enactment of a ritual, while the central actions of *Morountodun* and *Esu* are presented in the form of a festival.

In *Morountodun,* he reconstructs the Moremi myth and legend of the past to suit his revolutionary view of the political forces of oppression, injustice and corruption in contemporary Nigeria. Legend relates that when the existence of ancient Ife was threatened by the frequent military onslaughts of its Igbo neighbours, Queen Moremi abandoned her wealth and palatial splendour, infiltrated the enemy camp, studied their tricks and came back home to ensure victory for her army.

In *Morountodun,* Osofisan yokes this legend with the 1969 popular farmers' uprising, the Agbekoya Farmers' Rebellion, in the old Western Nigeria. In that year, the Yoruba peasant farmers revolted against the oppression and excessive taxation of the government of that region. In the play, the aristocratic Titubi, fancying herself a modern-day Moremi and egged on by the government agent Salami, infiltrates the peasants' ranks as a spy. But after being exposed to the peasants' way of life and experiencing their suffering, she, in a twist of the story, renounces her bourgeois heritage and becomes ideologically transformed to the farmers' cause.

The play's technique appropriates the folktale form which is pliably employed to accommodate all the structural peculiarities which Osofisan imposes on it. For example, the historic past and the present are simultaneously shown on the stage through cinematic and composite setting techniques. Similar techniques are used to recapture the historic past of Queen Moremi and her husband, Oranmiyan, at the dawn of Yoruba civilization at Ile-Ife,[27] and to present the streamside scene where Titubi was ideologically converted when she washed and sang with peasant women.[28] These techniques, taken together, constitute the acted-out narratives which are the core of the play as they show the transition process of Tibubi, a spy, to Morountodun, a conqueror.

The flashback technique is also employed to realize the theme and dramatic action in *Farewell to a Cannibal Rage* and *Another Raft.* Demystification, the dislodging of the illusory world of art for reality is employed in *Esu and the Vagabond Minstrels,*[29] and in *Morountodun,* the dressing room action is brought into the full glare of the audience:

Stage opens on the Dressing Area, marked out by mats and wooden frames, etc. of an evidently ambulant and somewhat amateurish theatre company. A bench. Tables and stools, and possibly a table with a long mirror. Lockers. A flurry of activities: actors making up, trying costumes, reading scripts, rehearsing gestures, miming some of the latter actions in the play.[30]

At the end of the play, the Director reminds the audience that '... you must not imagine that what we presented here tonight was the truth. This is a theatre, don't forget, a house of dream and phantom struggles ...'[31]

In *Another Raft*, Yemosa One is similarly open with the audience:

I am here to warn you about a number of things. Some of you come to theatre, expecting to see a marvellous world of dreams. A magic world, full of fantastic stunts and fabulous gadgets, machines flying dizzily through the air, like say in Arabian Nights .... Nothing you see will be real, or pretend to be. Nothing you hear will be true. All is fiction, the story is false, the characters do not exist. We are all in a theatre, as you well know, and we see no need to hide it.[32]

Almost all his plays contain this demystifying element. The plays are generally open-minded, challenging the audience to draw their own conclusions. As the stage direction at the end of *The Chattering and the Song* states, while the actors dance among the audience, 'the play does not end'.[33] In *Birthdays Are Not for Dying* and *Altine's Wrath*, Osofisan writes endings which the audience is expected to go on debating and even rejecting because 'I want an ending which tells them that the theatre doesn't solve anything ... because it is a fictional world. The problem has to be solved in the society .... But it won't be solved if we simply don't discuss it; we must discuss the thing and work towards solutions.'[34]

Further demystifying history in *Morountodun* Osofisan shows how Titubi wins the hearts of the peasant villagers and is subsequently renamed Morountodun and married by Marshall, and how she destroys the myth about the inviolability of authority by talking down to Superintendent Salami.[35] Legend is reconstructed dialectically to show its relevance and usefulness to achieve revolutionary ends. The arrest of Titubi is also a demystification of the rich whom she represents.[36]

Fluid changes allow the scenes to flow freely into one another with the actors becoming stage hands while some of them play multiple roles. This technique also constitutes acted-out narratives which show the process of transition of Titubi from a spy to Morountodun. Set-changes are usually carried out in full view of the audience as an integral part of the performance. In *Farewell* to a *Cannibal Rage*, where this technique is brought to a peak, actors form part of the scenery and 'create' sets with their bodies.

Traditional techniques like songs (often in Yoruba) and music, riddles, proverbs, and enacted parables are incorporated into *Morountodun* as in most of the plays to comment on the action and involve the audience emotionally enhancing the African flavour.

Structural Devices

The playwright also uses other structural devices like play-within-a-play, language, theme, characterization, radicalizing the familiar, dialectical confrontation between characters, contrasts, repetition and inversion, in a subversive manner to postulate his vision of change in the society as well as fashion out a theatre with a populist thrust.

The Chattering and the Song, Once Upon Four Robbers, Farewell to a Cannibal Rage, Morountodun and *Another Raft* rely structurally on the devices of the play-within-a-play. The core of *The Chattering and the Song* is the re-enactment of an historical drama of eighteenth-century Yorubaland. In this play-within-a-play, Osofisan reconstructs the recorded history for his own radical purposes. Alafin Abiodun is no longer the hero who has restored peace in his kingdom. Rather, he is presented here as a tyrant who has used the claim of custom and divine sanction to perpetuate exploitation of his people.[37]

Osofisan's drama seeks to precipitate social change by rallying its audience to action, using the vehicles of style, theme and language. The themes of his plays have direct relevance to, and touch on, the nudging problems of the social and political issues of Nigerian society.

Language, which plays a significant role in the plays of Osofisan, is also an important aspect of his dramatic devices. For one thing, his language is simple and accessible. For another, the style of his writing is not tortuous or convoluted. His language is the prose vernacular of everyday life. But the beauty of his simplicity is the subtlety that permeates his style. He employs language to differentiate characters; to develop an appropriate setting; to create a convention which achieves consistency and which is an integral part of the dramatic texture. Based on linguistic features, Osofisan's characters may be classified into three categories: the ruling class characters who use standard, formal English variety with occasional, appropriate modifications; gods and religious personages who use elevated style, marked by a distinctive syntax and use of idioms, imagery and proverbs; and the common man who uses pidgin or non-standard English. Besides, Osofisan employs effusive metaphors, symbols and allegories alongside dialogue that is sharp, terse concise and succinct.

His characters wrestle not with their families or their immediate personal concerns, but with complexities of the world in which they struggle to survive. In the tradition of Brecht and Molière, as well as Shakespeare, Osofisan's characters live in and deal with a social and political landscape. The socio-political theme of unemployment, hunger and other social ills in *Once Upon Four Robbers* has been discussed earlier on page 111.

His strategy of 'radicalizing' the familiar provokes and startles the audience into analysis and confronts them with images that suggest the possibility of empowerment and change. He radicalizes and reshapes history in *The Chattering and the Song*, myth and legend in *Morountodun*, murder mystery form in *Birthdays Are Not For Dying* and story-telling in *Once Upon Four Robbers*.

In *The Chattering and the Song*, the familiar performance mode of repetition and inversion is expropriated and reshaped for more radical purposes. The various games of iwori otura, 'whot' cards, the riddling competition at the outset of the play, which are repeated and inverted in the later play-within-a-play, demonstrate how Osofisan structures a series of repetitions and inversions to dramatize his view of life as a dialectical process.

Dialectical confrontation between characters is in fact a fundamental characteristic of Femi Osofisan's dramaturgy. The device is calculated to provoke debate, logical argumentation and subsequent reconciliation or synthesis among the characters on stage thereby challenging the audience to a critical examination and collective analysis of the issues being presented.

For example Latoye confronts King Abiodun's guards dialectically in *The Chattering and the Song* and is able to convince them and raise their consciousness, through logic, to free themselves from the tyrannical and oppressive reign of King Abiodun:

> Latoye: Look around you. Look into your past, look into your future. What do you see? Always the same unending tale of oppression, of poverty, of squalor and disease. Why? You and your people, you are the soil on which the king's tree is nourished, tended until it is overladen with fruit: And yet, when you stretch out your hands, there are no fruits for you .... I am begging you, please fly out of your narrow nests. Come follow me, raise a song of freedom now!
>
> Guards: Freedom![39]

The argument between the armed robbers and their executioners, the soldiers, in *Once Upon Four Robbers* shocks the audience into an awareness[40] of the unjust social system that produces armed robbery.

At the end of the dialectical confrontation between characters, the issues are resolved and the audience are integrated and rid of their passive acceptance.

Conclusion

Osofisan's work is consistently impressive because of its technical accomplishment. He does not only fashion a dramaturgy that is adequately equipped to express contemporary reality, but constructs plays that offer questions rather than prescriptions. The plays not only promote his political ideology which is a commitment to societal change for the better, but also constitute a populist thrust for the English language theatre in Nigeria. The message of art may be universal but form is an individual matter. What marks out the efforts of the artist is his ability to stylize his forms. Thus Osofisan is mostly concerned, for now, with the aesthetics of his art:

> At the moment, it is not the message that pre-occupies me most. It is experimenting with these forms. How do we create an African theatre form? .... Really, I am very concerned about the aesthetics of my works.[41]

More than its revolutionary ideology, it is the aesthetics of Osofisan's drama that bewitches at first encounter. And at the heart of this aesthetics is a dramaturgy that uses all the known elements of Yoruba or African playmaking processes. The dramaturgy has a hybrid brilliance, grafting different forms of comedy, realism, compressionism, absurdism, epic and traditional African theatres, and making them his own. Rather than being bound to a particular form, he creates comprehensive, wide-ranging structures that are eclectic in form but suitable for transmitting African dramatic enactments on all types of stages be they thrust, proscenium or arena.

Finally, his exploration of form and deployment of techniques certainly make him one of the most exciting African dramatists writing at the moment. His works to date represent extraordinary diversities in style, technique and form. But whatever the divergencies in approach, the thematic preoccupation of the works remains the same: a vision of a better society that is free from the shackles of oppression, injustice and corruption.

Thus the overall effect of the appropriation of the familiar traditional performance modes and conventional devices in the plays of Osofisan is the creation of a popular African theatre form through which he makes critical social commentaries about the state of the nation and through which opinions and ideas in the society are capable of being influenced. Consequently his drama represents contemporary Nigerian literature of protest that manifests the struggles of a people whose country is undergoing a painful process of transformation from colonial through neo-colonial to a wholly self-determining nation.

NOTES & REFERENCES

1. Femi Osofisan's first play, *A Restless Run of Locusts*, was published in 1975.

2. Femi Osofisan, *A Restless Run of Locusts*, Ibadan, Onibonoje Press, 1975.
   Femi Osofisan, *The Chattering and the Song*, Ibadan, University Press Limited, 1977.
   Femi Osofisan, *Who's Afraid of Solarin?*, Calabar, Scholars Press, 1978.
   Femi Osofisan, *Once Upon Four Robbers*, Ibadan, BIO Educational Publications, 1980.
   Femi Osofisan, *Morountodun and Other Plays*, Ibadan and London, Longman, 1982.
   Femi Osofisan, *Red is the Freedom Road*, Ibadan and London, Longman, 1982.
   Femi Osofisan, *No More the Wasted Breed*, Ibadan and London, Longman, 1982.
   Femi Osofisan, *Midnight Hotel*, Ibadan, Evans Brothers Nigerian Limited, 1986.
   Femi Osofisan, *Farewell to a Cannibal Rage*, Ibadan, Evans Brothers Nigerian Limited, 1986.
   Femi Osofisan, *The Oriki of a Grasshopper*, Ibadan, New Horn Press, 1986.
   Femi Osofisan, *Altine's Wrath*, Ibadan, New Horn Press, 1986.
   Femi Osofisan, *Esu and the Vagabond Minstrels*, Ibadan, New Horn Press, 1988.
   Femi Osofisan, *Another Raft*, Lagos, Malthouse Press Limited, 1988.
   Femi Osofisan, *Birthdays Are Not For Dying*, Lagos, Malthouse Press Limited, 1990.
   Femi Osofisan, *Fires Burn and Die Hard*, Lagos, Malthouse Press Limited, 1990.
   Femi Osofisan, *The Inspector and the Hero*, Lagos, Malthouse Press Limited, 1990.
   All subsequent references to these plays are from these editions and indicated in parenthesis in the text.
   Femi Osofisan also has four plays in the press:
   Aringindin and the Nightwatchmen
   Twingle-Twangle: A Twynning Tale
   Yeepa, Solarin Mbo and
   The Album of the Midnight Hotel.

3. He is at the time of writing, the Vice-President of the Continental Pan African Writers' Association (PAWA) West Africa Sub-region.

4. The first generation of Nigerian playwrights are James Ene

Henshaw, John Pepper Clark and Wole Soyinka; while the second generation include Ola Rotimi, Zulu Sofola, Wale Ogunyemi, Bode Sowande and Femi Osofisan.

5. Personal interview with Femi Osofisan on 19 July 1986.
6. Dan S. Izevbaye, interview with Joy Umejei, 'The Social and Political Dimension of Femi Osofisan's plays.' Unpublished M.A. thesis submitted to the University of Ibadan, 1982.
7. Richard Southern, *The Seven Ages of the Theatre*, (Faber and Faber, London, 1962): 268.
8. Personal interview with Femi Osofisan on 19 July 1986.
9. Joel Adedeji, 'A Profile of Nigerian Theatre, 1960–1970,' *Nigeria Magazine*, 107–109, December–August, 1971: 3. He describes the concept of African 'total theatre' as 'an ensemble where the conscious and the unconscious, the real and the unreal, poetry, song and dance, intermingle with elements of traditional theatre both sacred and secular.'
10. Personal interview with Femi Osofisan on 19 July 1986.
11. *A Restless Run of Locusts*: 30.
12. Odun Balogun, 'Gogolian grotesque Humour and Chekhovian Slice of Life: Creative Originality and Artistic Faithfulness in Osofisan's Adaptations Of Two Russian Plays.' A paper presented at the 3rd World Congress For Soviet and East European Studies, Washington, DC (1985): 17.
13. *Midnight Hotel*: 65.
14. *The Oriki of a Grasshopper*: 28.
15. J.P. Clark, *Three Plays*, (London: Heinemann, 1964).
16. *Another Raft*, 45.
17. Ola Rotimi, 'Much Ado About Brecht', in *The Dramatic Touch Of Difference*, ed. Erika Fischer-Lichte *et al.* (Germany: Gunter Narr Verlag Tübingen, 1990): 259.
18. *Once Upon Four Robbers*: ix.
19. *Once Upon Four Robbers*: 11.
20. *Once Upon Four Robbers* Programme notes: x.
21. *Once Upon Four Robbers*: 72.
22. *Once Upon Four Robbers* Programme notes: viii.
23. *Once Upon Four Robbers*: 5.
24. *Once Upon Four Robbers*: 15.
25. *Once Upon Four Robbers* Song of the robbers (p. 7).
26. The traditional African techniques he employs include folklore, oral history and beliefs, myth and narrative, magic and incantation, mystery, ritual and sacrifice, festival, proverb, music and song.
27. *Morountodun*: 31.
28. *Morountodun*: 61.
29. *Esu and the Vagabond Minstrels*: 70.
30. *Morountodun*: 5.
31. *Morountodun*: 79.
32. *Another Raft*: 2.
33. *The Chattering and the Song*: 56.
34. Femi Osofisan in an interview with Sandra L. Richards on 21 January 1984.
35. *Morountodun*: 11–13.
36. *Morountodun*: 10–14.
37. *The Chattering and the Song*: 45.
38. *The Chattering and the Song*: 42.
39. *Once Upon Four Robbers*: 63.
40. Personal interview with Femi Osofisan on 19 July 1986.

Contemporary South African Theatre & the Complexities of Commitment

Femi Ojo-Ade

– Morena, I must tell you, I'm among those who have stopped waiting. One day we'll have to help you! Power to the people![1]

– Death, is when you start to hate to be black![2]

– Hope must forever burn in our hearts.[3]

– We the Black nation will die for our land taken from us by the Boers.[4]

Introduction: *of Theatre & Commitment*

Until recently, most references made in the West to South African theatre began and ended with Athol Fugard, a white who, his empathy for the Africans' plight notwithstanding, cannot be expected to, as it were, enter the black skin and live the trauma and tyranny of apartheid from within. *Woza Albert!* and other award-winning plays penned and performed by Africans have forever changed the theatre-goer's perspective. The present critique is meant to look closely at these plays, particularly the six making up the anthology, *Woza Afrika!*, published in 1986, with a view to determining how adequately they represent reality and the aspirations of the people for freedom from the last bastion of racism and colonialism in Africa.

'Drama,' affirms Amiri Baraka (quoting George Thomson),[5] 'is a form that rises to its most effective expression during periods of sharp social transformation.' Indeed, in Africa where life itself has always constituted a form of drama, one can imagine that that statement would be absolutely true. Theatre, an extension of Oral

Tradition, has existed for centuries and the work of the playwrights of the eighties has a point of reference rooted in the soil
of the motherland. As Wole Soyinka, Nobel Laureate, has rightly
stated, 'the art of creating is firstly an act of affirmation'
(foreword to *Woza Afrika!*, p. ix). With its traditionally communal
orientation, that affirmation is geared towards existence and
survival. Clearly non-materialistic in outlook, that theatre was

> not regarded as a totally separate and commercial entity. It
> was a way of passing on information from one generation to
> another, or, in the case of (South African) township theatre, a
> way of trying to forget the frustrations of life in South Africa.
> (Duma Ndlovu, p. xx)

To the African ethos of communality is added commitment, a
word that is often used with frivolity by many who hardly understand its meaning. Commitment emanates from a positive but
pained state of mind – suffering, sacrifice, selflessness, determination to defy misery and triumph over travails – given life through
action. The Self coalesces with the Other into a macrocosmic Self
that is Society. Commitment is concomitant with Resistance; for,
the reality necessitating commitment is an inhumanism, and there
are words galore to describe the inhumanism. Commitment is made
meaningful by such plagues as racism, repression, oppression,
exploitation, determination to destroy the helpless, innocent victim.
More than any other place in the world today, the South African
situation demands of the African nothing short of commitment.
Now, some might say that commitment to individual self is natural
and acceptable, but such spurious posture would at best prove the
so-called human failing of narcissism with the destructive forces
still in place and most capable of killing even the selfish self.

> In South Africa commitment is not a problem. You do not have
> to be a hero to be committed, you are compelled to be commit-
> ted, you are involved in a situation so fraught with evil that you
> are brought into collision with it. That is the only way of asser-
> ting certain human values and the fundamental value that the
> writer is so insistent on claiming for himself, the value of
> freedom, freedom of expression – what else is he seeking in his
> writing but precisely this freedom?[6]

Dennis Brutus, the author of the above statement, is a poet;
hence, we could understand the individualistic tendency of the
point of freedom. Yet we know that even the poet is not allowed
to hide in the haven of his muse: Brutus was imprisoned in
apartheid hell and he quickly realized that poetry is an aspect of

the politics of existence and that, willy-nilly, the poet must be the voice of his voiceless people. For his part, the dramatist has never had any delusion of grandeur because, from the first, his art is popular and communal. It is therefore not surprising that the plays of *Woza Afrika!* immediately strike the reader as expressions of the total reality of South Africa, not from an individualistic perspective but from the viewpoint of the oppressed majority. As we shall soon see, as in the Oral Tradition, theatre – and we should add a rider here that its essence is performance – is only viable when the artists and their audience participate in the symbolic, existential experience.

In introducing one of the plays, *Asinamali!*, Ndlovu declares that 'it is not just a play, but a venture into the reality of apartheid' (p. 179). The same statement is valid for all six plays. Reality is the passbook, principal symbol of apartheid oppression, controlling and restricting the Africans' presence and movement in their own land. Reality is the series of acts and laws (Migrant Labour, Influx Control, Bantu Education, Native Land, Bantu Authorities, Internal Security, Terrorism, etc.) legalizing illegalities blatantly perpetrated by the white minority. Reality is the reign of terror that has taken, and continues to take with impunity lives of black adults and children. Finally and most significantly, reality is Black Consciousness, fight for freedom, defiance and resistance. These plays document and dramatize this tragic reality, using real names of people and places and events. From the Sharpeville massacre of peaceful anti-pass protesters to the nightmarish re-enactment in Soweto of the same disrespect for human life in the persons of innocent children, the plays project a picture of *déjà* vu with emphasis on the people's determination to survive. The list of heroes and heroines mentioned is endless, including Biko, Dube, First, Luthuli, Mandela, Mbeki, Sisulu, Sobukwe, Tutu, and the editor of the anthology has deemed it fit to insert a glossary at the end of the text. One might be tempted to complain about this use of a who's who of anti-apartheid movement and of apartheid villains, too. This critic's opinion, however, is that knowledge of historical facts and figures is the reader-audience's commitment to the theatre. The human drama unfolding on stage and on paper is not mere entertainment; a function of a people's essence and existence, it demands the audience's reaction and, indeed, action, so that people may regain the lost humanity.

Dramatic Art, Language & Commitment

The very titles of the plays and that of the collection, are: a call to action, a revolutionary cry of defiance, an affirmation of existence, accusation of the oppressor. It is interesting that the playwrights, instead of representing on stage specifically the lives of known heroes, such as Biko and Mandela, have used their lives as inspiration for presenting other, fictitious lives. This, to my mind, adds to the plays' plausibility and authenticity: heroes are a rare breed and it is only normal that the majority of ordinary people remain down-to-earth while trying to use their heroes as models. The underpaid workers and suffering masses of *Woza Afrika!*, the unjustly imprisoned protagonists of *Asinamali!*, the young activists of *Children of Asazi* and the interracial ones of *Born in the RSA*, the black police collaborators of *Bopha!*, show the potential and pitfalls of everyone's everyday struggle. The only play with a hero approximating a real-life figure (Biko) is *Gangsters*. The viability of this strategy would be the need to show the public, through dramatization, an example of commitment *par excellence*.

Now, the use of English as basic vehicle of communication in these plays could constitute, as it often does in African literature, a matter for debate, especially given the fact that the vast majority of Africans, who would be expected to be the immediate audience, do not use English as a first language. The language issue is, however, not as controversial in theatre as it is in other genres; for, there is a theatrical language beyond words, that is made of motion and movement and mime, of rhythm and action, of music, song and dance and, more than in any other forum, theatre provides myriad possibilities of communication. In the plays of *Woza Afrika!* African languages, Zulu and Sotho, are interjected into conversations; Afrikaans, too (the language of the Boer victimizer). And the African languages are used in all the songs. Besides, the English is often 'Soweto English'.

None the less, all that would not explain why English is used as the major vehicle. The explanation is that the plays are actually also meant for an international (Western) audience. A criticism would be that, as usual, Africa is defining herself, or compelled to define herself, by the yardstick of the West; that, once again, she is trying to prove a point to the master, to seek his help in solving her problem. Such criticism would be valid, to a certain extent. As another aspect of the African dilemma, the plays would therefore be the servants' show of weakness before the all-powerful master who has control over her destiny. What would obviate such thought of inferiority complex is the critical consideration of Western cooperation and connivance with apartheid and the accusatory tone of the plays.

The audience, as mentioned earlier, is made to participate in this theatre. Significantly, the audience often is portrayed as the enemy, as the very symbol of apartheid that the characters on stage are condemning. When, in *Bopha!* (meaning, 'arrest'), Njandini describes the South African Police Passing Out Parade, 'another proud moment in the Republic of South Africa' and proudly presents 'to you [the audience] The Commissioner of Police' (p. 230), he is asking them to witness the formation of monstrous men in uniform the beastliness of whom the audience supports. In *Born in the RSA* the audience becomes integrated into the court deliberations where human beings fighting for their rights are summarily condemned. In *Woza Albert!* Zuluboy, protesting against the non-violent attitude of turning the other cheek to the violent enemy, turns on the audience with his knobkerrie (fighting stick) and screams, 'Forgive them, they do not know what they are doing? They know! They know!' (p. 40). Here, the audience is all of white South African society. In the same play, a police character, talking directly to the audience, intones: 'Do you know about Section 29? That's a nice little law specially made for loafers like him ...' (p. 5) So, in case the audience is non-South African, they are given quick lessons on the system so that, finally, they agree with the authorities that 'these kaffirs can lie, hey?'

Two scenes of audience involvement are of particular interest. One, in *Woza Albert!* where one of the characters suddenly sees Morena (Jesus) in the audience:

- It's Morena – that one there with the white shirt.

- Morena? Ay, nonsense.... Is it Morena?

- It's him – I saw him in the *Sunday Times* with Bishop Tutu. It's him!

- Hey, speak to him.

- (nods with the invisible Morena) Excuse. Are you not Morena? Yiiiii! Hosanna! Morena! (The actors embrace joyously. Then follow Morena, frantically showing their passes and pleading.) (p. 23)

The two finally throw away their passes, after pleading unsuccessfully with Morena to take them to heaven. The scene is full of humour and satire; for, the truth is that Morena is a tool in the hands of the enemy luring his unwary victims into a sleepwalk on earth with their eyes and minds pointing up toward heaven, while he, firmly rooted in their land, is exploiting its earthly riches.

The other scene comes from *Asinamali!* ('we have no money') where, in the burial procession for the rent-protest hero, Msizi Dube, 'a man among men', all the characters cry out, *ASINAMALI!*, and Bhoyi, the main character, says:

– Shhh ... and the government informers killed him. I think I see an informer in the audience.

ALL – WHERE?
(They all jump and go to different places in the audience picking out people indiscriminately and warning them. After a few hot moments they all come back to the centre of the stage.)

Bhoyi – That anger was not only the problem of Lamontville township. But it became the problem of the whole of South Africa. But now, understand. It is not only about the language Afrikaans. It is not only about rent increases. It is not only about job reservations and working conditions. It's not only about gold (. . .) Not only about the vote. What is it? hey! What is it? You. (points to a white member of the audience). You, stand up. Go for him boys!

ALL – (Jump up and go towards the person in audience) STAND UP!!!

Bhoyi – What is it? Talk! You think I'm playing games with you. You think I'm acting. Sit down. My friend. You've got to look for it. It's deep down in your heart. (pp. 211–12)

Mbongeni Ngema's *Asinamali!* is perhaps the play most marked by passion and anger against Western/white collaborators of apartheid and, as the above scene clearly confirms, no one can claim to be innocent; for, sitting on the fence, indifference, is proof of support for the genocide being perpetrated against Blacks. The quoted scene questions the West's humanity. As a kind of total theatre, it involves everyone and every aspect of humanity in the contestatory process; in essence, it demands to know what is being done to maintain human life.

It cannot be overemphasized that these plays are not simply a matter of dialogues, monologues and accusations. The thrust, as we have stated, is the community. Besides *Gangsters* in which nothing categorical is said about the actor playing the role of Whitebeard (the white policeman), all the other plays indicate that Blacks play white roles, using moustache and pink nose. Of course, segregation is the norm in apartheid hell and the absence of white actors is a statement. In spite of the international audience, the plays can still be categorized as 'popular' theatre, using performing arts to help people develop a critical awareness of their situation and a commitment to collective action.... Art is used in a deliberately functional sense – not as an end in itself, but as a medium of social transformation.... This more functional and participatory use of the performing arts has been called 'popular theatre', which has been defined as 'people's theatre speaking to the common man in his language and idiom and dealing with problems of direct relevance to his situation'. It is 'popular' because it attempts to involve the whole community, not just a small elite determined by class or education.[7]

The African community can relate to the plays represented without acts, just scenes, often only one long scene, with the action flowing freely to and fro, back and forth, on the streets, in the cities, prison, police-station, court, township homes, in scenes and scenarios of everyday life. Soyinka calls it 'theatre of poverty', with very few props, and a few actors playing multiple roles: in *Woza Albert!*, for example, the two actors play some 20 different roles. Not only is the language violent, the imagery captured by words, expressions and songs, is vivid and shocking and no symbol is more poignant than that of the bulldozer in *Children of Asazi*, becoming the apartheid monster itself, razing Black houses, destroying destinies and hope for happiness. Simultaneously with the confused sounds of demolition are the angry, confused voices of the victims. But, suddenly, the cacophony is blurted out by choreographed, harmonious sounds of human voices and the movement of objects: this is symbolic of the people's reorganization and resistance and, indeed, commitment to their cause. So also is Diliza's recital accompanying the saxophone-blowing of Mabu: 'Blow the hell out of the bulldozer/Blow for Afrika' (p. 127).

According to Duma Ndlovu, these plays have been created for township audiences, offering a vision of hope, contrary to white South African plays' tendency to 'sound a note of hopelessness'. 'These plays give direction, ask questions, provide answers, and tell us, yes, there will be change in the country, sooner than most people think.' (p. xxv) The editor also informs us that *Born in the RSA* is the only play of the six to come out of a theatrical institution, Barney Simon's Market Theatre. Yet this critic is not completely convinced that the balance, as far as audience is concerned, is not tilted towards the oppressor group (the West). The reality of South Africa probably has prevented the township audience from witnessing these plays and the saga of *Woza Albert!* is an eye-opener: Percy Mtwa and Mbongeni Ngema, the playwrights, spent three years literally on the run, from South Africa to the supposedly free and liberal Transkei, rehearsing and running the risk of never reaching their goal, until they contacted Barney Simon. Reminiscent of the paternal figure of Athol Fugard, Simon's name spelt success, especially overseas. One might say that the whole matter is one of reality and realism. All the same, a theatre of commitment must begin to face another reality, that Africa is not yet determinant of her own destiny and, as long as catalysts and mentors continue to come from the other side, real change might never occur.

The final song of *Children of Asazi* is a take-off on Martin Luther King's famous March on Washington speech:

Yes I had a dream
that one day
there'll be this time
This time of togetherness ... (p. 127)

And, on one or two occasions, references are made to pan-Africanism (for example, p. 241). These two allusions are significant: they point towards possibilities which, unfortunately, the plays have not fully exploited. Presenting a bland imitation of a great speech is in bad taste. Throwing out pan-Africanist jargon is a sign of shallowness when the natural bonds between Africans of the continent and those of the diaspora could make not only for interesting but progressive, essential theatre. One has often wondered what Africans outside of South Africa are ready to do in the liberation struggle. All that is visible is the sham solidarity of governments paying lip-service, setting up public funds that go into private pockets.

The Complexities of Commitment

Regarding commitment within South Africa itself, there is no doubt that, overall, the six plays paint a picture of courage and trace the process of awakening in certain individuals that originally lack consciousness.

Among the most interesting symbols of commitment is Morena (Jesus) depicted in *Woza Albert!* Mtwa and Ngema, the authors, wonder about the second coming of Christ, how black South Africans would receive him, their expectations, the reaction of apartheid government.... So, we have a series of scenes where people are told of Morena's return, and their reaction. Each person makes personal demands and, true to form, Morena brings days of joy, bread, peace, harmony and relief to the barber, Auntie Dudu, workers Zuluboy and Bobbejaan, the meat-seller and others. However, the joy may be short-lived.

We will all go to Morena for our blessings (...) And then ... the government will begin to take courage again.... The police and the army will assemble from all parts of the country.... And one night, police dogs will move in as they have done before. There will be shouts at night and bangings on the door ... (p. 26)

That notwithstanding, the end of the play is uplifting: Morena leads the protagonists to the cemetery and resurrects the dead heroes of the Struggle (pp. 51-3). On the other hand, Morena is rejected by the apartheid authorities who, calling him a communist terrorist, try unsuccessfully to imprison and to kill him. While the point of using the symbol is well taken, the detractors of Africa might use the example to make new claims to the necessity for their long condemned 'civilizing mission'. Christ has been, so to speak, africanized through the name-change, which does not mean that he is African and, no matter how many honorary degrees are awarded to the Tutus of South Africa, the Christians have shown no sign that they are willing to help overthrow apartheid. That, in essence, would be the thrust of the prisoner's cry to Morena: 'Power to the people!' In addition, we should re-affirm the satirical use of the Morena symbol.

The resurrection of leaders at the end of *Woza Albert!* is to be seen in the same light as the exuberant ending of *Asinamali!* where Bhoyi, the activist follower of Msizi Dube, asks: 'Where are our leaders today.' (sic) All the prisoners jump up and, in unison, shout out names of heroes past and present. Ndlovu considers this roll-call 'judgment that these heroes did not die or languish in jails in vain' (p. xxv). The challenge is for the living not to believe that the dead would really return, for the living to derive courage from the heroes and move ahead with the Struggle. The plays under discussion, beyond the passion of the instant, have not captured that poignancy that would make the living's commitment authentic.

The same would not be true of *Gangsters*, the play based upon the life of Steve Biko. The hero, Rasechaba, is a poet jailed, tortured and murdered. As a poet, he runs the risk of being a man of many words and no action. As is affirmed in another play, *Children of Asazi*, 'We don't sleep or eat words, my son. Don't let words become your master' (p. 100). Maishe Maponya makes sure that the poetry of his hero is militant and meaningful to the masses, that it is a call to action and, indeed, an aspect of revolutionary action. The poems are strategically placed in the play, to serve particular purposes: as proof of 'life become unfair to black soul' (p. 65); defining the state of death of the African sold to apartheid slavery (p. 69), and the africanity of the poet (p. 72);

relating the poet's arrest at his home by 'messengers of darkness' (p. 81) and, finally declaring Rasechaba's love for the land:

> So deep is my love for my land that those who fail to understand seek to destroy me.

> Perhaps, finally at the very end
> When the curtain falls
> On the last act of your pillage
> You will come to understand
> How deeply
> We loved this land
> And cared for all its people.
> (upright and now facing the audience)
> White and black
> Free and unfree. (p. 86)

In short, Rasechaba is, like Biko, totally committed to the Struggle. He shows immense courage and, significantly, a genuine solidarity with the people. He affirms: 'My leader is the people' (p. 75).

If Rasechaba symbolizes the adult hero, Diliza, the young schoolboy poet in *Children of Asazi*, is proof of the important role being played by children in South Africa. Diliza's poetry is more prosaic than Rasechaba's, but the ultimate objective attained is no less authentic. When he asks, 'Where are the men?', Diliza is making a serious comment upon the quality of men and the seriousness of the work to be done. The graphic descriptions of children being mowed down by police remind one of Soweto. Also of interest is young Diliza's success in conscientizing his father Nduna, a reactionary who finally joins the resistance. Furthermore, this play shows that commitment is realized with the family, nucleus of the nation, serving as springboard. Diliza reconciles his separated father and mother just as in *Bopha!* the schoolboy Zwelakhe succeeds in goading his father Njandini to resign from the police. The politicization of the father goes hand in hand with that of his brother, Naledi. The criticism is that this ending is somewhat unconvincing and ill-contrived. For one thing, Naledi is not truly freed from apartheid's dehumanization since he is expressing joy at having regulated his passbook. For another, Njandini's action is left undefined.

The love affair between Diliza and Charmaine constitutes one of the few attempts to portray woman. Charmaine is rather self-centred and apolitical, mainly concerned with 'when the boy would have time for her'. *Born in the RSA*, on the contrary, makes a more serious effort to present female characters involved in the

anti-apartheid movement, and it is the only occasion when black
and white work together in the persons of Thenjiwe, black trade-
unionist leader, Susan, her white friend, and their white lawyer,
Mia. Interestingly enough, Barney Simon is one of the authors of
this inter-racial play, just as he participates in the production of
Woza Albert! The attempt to move beyond black and white is com-
mendable and one is struck by Mia's appreciation of Thenjiwe:
'This ... will be the first woman president of South Africa!!!'
(p. 140) The lawyer herself is symbol of total commitment; she has
no family, is a divorcee, and has been political all her life. The
Mia character leads to some thinking on commitment: how successful and authentic would it be where one is not as 'free' as
Mia? Would one really feel this 'desperate need to change the
world we live in'? (p. 135)

Thenjiwe is well portrayed as a woman of courage and she
would be in the class of Rasechaba. None the less, one wonders
why she is restricted to the role of women's leader. One might
even ask why no women are involved in the artistic effort of the
anthology. The unique figures in *Born in the RSA* do not make one
forget the all too often derogatory, chauvinistic allusions to women
in *Woza Albert!* (e.g., pp. 6, 13, 15, 16, 27, 29). It is true that
workers generally use low-down language and refer to the female
body in jest; yet it is important that serious theatre find other
means of exhibiting earthiness. What is supposed to be good comic
relief could be an unwary submission to stereotypy, harmful to the
whole community.[8]

Several instances of forced show of commitment are seen in
these plays, although we agree with the editor that the final,
positive, statement of hope is essential. The roll-call at the end of
Asinamali! is glaring for its inconclusive impact. It were as if
recognizing the heroic leaders would transform the prisoners into
committed figures. An explanation in support of the playwrights'
artistic ploy would be that everyone should have a chance to
change for the better.

Of Masters & Their Collaborators

As is to be expected, the apartheid masters are not portrayed in
that positive light. In fact, among the most realistic portraitures
are those of the oppressors. The white-black relationship is
absolute as far as officialdom goes. Even when a black policeman
is senior to a white one, the latter is considered superior to the
former. Whites wear blue caps; Blacks, brown. *Bopha!* gives

details of police training and black policemen are most dedicated
to duty, most insensitive, most objective in their work:

> The law is the law. The police are not the law. The police are
> the protectors of the law and the law is made by the white man
> there in Pretoria (...) I'm proud to be a sergeant today. A true
> gentleman. A man amongst men. A policeman of strength and
> loyalty. (p. 233)

And the same character intones: 'If you can't beat them, join
them.' In a very successful use of comparison and contrast,
Bopha! throws the lie at the face of this slave and he learns soon
enough that he is only a 'man' in as much as he follows instructions to kill his own children, murder his own brothers and sisters
and remain a tool in the hands of the master.

Such a collaborator is Jonathan in *Gangsters*. He is at the
mercy of Whitebeard who is there solely to ascertain that the
black policeman carries through the action of murdering by
torture the poet Rasechaba. The tragic drama is made to show the
murderers in their despicable inhumanity and most convincing is
the portrayal of Jonathan as the guilty one. Thus, the collaborator
is shown to be in an absolute state of self-hate while his 'lord' and
'king of kings', Whitebeard, proud in his innocence, teaches him
how to hide the marks of torture on the poet's dead body and to
explain the death to the court. Jonathan is certain that the Whites
will always be in power and he is one black person not won
over by Rasechaba's poetry. The play is so well crafted that this
exclusion from the poet's reach is explained by the fact that
Whitebeard deliberately hides the poems from Jonathan.

This act on the part of the white policeman is used to make
another important statement, that Whites are actually afraid of
the Africans. Whitebeard shows respect for Rasechaba when they
are together. Thenjiwe dominates her prison-guards in *Born in the
RSA*. In *Bopha!* policemen panic and shoot children in the back.
The element of fear, coupled with the more sophisticated way in
which murder is being committed, is already a big dent in apartheid's armour. We quote here from Soyinka's Nobel speech
dedicated, by the way, to Nelson Mandela:

> Every act of racial terror, with its vastly increasing sophistica-
> tion of style and escalation in human loss, is itself an
> acknowledgment of improved knowledge of, and respect for, the
> potential of what is feared, an acknowledgement of the
> sharpening tempo of triumph by the victimized.[9]

The panic and fear of the police do not respect any racial law.
Black policemen are even more fearful than Whites; of course, we

know and they know that the petrol-laced necklace could suddenly transform their body into a blazing inferno. And Blacks could be more brutal than Whites. It is remarkable that, in all six plays, the only official work done by Blacks is in the police force and the irony is not lost on the reader when, in *Bopha!*, the Police Commissioner berates other countries for being jealous of South African police achievement in crime prevention. It is in the police that brother goes against brother; father goes against son; men torture children to coerce them into signing false statements. As the headmaster in *Born in the RSA* says: 'They are devils' (p. 168). What the master uses to enslave Blacks in the force is the false security offered them: 'Remember you'll have to feed your family on a policeman's salary' (p. 241).

The figure of a white collaborator, Glen Donahue, in *Born in the RSA*, is further proof of how racism is ever present even among interracial devils. Glen is a former graduate student turned informant, then police-officer. With a straight face he claims that 'racism is a problem everywhere, it's primal man . . .' (p. 160). The nausea that one feels at that statement would be comparable to that aroused by the policeman in *Bopha!* laughing hilariously at the sight of a man shot and rolling on the ground, in death-throes. The officer says that the man is doing break dance! (p. 251)

In spite of such nonchalance, such total block-out from what Soyinka has called the 'human otherness' of their victims, one comes away from the plays in Ndlovu's anthology with a certainty that both the masters and their collaborators are destined to fail. Witness the statement of the apparently phlegmatic Glen:

> I've often thought of becoming a game ranger or a forester or something. No, I'm being serious. You must go to Soweto, you must look at these kids, look into their eyes. It looks like we are all going to have our houses burned down pretty soon so I think the best place to be is in a place with no houses, you know – like a forest. (p. 173)

Conclusion: *Of Commitment & its Pitfalls*

Glen's desire to desert the land stolen by his ancestors is the ultimate proof of Black Power and the hope suffused in the theatre of commitment. Hope here is not a sublime state, cold and static, like a museum piece; it is a functional marker of revolutionary action. The individual may die so that the community may live; it is all in the cyclical culture. One pitfall is that the individual may have a fear of death, and of living. As the poet states in *Gangsters*, death of the soul is worse than physical demise:

Death is when your mouth can utter no cry.
Death is when your eyes cannot see the light beyond the
   darkness.
Death is when your ears cannot hear the call filtering
   through the noise.
Death is when your feet can no longer carry you through
   the distance.
Death is when you stop to be you!
And above all,
Death, is when you start to hate to be black! (p. 69)

When heroes die physically, we celebrate, convinced as we are
that their lives have not been wasted; yet, in celebrating heroes
dead and alive, there is the danger of messianism. In South Africa
today, the burden of heroism is a matter of controversy. The halo
might be too heavy; broken, it might reveal a head more ordinary
than extraordinary, more human than heroic. To a large extent,
the plays studied in this essay have avoided the pitfall of hero-
worship. They affirm that everyone brought down by an apartheid
bullet is a hero, that 'every grandmother that gets shot gives birth
to a thousand freedom fighters' (p. 163).
   The names may change, but the struggle remains the same.

When we clothe and house ourselves we must think of the
homeless and the unemployed of this township.
Yes we must think.
Think about how we can share the joys and sufferings
of this earth. (pp. 125-6)

We have confirmed that theatre, with its artistic malleability
and its habitat in the community, is the best vehicle for commitment. It is not absolute or absolutist like poetry and fiction and,
even in the worst representations, not as liable to definitive
obscurantism as the other genres. A change in scene or word can
make a whole lot of difference in theatre; and we note that some
of the plays in the anthology did not have a script to start with.
   The firm statement made in all the plays is that the final objective is freedom, and peace:

Let peace be the pulse of the heartbeat of this land.
Let it blossom in the hearts of all men
Perhaps those who destroy will understand what goes
with building. (p. 102)

Unfortunately, the optimistic endings have not succeeded in hiding
the reality of a still arduous journey ahead. It is the lawyer, Mia,
who declares in *Born in the RSA*:

They say we haven't even begun to feel the force of the government. That there are mountains of arms and mine shafts full of fuel (...) They talk about releasing Mandela and yet arrest people like Suzie and Thenjiwe! (pp. 170–1)

Anger at apartheid's bad faith leads some to seek total elimination of Whites: 'Time will come when we'll chase these whites away!' (p. 40) However, that position is not common. It would seem that a more conciliatory stand is generally accepted by the playwrights. Duma Ndlovu laments the present situation of tension:

It is unfortunate that ours is a country where one can never seem to escape describing work, art, theatre, dance, religion, any aspect of life in black and white. But maybe this tension is the very reason that South African art is as dynamic as it is. (p. xxviii)

Whatever happens, one thing is clear, that South Africans themselves must determine their destiny. Amilcar Cabral, the much regretted Guinea-Bissau revolutionary, cautioned the committed, reminding them that it is only in stories that you cross the river riding on a crocodile's back; for, in real life, crocodiles kill and devour human beings. In reading or watching these South African plays, one has the feeling that the victims of apartheid are prepared to fight to the very end. To the well known battle-cry, *Amandla!* (Power to the People), is now added a new one, *Sonqoba Simunye* (United We Will Conquer).[10]

NOTES & REFERENCES

All the six plays studied in this article make up *Woza Afrika! An Anthology of South African Plays*, edited by Duma Ndlovu, New York: George Braziller, 1986 edition. References will be made to pages from this original edition, in addition to the title of the particular play.

1. *Woza Albert!*: 46.
2. *Gangsters*: 69.
3. *Children of Asazi*: 101.
4. *Born in the RSA*: 176.
5. Preface to *Woza Afrika!*: xiii.
6. Dennis Brutus in Per Wästberg, ed., *The Writer in Modern Africa* (New York: Africana Publishing Corp., 1969): 33–4.
7. Quoted from UNICEF publication, in Robert Kavanagh, *Theatre and Cultural Struggle in South Africa* (London: Zed Books, 1985): 211–12.
8. The lack of adequate consideration of woman's role is a serious failing in these plays, particularly since women have contributed immensely. See Hilda Bernstein, *For Their Triumphs and For Their Tears* (International Defence and Aid Fund, 1985).
9. Wole Soyinka, 'This Past Must Address Its Present', *MPLA* 102–5 (October 1987): 764.
10. Every play in the collection ends with the affirmation (pp. 53, 87, 127, 176, 224, 257).

Folklore & Tradition
in the Drama
of Cliff Lubwa p'Chong

Sam Kasule

Lubwa p'Chong is the leading Uganda playwright in English. His works include *Generosity Kills* and *The Last Safari* (1972),[1] and *The Minister's Wife* (1982).[2] Yet to be published are *The Bishop's Daughter* (1988)[3] which discusses moral decadence and hypocrisy in the church today, *Do not Uproot the Pumpkin* (1987)[4] a stage adaptation of Okot p'Bitek's *Song of Lawino*,[5] *Kinsmen and Kinswomen* (1988)[6] which deals with issues of extended families, and *The Madman* (1989).[7] He has described all these plays as being 'very very, political'.[8] He has also published a collection of poetry, *Words of my Groaning* (1975).[9] He is a realistic and direct dramatist who belongs to the 'song school'. The 'song', being emotive and the most popular traditional performance genre, became the major motif of the writings of Okot p'Bitek and many Ugandan writers. This form adapts and transforms idiomatic expression into English making the end-product appeal to literate and semi-literate audiences alike. It develops the stylistic features of traditional orature as a means of re-awakening communal and collective responsibility in society. Lubwa p'Chong's sensitivity to socio-political issues and 'humaneness', as alternatives to political absolutism, is evident in the play texts discussed in this article.

Generosity Kills

Generosity Kills,[10] like *The Last Safari*,[11] a dramatization of a legend, belongs to Lubwa p'Chong's earlier works contextualizing the disorder in Uganda's history. It was written for performance during the Makerere Arts Festival Week of 1971. In the plot, Latina discovers a new recipe for beer and, in her excitement, she brews it and generously serves the whole community. The chief of the village consumes a substantial amount and passes out and is mistaken for dead. On waking from his stupor he demands to see Latina to congratulate her, only to be informed that she has been killed, an act fulfilling the Acholi proverb 'Generosity kills the generous ones.' Latina's brewing skills, her inventiveness and generosity lead to her death. Lubwa p'Chong adapts the form and structure of the folktale illustrating how excessive well-meaning behaviour can be detrimental to an individual.

The Prelude to the First Movement begins with excitement as a group of people drink beer at Latina's house. It is a traditional evening setting complete with story-telling, dance, and music. The characters in this scene are only referred to as 1st Man, 2nd Man, 3rd Man, who are villagers or representatives of a community whose voices may easily be mimicked by the narrator. On behalf of an Elder, who arrives too late to share the brew, the Boy warns the Girl to '... leave a remnant/In the bottom of the pot'. After goading the Elder to explain how 'generosity' which has '... no hands/For holding knives, stick or Spears/To kill ...' could have killed Latina, the Elder becomes the Narrator-cum-Diviner and the scene is transformed into a re-enactment of Latina's legend. He uses a diviner's 'cloak' and 'gourd rattles' to invoke the spirits of Latina and her adversaries. Weird sounds signify the response of the spirits to the invoking sounds of the rattles. In performance the Elder and his audience join the secondary audience in the circle off the stage to witness the re-enactment of the legend. The Elder, as Diviner, appeases Latina's spirit approaching earth from the underworld beckoning her to 'Come in peace ... Slowly, slowly ...' Latina, and her daughter, Lawino, appear centre stage and are later joined by Oluma the husband. After Lawino has accomplished her 'creation', Oluma drunkenly dances and laughs while Lawino yodels to climax.

Dramatic irony is achieved when Twon-coo and other neighbours initially dismiss the brew as 'soppy bread' or 'the sickly vomit of a dog' only to discover its potency. The point to note is the communal spirit of the society which collectively responds to the alarm (ululating) – this time resulting from excitement – and are willing to share the achievements and shortcomings of their neighbours. Latina observes communal ethics when she takes her brew to the Chief for,

> ... our people say
> If you kill an animal, however small it may be
> One leg belongs to the Chief.
> Chief ... here is your share. (p. 15)

The Chief gulps the drink and talks wildly, reciting his heroics to the background of exciting music. Lubwa p'Chong's ridicule of the Chief is highlighted in the following extracts.

(*He [the Chief]* again drinks it non-stop. He begins to sway. Gets up, dropping the calabash, and begins to talk wildly)

I went to hunt,
A buffalo came,
It came as if singing:
'Children, children, children.
See, see, see,
My liver, my liver, my liver ...' (p. 16)

and later,

(*He looks at one of the court jesters who is not even standing near any of the Chief's wives*)

Chief:	You, you, what are you doing?
The Court Jester:	Nothing, Nothing, Chief.
Chief:	Nothing, Chief, nothing, Chief.
	Do you think I am blind?
	Do you think
	I did not see
	What you were doing?
	(*staggering towards him drunkenly*)
	How dare you, a commoner,
	Touch the Chief's wife? (p. 1)

Laughter is provoked from the audience by his attempt to chase the Court Jester round the stage. As the Chief strikes the Court Jester the latter ducks and he falls on the floor. More laughter is 'milked' from the audience by his abortive attempts to stand before he finally lies prostrate, dead drunk. Like a 'commoner', he is embarrassingly awakened from his stupor by the throbbing drums and the cold water poured over him. The awe, embarrassment, shock and communal guilt is expressed by the silent moment, as the Chief looks round searching for Latina. The projection of the Chief in this state is meant not only to criticize chiefs who behave in a manner contrary to their positions of responsibility in the community, but to caution people against the evils of taking strong drink.

Lubwa p'Chong intends to recapture in English the aesthetics of Acholi. The poetic effect of the play is realized through images, symbols, similes, proverbs and metaphors which relate to the cultural environment and are very much part of the audience's life. For example, describing the potency of the beer, the 3rd Man says, 'See how it [the beer] vomits clean froth.' Latina describes Lawino's emerging breasts as 'pawpaws'. The lyrics in the language are highlighted in Oluma's description of the brew as,

> ... not *gasia* (*tastes*)
> This is sour-sour. (*tastes*)
> Bitter-bitter. (*tastes*)
> Sweet-sweet. (*shakes his head*)
> Strong-strong ... (p. 8)

Similes, praise-names and other images are used by the characters to describe each other, such as Oluma's description of Latina as, '... the mother-in-law of birds ...' whose mouth has been beaten with 'the testicles/Of a he-goat'.

Glorious mention of one's roots by the naming of clan and praising of parents is an instinctive response in the people's daily life. It is done to summon one's courage in moments of danger, to show pride, warn off potential antagonists and display determination:

> Oluma: Woman shut up!
> Let me drink this drink in peace,
> (*Drinks and belches*)
> I am the son of my mother!
> I am the son of the woman
> Whose teeth are white
> Like dry season moon!
> I am your wife beat you with pestle ... (pp. 9–10)

It is the praises, and the subsequent cajoling adjectival phrases, which make the scene in which Oluma's neighbours share his brew light-hearted, humorous and memorable.

> *Oluma holding the calabash in one hand, shakes*
> *hands with him [Twon-coo]. They call each other praise names.*

> Oluma: *Yaa* Twon-Coo!
> Twon-Coo: *Yaa* Oluma yaa!
> Oluma: *Yaa* a dog urinated in your wound!
> Twon-Coo: *Yaa* your wife beat you with pestle!
> Oluma: How are you man?
> Twon-Coo: Healthy as sunrise.
> Oluma: Put your buttocks down man.
> Twon-Coo: (*sitting*) Thank you, friend.
> What are you drinking?
> Oluma: We are drinking millet bread
> Which our child dumped in water.
> Twon-Coo: So you drink *Gasia*, rubbish? (p. 1)

In juxtaposing ritual, divination, invocation, and legend Lubwa p'Chong transforms the traditional story-telling genre into a theatrical mode. The result is a mutually shared experience of the legend by both audiences – the primary audience assisting the narrator to animate the story and the secondary audience watching the dramatization.

The Last Safari

This is a dramatization of a folktale existing both in Acholi and Buganda, centred on Ketimo (or Mpoobe in Buganda), a hunter of great repute, who defies the ominous signs of fate. When Ketimo goes hunting, he ends up in the Kingdom of Death in the underworld. Death releases him on condition that he should never reveal his experiences. When he breaks the promise Death strikes him.

Lubwa p'Chong focuses our attention on the spear, the strongest symbol of the homestead in many Ugandan communities. It is the pride of the homestead, source of food, and 'guard/over all!' Neglected and rusty, the spear is discovered by the Young Man who raises the alarm, calling the whole cast to the stage. The Old Man interprets the sacrilege as the cast bursts into a mournful dirge indicting the community for having neglected the 'shrine of my father' and left the 'hippo-spear sleeping out'. The Old Man proclaims that social chaos, disorder, rape and robbery will prevail and the community will have to pay the price. The dirge highlights the shared social guilt. It is a dirge for a community plunged into chaos by reckless individuals who should have been guardians of the people's conscience, physically symbolized by the ancestral shrine. The whole community has participated in the erosion of the human essence, the cultural mores which made it whole. The state of the neglected spear is parallel to the state of a community which has become powerless, defenceless and helpless.

The First Movement is full of ominous signs such as the sounds of cock-crow, hoots of the owl, and Ketimo's sneeze as he cleans his hunting spear. His wife, Binen, dreams of Ketimo sitting under a 'big *Kituba* tree/While young men were digging a grave' (p. 27). Contrary to her interpretation of the dream – Ketimo should not go hunting – Ketimo predicts a successful hunt. Further, Binen draws her son's attention to the multiplicity of ominous signs hovering over the homestead:

Binen: Mh, my son, do you call that
success.
Don't you know

Meat is red
Like grave soil?
To make the matter worse,
An owl was hooting
Just before you sent for me.
When owls hoot at dawn,
It means death, sure death.
Therefore, this owl
Was announcing someone's death;
And that person
Must be close, close,
For the owl was sitting on your
roof. (p. 30)

It is signals such as these that Lubwa p'Chong exploits to create
a fresh indigenous theatrical shorthand.[12]

The play is a multidimensional reconstruction of Acholi
attitudes, thought-systems and social ceremonies relating to death
and human destiny. Tragedy is a communal concern to be shared
by friend and foe. Through imagery Lubwa p'Chong reminds the
audience that they should not laugh at victims of death like Cock:

Elder: (*cock crows*) *Diki Wang ca rommo neno pala!*
A Man: Tomorrow the knife
           will sink past
           The ram's throat!
Clan
Leader: And the ram answers:
           In kono ibi dok kwere ki abila pa kwara?
A Man: What about you, cock,
           How will you escape
           Being sacrificed at the ancestral
           shrine?
Clan
Leader: (*addressing everybody*) The death
           That killed your brother
           Will be the death
           That will kill you. (p. 41)

The ubiquitous nature of death (fate) is further expressed in the
extended eulogy by Binen and the thematic content of the dirges.
Binen, using hyperbole, refers to her tragic loss of a son as,

... the sharp axe
Of death, the unkind one
Has felled Ketimo ... (p. 39)

and

Then my son must be dead.
My clansmen. Come and see me,
This cruel world has knelt on me
And crushed me completely. (p. 39)

She personalizes death, drawing a picture of a cruel, beastly, and blood-thirsty person who fells people like trees. Okot p'Bitek[13] notes that, among the Acholi, Fate is described with hunting images of 'kneeling and crushing'. These derive from the manner in which a wounded buffalo, for lack of strength, falls and crushes its victim with its massive weight.

The climactic conclusion to the tragedy is a synchronized mime of omnipresent Death and his assistants dancing to the rhythm of an Acholi dirge, stalking, shouting and wooing Ketimo to his Death. The Acholi metaphysics visualize Ketimo being locked in battle with death while his people helplessly watch him receding beyond the horizon. The audience may

> ... just sit there stone still in their seats though alive in every fibre of their being to every little movement or sound or impression that is being projected to them by the actors ... intensely silent, but intellectually and emotionally active [in] participation ...[14]

The ritual presented in its entirety in the play is the blessing of the hunters' spears by Binen. Ketimo and his friends hold their spears and stand forming an arc, while the elders stand behind them. A liturgical prayer intended to placate the ancestors, inspire the hunters and woo animals to their traps, is chanted in a litany. As Binen sprinkles ritual water on the spears, she leads the chant and the elders respond with the last line of her incantation. The hunters do not respond till the last lines of the prayer. Binen prays to the ancestors to bless the spears so that they may 'Drip red with animal blood'. She asks the evil spirits which live in rivers, big trees, dark mountains, shady forests, caves and holes to give way to the hunters. This part of the prayer illuminates the metaphysical and cosmic nature of Acholi belief and the possibility of communing with evil as well as good ancestral spirits.

Sacrifice and ritual are important facets in the development of the plot. Ketimo's return from the bush is a representation of a funeral crowd 'unfearingly' speaking their minds for the good of the victims of death and the community. The elders emphasize to Ketimo the importance of instant sacrifice for falsely shed tears – to be instantly washed away with a bull's blood – else he would end up in the 'stomach of the earth'. Using mimicry, the Elders recall Lekamoi's words:

I still do not have a bull,
I still do not have a bull ...
Now where is the young man?
Is he not in the stomach of the earth? (p. 45)

The men led by the Clan Leader use strong images to make their point.

Clan Leader: If you want to kill a snake
　　　　　　safely, kill it in the egg,
　　　　　　Don't wait till it breathes. (p. 45)

and

Elder:　　　Evil is like
　　　　　　Dog's dung, [it] must be removed
　　　　　　From the floor
　　　　　　While it is still steaming.
1st Man: 　True, if you wait till it gets
　　　　　　cold,
　　　　　　It stinks. (p. 45)

Lubwa p'Chong uses language with intensity, as in the speech when Binen mourns her son's death with the poetry of a funeral ceremony declamation. She draws attention to her plight by dramatizing her sorrow as she imagines her son, '... rotting/ Somewhere in the grass/Like a dog!' (p. 39). In anguish she decries the hyenas, bald-headed vultures and worms laughing at her son's body, breaking bones, eating out the intestines, burrowing into his beautiful eyes, ears and mouth (p. 40). She further carries the audience into the abyss by alternating images of Ketimo's body being ravaged by land as well as aquatic creatures. The images used by Binen intensify the tragedy because they are within the immediate social experience of the people as, again, they are allegorically referring to their experiences under the Amin regime.[15]

The Madman

This play, written after an interlude in which Lubwa p'Chong changed his style, marks his maturity as a playwright able to mix the contemporary and myth, legend and fantasy. His argument in The Madman is that ultra-egotism and myth-making have contributed to the state of dictatorship and the gun culture endemic in Uganda's politics. The play laments Fruits of Independence, Matunda Ya Uhuru, which have not been delivered thus causing a paralysis in a society where human and temporal clocks have stopped:

> The clock at the prestigious Mulago Hospital's eye-nose-throat clinic reads 4:56. On the tower of Makerere University's administration building the clock reads 12:20. Above the main entrance to the high court in downtown Kampala it reads 11:14. Inside the main post-office it reads 12:27. All over Kampala clocks have stopped – at different times.[16]

It is a society where the élite at the national university drive their '... Mercedes on the sidewalk right up to the door of their office building ....'[17] In Uganda the euphemism for this institutionalized madness is 'Aminism' or 'Oboteism'.

In *The Madman*, the legend of Walukagga has been so dramatized that at each stage the equation with the modern situation can be recognized (the same legend has been treated by Eli Kyeyune in *Bemba Musota*). In style and form, the play illustrates the theatrical trend in Uganda by which artists use folklore, pre-colonial themes and traditional structures to interpret and criticize contemporary conditions. As in the earlier plays, the Narrator plays a central role in the plot. He outlines the conflicts in the plot underlining the fear experienced by the villagers, '... for each morning the sun rose with news of some new orders ... and nobody's life was safe' (p. 5). He highlights the misdeeds of the Chief, noting his manipulation of the people through plunder, torture and murder. His warrior vigilantes follow his instructions without '... caring about right or wrong .... They operated anywhere at any time, and in full public view ... ran wars of intimidation and terror ... looted and destroyed property, killing and maiming, raping young and old women ... widows ... sowing yaws [AIDS]!' (p. 6). The people reached their nadir when the royal warriors, in executing their 'painful duty' of collecting human tears and hair, broke bottles and used the pieces to shave heads. In the end 'popular anger' forced the Chief to relinquish power to a committee of elders. The end-form of folktales in Buganda is used by the Narrator when he describes how the people celebrated the Chief's downfall:

> ... I came away to tell you the story. (*plays a tune briefly* [*on his bowl-lyre*]) And up to this day in Uganda, there is a proverb which says: A man will take his problem to a madman when sane men fail (*Wokubira omulalu mu kyama nga omulamu gwolaba*). (p. 109)

One of the characters in *The Madman* is Walukagga, the

Blacksmith who, in *Ganda* printed literature is a folk figure.[18]
Lubwa p'Chong exploits the conflict between a megalomaniac,
self-centred Chief and the peasant Walukagga. The latter represents the *Will* of the people, the unspoilt elements of harmonious
communal existence and humaneness. The Chief represents
despotic rulers.

Chief mistrusts crowds and only visits at short notice. When
he eventually appears on stage he rolls his 'frightened ... eyes
terribly' to frighten the villagers. This parodies the manner in
which both Obote and Amin faced their audience at the ebb of
their rule. Using phrases and words relished by dictators, he
orchestrates forced applause from the villagers. The people are
his 'masters' and he is their 'humble servant', the 'shamba boy',
labouring in their gardens for their own good. For this reason they
are 'fat' and *must* 'Clap for your happiness'. His images and
metaphors are beastly and obscene, showing a person whose
brain has been crippled by power, wealth and innocently spilt
blood. For example, he illustrates his contribution to the welfare
of the villagers, by comparing their physical state at the beginning
of his reign to 'chickens drenched by some heavy rains ... cows
suffering from dysentery' (p. 23). But now they are 'sleek like lion's
cubs! ... like well-fed puppies ... bubbling with life like well
brewed *kwete* beer!' (p. 24).

Chief's intellectual dwarfism and gullibility is further exhibited
in the riddle he gives the women to solve. He is oblivious to the
sufferings of his people, failing to interpret the women's answer
to his riddle in which they echo the suffering unleashed on the
community because of his greed. They tell him, that after eating
a lot of 'saliva-bringing food', his hunger goes to a poor person in
his kingdom, and so does his illness after he is cured of an illness.
The women's solution to the riddle means that the Chief's rule has
merely putrefied society. Chief makes a decree that no one else
in his Chiefdom is to be referred to by the title 'CHIEF'[19]
any more, and all holders of the title will henceforth be called
'Clan-overseers, Village Heads, [and] Communal organisers ...'
(p. 25). Dramatic irony is effected when we realize that the 'Chief
Hunters' will effectively become 'Head Hunters'. The pun is
not lost on the audience as the villagers, at 'spear-point' (gun-
point), chant refrains parallel to contemporary party songs, 'One
Chiefdom, One Chief.'

The ritual of peasants offering gifts to visiting 'dignitaries' is
structurally used to precipitate the conflict between Chief and his
people. Village Head 1 offers a 'Hammer' to the Chief. Village
Head 2 offers a 'Chain'. Village Head 3 a '*Panga* (Matchet)' and
Village Head 4 offers a 'Spear'. Chief is the 'Chief Murderer', the

master blacksmith, forging dead bodies out of his human subjects. The audience is aware of the apparent misuse of these symbols of torture and cruel death, so that the euphemism for Amin is 'Matchet' (*Kijjambiya*) and his regime is the 'Matchet's reign' (*Omulembe gwa Kijjambiya*). The intended parallelism of the Chief's regime with Amin and the post-Amin state security organs (Head Hunters) is quite clear.

Chief, incensed by the display of praise for Walukagga, dares, '. . . our clever blacksmith [Walukagga] . . . to forge me a man who can eat and starve, can cry and laugh, can love and hate, can kill and be killed . . .' (p. 39). Because jealousy, rivalry, ambition and greed have become a way of life in the community, abductions and extermination of work-mates, neighbours and relatives are commonplace. In the conflict between Walukagga and the Chief, the latter is supported by the evil blacksmiths. Walukagga's adversaries preoccupy themselves with mud-slinging, spreading '*ladit*' (nepotism and corruption), backbiting, bickering, gossiping and rumour-mongering.

Lubwa p'Chong's dramatic vision is evidenced by his choice of folklore material from east, west, south, north and central Uganda to represent the 'various types of madness of our time and place'.[20] In an interview given after the première production of *The Minister's Wife* he remarked that '. . . particularly after the fall of Amin . . . about 90 per cent of Ugandans' heads are not correct . . .'[21] In using 'madness' as a motif he is contemplating the plight of Ugandans who continue to suffer at the hands of a few mad politicians. He traverses post-independent Ugandan history identifying positive and negative forms of 'madness' in society. His target is the negative and destructive madness of politicians which has moved the leadership in Uganda from reconciliation to intimidation, to the systematic elimination of citizens in the Amin regime, and the near-genocidal massacres under Obote. The addition of the madman in the play is a thematically important feature. He represents the people's past, present and probable future. He is a living example of those people who have paid a price for resisting the Chief's orders. He enters, '. . . wearing some human bones around his ankle like ankle bells, and carrying a human skull in one hand laughing at (and) with the skull' (p. 52). He cross-examines the human skull, his only companion, and the symbol of death and terror existing in society:

To whom did you belong? What was your sex? Place of birth? Age? Work?
Tribe? Religion? Marital status? How did you meet your end? (p. 52)

The question about the 'skull's' identity echoes the statement made by a former Ugandan Vice President to the effect that he should not be charged with the atrocities (in the 'Luwero Triangle') because the skulls in Luwero are unidentifiable.[22] The drum is replaced by the skull as the symbol of the kingdom. The Madman

> ... (*lifts up the human skull*) This is Chief's royal drum! (*beats it briefly ...*) (p. 61)

The substitution of the skull – which he presupposes to have belonged to his wife who with his children 'disappeared'[23] from his home – as 'the Reality of this chiefdom', marks the denouement.

The character of the Madman has multi-layered metaphorical significance in this play. Like Serumaga's Majangwa (in *Majangwa*),[24] the Madman is the 'conscience' of society, indicting the audience for mis-treating the sick in their midst. They,

> ... throw cruel jokes at me! You set your dogs on me! One of you one night scratched me all over the body with his barbed arrow for sleeping on his verandah! Your children throw stones at me but you don't reproach them! A bad animal comes from a bad bush. You and your children are the same: mad! You are like Chief! Mad! You enjoy inflicting pains on people. Like Chief! ... (p. 61)

He underlines the 'mad sense of humour' prevalent in the community which makes people,

> ... Nyah, nyah, nyah, nyah! (*laugh*) at the misfortunes of others, at everything ..., Even when Chief says or does something that pulls our hair, and makes anger choke us, we burst out, nyah, nyah, nyah! Nyah, nyah, nyah, nyah ... nyah! (p. 68)

Society expunges its frustration, moral and physical corruption, on the mentally sick, turning them into 'carriers' of evil. There is dramatic reversal when the Madman comments that the 'madness' in society has reached such abominable depths that ancestral prayers relating to society's cosmology have changed.

> North is [now] south, and south is now north. The sun rises in the west and sets in the east ... (p. 60)

Contrary to the Acholi world-view by which people pray for evil to descend with the setting sun, the prayer asks:

> All the evils
> That are coming,
> Let the setting sun

Take them down
In the East!
And so they are taken down
In the east! (p. 60)

The Madman's image of the 'man' who can effectively tackle Chief is Lubwa p'Chong's metaphor for a strong ruler, capable of purging the country of all the evils symbolized in the Chief. He offers Walukagga a solution to his dilemma through a riddle to be given to the Chief. Sarcastic about Walukagga's troubles, he states that Chief's virility may be on the wane otherwise he would not require a 'man' forged from steel. In this mood he requests Walukagga to:

> ... forge us a man who will tackle Chief head on. A real man who will wrestle with Chief and throw him down. (*grabs Walukagga and throws him down*) Like that! To teach Chief some sense. Stupidity has built a permanent house over Chief [25] ... a man not with two balls only but five balls, who will grab Chief's big balls and pull them hard for us. Chief has fondled our balls for too long! (p. 56)

If Chief wants Walukagga to forge a man, he must provide him with 'a full five big sacks' of charcoal burnt from human hair and five big pots of 'human tears'. Chief orders his warriors to collect the items from all '... four corners of the chiefdom ... today before the sun sets' but they only manage to collect a pouch-full of hair and a bowl of tears. Dissatisfied, Chief orders everybody to 're-shave hair, and re-shed tears'. Should the villagers refuse, the warriors must

> ... slaughter all the people therein! Raze their huts and granaries to the ground! And drive all their livestock to the royal herd!.... Kill everyone then hang yourselves on the nearest tree! I must see only corpses tomorrow! (p. 86)

This is the turning point in the plot, for 'popular anger' turns the villagers against the Chief and they demand his resignation. In spite of promises for reform, Chief and his Chief Murderer Ssenkoole are tied up and elders take over the reins of the state. Lubwa p'Chong is optimistic that society will one day say 'NO' to dictators.

The use of indigenous images and phrases makes it easy for Lubwa p'Chong to make believable his themes and effectively communicate with the audience. Two women in the play (called Woman 1 and Woman 2) give us the impression that the issue of a multitude of edicts, decrees, legal notices and pronouncements is the Chief's delight.[26] Ethnicity is used by the Chief to manipulate his subjects as illustrated by his latest order by which everyone must stick to their places of ethnic origin. Woman 2 graphically describes the divisive and isolationist strategies of the Chief as a game of 'dividing, sub-dividing and sub-sub-dividing' society. The women are sarcastic about the nature of obedience prevalent in society:

Woman 1: Our children are now like little machines ...
Woman 2: When Chief presses Button A ...
Woman 1: They move ...
Woman 2: When Chief presses Button B ...
Woman 1: They stop ...
Woman 2: Like well-oiled little machines!
Woman 1: Obedience!
Woman 2: Obedience!
Woman 1: Obedience has become madness in this chiefdom.
Woman 2: We have become obedient like bulls trained for ploughing.
Woman 1: We are submissive!
Woman 2: So subordinated that even Chief's favourite expressions have become fashionable throughout the chiefdom.
Woman 1: Everyone wants to be his Master's voice!
Woman 2: Everybody dies to talk like Chief!
Woman 1: To smile like Chief!
Woman 2: To walk like Chief!
Woman 1: To stand like Chief!
Woman 2: To dress like Chief! (p. 12)

The climax of the 'play-in-play' is achieved when both women turn to the audience and in unison consult it on whether they should turn their Chief into a 'Chiefdom deity [President for Life]'. The scene illustrates the power with which Lubwa p'Chong uses folklore motifs and expressions to enhance his drama.

Absolutism and the demagogic position of the Chief in society is symbolized by the 'stick' he carries, for every person straying from 'the herd ... is beaten back'.[27] Implied in this image is the contemporary African leaders' ridiculous use of fetish-like paraphernalia such as sticks, fly whisks, and handkerchiefs. Talking through riddle and metaphor, the women satirize the maddening aspects of power, comparing it to the fangs of a poisonous snake.

Woman 2: ... the longer the person stays in power the longer his fang grows.
Woman 1: Until it grows out of his mouth like the teeth of a warthog.

Woman 2: Yes, power possesses man, with evil spirits!
Woman 1: And when a man is possessed with some evil spirits of power, he can wake up one day and tell the people under him, 'I want this mountain levelled down!
Woman 2: Yes, when power has possessed a man in power, the unthinkable becomes thinkable!
Woman 1: The impossible becomes possible!
Woman 2: And the useless becomes useful!
Woman 1: I tell you, power turns us into mad people.
(*They both burst out laughing*) (p. 22)

The theatrical devices include music, song and dance. Most outstanding is his use of the Luganda (sacred) folk song 'Walugono'. The villagers perform this song during the preparations of the village ground for Chief's visit. Walugono is a pugnacious god whose relationship with the community is as demanding and retributive as Chief's. In: '... mother's womb/Walugono twists babies' hands/He enlarges heads of babies/When they are born/ They are deformed' (pp. 16–17).

Throughout the performance the actors involve the audience to imply that they share the guilt for the country's decadence and must therefore help to remove the ogres in their midst.

Lubwa p'Chong effectively articulates the problems of society. However, because he writes in English his plays have a limited audience and one can only hope that they will begin to be translated into Acholi, Luganda and other indigenous languages.

NOTES

1. Cliff Lubwa p'Chong, *Generosity Kills and The Last Safari* (Nairobi: East African Publishing House, 1975).
2. Cliff Lubwa p'Chong, *The Minister's Wife* (Kampala: New Expression Press, 1983).
3. Cliff Lubwa p'Chong, *The Bishop's Daughter*, (Unpublished, 1988).
4. Cliff Lubwa p'Chong, *Do not Uproot the Pumpkin* (Unpublished, 1987).
5. Okot p'Bitek, Song of Lawino and Song of Ocol (London: Heinemann, 1984).
6. Cliff Lubwa p'Chong, *Kinsmen and Kinswomen* (Kampala: Crane Publishers 1988).
7. Cliff Lubwa p'Chong, *The Madman* (Unpublished, 1989).
8. Lubwa p'Chong made these comments in a letter to the present writer in May 1991.
9. Cliff Lubwa p'Chong, *Words of my Groaning* (Nairobi: East African Publishing House, 1975). (Dates in text are of first performance).
10. Lubwa p'Chong, *Generosity Kills.*

11. Lubwa p'Chong, *The Last Safari*.

12. This style is close to that used by Okot p'Bitek and Tom Omara.

13. Okot p'Bitek, *Horn of My Love* (London: Heinemann Educational Books, 1974): 150.

14. J.C. de Graft, 'Dramatic Questions' in *Writers in East Africa*, eds. Andrew Gurr and Angus Calder (Nairobi: East African Literature Bureau, 1972): 33–67.

15. Forests, lakes and rivers became dumping (burial) places for victims of state terrorism. Namanve, eight miles from Kampala City on Jinja Road, is a forest reserve which was the most favoured dumping spot. After the fall of Idi Amin it was declared a 'National Cemetery' by President Binaisa in 1979.

16. Adolf Enns, 'The Clocks Have Stopped in Uganda', in *Crisis in Uganda*, eds. P. Dodge Cole and Paul D. Wiebe (Oxford: Pergamon Press, 1985): 53–6.

17. Enns: 54.

18. Sir Apollo Kagwa, *Engero za Baganda (Baganda Folk stories)*, (London: Sheldon Press, 1956): 1–7. Zirimu's translation is quoted by Lubwa p'Chong in the introduction to the *The Madman*. Eli Kyeyune uses the same legend for his play, *Bemba Musota*.

19. This echoes Idi Amin Dada's Decree which forbade anybody other than himself to be referred to by the title, President.

20. See Lubwa p'Chong's Introduction to *The Madman*.

21. Interview with Alex Tetteh-Lartey of the BBC African Service Programme, *Arts on Africa*, (London) 7 June 1985.

22. The statement was made in 1989 before the 'Uganda Human Rights Commission' by Paulo Muwanga, a former Vice-President and Minister of Defence in Milton Obote's government.

23. 'Disappeared' (*yabula* or *yabuze*) is a euphemism coined to describe the method used by the state to exterminate its opponents. For more information see, Ali Mazrui, *Soldiers and Kinsmen in Uganda* (California: Sage Publications, 1975): 161.

24. Robert Serumaga, *Majangwa and A Play*, (Nairobi: East African Publishing House, 1974).

25. Here Lubwa adapts and directly translates the saying, '*Obusiru bumuzimbyeko akayumba*', in popular use at the time of the writing of *The Madman*.

26. This is a parody of the 'unconstitutional' laws imposed on Ugandans under the umbrella of 'Presidential Decrees'. We note that whereas Amin ruled by 'decrees', the post-Amin liberation governments have used 'Legal Notices' to impose laws outside the rule of parliament.

27. King Bemba earned the title of *Musota* (Snake) because of his murderous character and, the saying, 'King Bemba never pays a friendly visit, he always raids' was coined to describe his reign.

The Poetry of Syl Cheney-Coker: *The Blood in the Desert's Eyes*

Ernest Cole

Syl Cheney-Coker has published three collections: *Concerto For An Exile, The Graveyard Also Has Teeth* and *The Blood in the Desert's Eyes*.[1] In *The Blood in the Desert's Eyes*, the most recent, one notices the poet's mastery of the poetic techniques and other literary devices earlier employed in his work. His brilliant exploitation of imagery and symbolism, dense images, biblical allusions, his exploration of Greek and Roman mythologies, his linguistic competence and precise diction are even more evident in this work. There is indeed a tremendous improvement and development in his handling of literary techniques. Most of the themes in *Concerto For An Exile* and *The Graveyard Has Teeth* recur here with freshness and vivacity: his religious concerns, his disgust with political rulers, social issues such as corruption, neglect of the masses, poverty, crime, abuse of power and class discrimination.

The prefatory epigraph from William Blake's 'Jerusalem'[2] provides a clear insight into the poet's concerns. Jerusalem is the Holy City held sacred by the adherents of the three monotheistic faiths. Pursuing this unifying role of Jerusalem, William Blake stresses the need for the unity of all, irrespective of race, and proposes divine guidance, humanity and love, as the basis of life: 'For man cannot unite with man but by their Emanations/Which stand both Male and Female at the Gates of each Humanity.' He conjures up a picture of bliss and heavenly glory on earth: 'When Souls mingle and join thro'all the Fibres of Brotherhood/Can there be any secret joy on Earth greater than this?'

Significantly, it is this state of bliss which Cheney-Coker acutely longs for in his homeland. Having experienced several traumatic incidents in his country, he ardently desires that Sierra Leone should achieve the status of the 'New Jerusalem'. In effect the 'Blood' must be wiped out from the 'Desert's Eyes'. The image of the desert connotes a picture of suffering and torment, death and decay which the poet is superimposing on to the political, social and religious activities in his country. He calls upon God to purge the land of its pestilence. As such, images of the Feast of the Passover, the Last Supper, and the Crucifixion of Christ for mankind's salvation recur. In addition to the deathly image of the desert, with all its implication of sterility and barrenness, there is that of blood, which underscores the impression of suffering and death. The fact that the blood is seen in the 'Eyes' of the desert connotes the visualization of horrible occurrences and the loss of a sense of sight and direction. His religious poems include 'Apocalypse', 'The Outsider' and 'The Philosopher'.

The title, 'Apocalypse' (p. 1), itself has a religious connotation, referring as it does to the last book in the Bible, Revelations, in which God in a vision reveals the future of the world to the prophet St John. However, in strict biblical terms, the Apocalyptic doctrine is represented in both the books of Daniel and Revelations. In passages within these prophetic books the eschatological future is envisaged in terms of direct divine intervention, a universal judgement of nations and a new age of salvation in which the cosmos will be radically transformed.

The doctrine of the resurrection of the dead is also found within these prophetic books which reveal the secrets of God's plan for history and for his coming triumph at the end of history. It uses dreams and visions to portray a future salvation. It amounts to a new creation in which all forms of evil and suffering will be eliminated; even death will be conquered in the forms both of spiritual immortality and of bodily resurrection. The new creation is a renewal of this world with the Kingdom of God replacing all earthly empires for ever. Thus the first poem 'Apocalypse' expresses the poet's longing for and belief in the power of the Almighty to destroy evil and foster unity and salvation, while the body of the work discusses the various evils and sufferings of mankind, and the last poem 'End of the Game' looks forward to the fulfilment of the vision of the prophets as recorded in the books of Daniel and Revelations.

'Apocalypse' both presents his disgust with the state of affairs in his country and invites divine intervention and guidance. Images of sickness and death show his contempt for the practice of religion: 'disjointed bones', 'lepers [who] enunciate their combustible chests with a prodigious absence of fingers', 'skeletal beggars' and 'ferocious cannibals' (p. 1). The Sierra Leonean society is presented as one in decadence and decay in which man has lost the benefits of Christ's death for his salvation. Hence 'the cup of life' is compared to 'the cries of labour/heard in those white rooms composed of women'. It is a society characterized by commercial exploiters who rape the resources of the country whilst the masses grovel in abject poverty and need. Such a society, the poet maintains, breeds diseased and demented people:

> those valleys of entrepreneurial vultures
> where delirious from want, the lepers enunciate
> their combustible chests with a prodigious absence of
> fingers! (p. 1)

He lambasts the hypocrites who use religion to destroy their fellow men. We are given a picture of a religion that produces and nurtures 'skeletal beggars scratching their soup bowls' implying its destructive and life-denying tendencies. The satire becomes more biting in the picture of a congregation proceeding for the Eucharist where the priests are presented as a 'confluence of hands over the unleavened bread' inviting the congregation to the altar. It depicts a procession of worshippers 'in hunger', comprising 'labourer, student, the miners who cough coming from their shift:/exposed animals without masks to keep their hearts from dying', in a reverent mood, delivering their contaminated offerings to God,

> they come on their knees summoned in mid-life, they
> declaim their earnings in pustules, portraying their elements,
> their ferocious cannibals at his table! (p. 1)

The Christian congregation are lost sheep 'going from their source to wilderness/without cane or camel', further diverted from the path of God by the alien music of Antonio Vivaldi. Followers of such a religion are 'paralytic children' in mission houses plagued with disease who '... cough so much,/stretched out, adumbrated and confused like extinct apes'.

Nevertheless, the poet hints at a possibility of rebirth and regeneration in the images of the 'cup of life' and the 'unleavened bread'. Throughout the Bible, 'Cup' is used figuratively as containing the share of blessings or disaster allotted to a man or nation, or his divinely appointed fate. In this poem, the image of the cup of life depicts the disasters, sufferings and torture which have befallen his country and hence its juxtaposition with the pains of labour. However, since the cup of life could assume a dual interpretation of Christ's Last Supper with his disciples, in which the gifts of his 'body and blood' were offered for man's salvation, it could be suggested that there is the underlying impression of an impending purification of the ills of this society, and the title of the poem 'Apocalypse' reinforces this idea. 'Unleavened bread' recalls the Feast of the Passover in which the Israelites were delivered from bondage in Egypt, through eating the flesh of the

sacrificial lamb with unleavened bread. It thus suggests a call for
the Almighty to rescue Sierra Leoneans from their sufferings.

'The Philosopher' (p. 4) is based on the crucifixion of Christ and
mankind's refusal to partake of the fruits of salvation, the blood
oozing from Christ's wounds being compared to water in a stormy
sea. We are presented with an appealing portrait of a monk, who
alone realizes the significance of the crucifixion for mankind. In his
state of disillusionment over man's negligence of spiritual values,
he sees life as a desolate and abstract phenomenon. In his desire
to live a pure uncontaminated life he is regarded as a castaway and
an outsider. The poet however, signals his own approval of the
rightness of the monk's vision by consecrating him 'Seer':

> Like a castaway an old man kept his books in a cave
> desolate his memory of life a portrait
> Like an abstraction of years, he lived
> forgotten by others before the last tidal wave
> I consecrate him seer his beard was a white book
> where we read about prophets and kings
> planners of the ruins astride our stormy conscience ... (p. 4)

The sufferings of Christ at Calvary and his neglect by mankind,
the pain, torture and torment he undergoes are the 'whirlwind,
that licked over your body'; but regardless of such a sacrifice,
mankind still clings to false beliefs neglecting 'the way, the truth,
and the life'. In the Old Testament the 'word of God' is to be
heeded by angels and men (Isaiah 40:8). In this poem, however,
the poet is looking at 'the word' from the perspective of the New
Testament especially from the Fourth Gospel. Here, the word is
a message revealed from God in Christ, which is to be preached,
ministered and obeyed. Neglect of the 'word' becomes a neglect
of the spiritual as epitomized in Christ with its implication of a
denial of truth, life, salvation and reconciliation with the Godhead.
Christ becomes translucent rather than transparent. The image
of light passing through a glass object connotes an acceptance
of the Lord and his teachings, hence transparency; while a neglect
of his personality and significance implies translucency as light
passing through frosted glass. This is the source of the poet's
disillusionment.

Images of nature in turbulence – the 'whirlwind' and the
'cyclone' – show the sufferings of Christ on the cross for which
mankind should be grateful. The 'cup of wounds like a chasm of
revolt' and 'the sea of red blood' complete the picture of suffering.

The poet is bitter against the kings and false prophets who mis-
lead society, society's adherence to false beliefs and the intellectual who philosophizes about the nature of God and existentialism

in abstract meaningless words and phrases. Mankind has to go through penance to obtain forgiveness and benefit from Christ's crucifixion. The Ascension is used to demonstrate God's omnipotence, Christ's potential and man's loss of paradise. Christ becomes the phoenix and like the mythical bird is eternal:

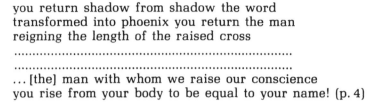

you return shadow from shadow the word
transformed into phoenix you return the man
reigning the length of the raised cross
....
....
... [the] man with whom we raise our conscience
you rise from your body to be equal to your name! (p. 4)

The persona in 'The Outsider' (p. 3) is another of Cheney-Coker's lonely figures as Christ himself who is pictured at the foot of Golgotha suffering guiltlessly for man's salvation. Identifying with Barabbas, the prisoner released by Pontius Pilate, the poet prays for a similar deliverance:

in the hour of your trial Lord
deliver from your cross your brother Barabbas!

'The Blood in the Desert's Eyes' (p. 5), the first of the political poems which, as a group, are the best in the collection, is a biting satire on the political situation. The Society is presented as a desert with blood flowing through with the images of the desert and blood implying aridity, sterility, barrenness, hunger and thirst, poverty, pain, suffering, death and decay. The political leaders are depicted as opium addicts crawling like 'those Methusalahan turtles/that grow melancholy with age' and agents of destruction with an insatiable greed for the country's resources. Animal images of the turtle, the jackass and the proboscises of the elephant cluster to bring out the bestiality and greed of these voracious rulers. Primitive instinctive animals, their depredations precede and even frustrate birth:

... the animal in man triumphs over these men
seizing them in their centrifugal rage
advanced dementia of reason, the thoracic longing
that kills rib to rib the archetypal mother
clutching her belly (p. 5)

The mad rush for personal material aggrandizement, 'the thoracic longing', the 'ulcerative longing to eat', destroy the nation prematurely (the abortion image above is very suggestive) and he admonishes his countrymen:

let us be done with the desire to be a father

before the son, the want that takes the child
from birth to death; (p. 5)

The poet extols the virtues of stoicism as a defensive force against such a deathly situation. The individual in such a society sees his world 'upside down' as he is strait-jacketed to follow the tide along paths already mapped out for him. Meanwhile the leaders are basking in opulence and splendour using political strategies to suppress the masses strongly suggested in the 'mocking grand father sun', the symbol of the governing All Peoples' Congress party, whose colour is a reflection of the sufferings of the people, and a direct relation to the blood in the desert's eyes.

'Cactus Needles' (p. 6), vents the poet's spleen against Sierra Leoneans who allow a gang of thugs and thieves to destroy their homeland. The image 'Cactus Needles' shows the pain and torture inherent in a one party system of government. Brutality and torture are dramatized in the striking opening images of the jails, the overcrowded hospitals, the tear gas, the gun smoke, the red blood, the rope of the gallows, the puerile laws of the judiciary, and the prodigious appetite of the cemetery (p. 6). He ridicules the professors, the lawyers, the politicians and the doctors and condemns them for their neglect of the masses. Although he depicts the brutalization of the masses with the suggestions of 'ferule', 'rustic bread', 'dregs', 'cactus', 'hunger', 'sweat', and 'poison', he ends with a note of hope and looks forward to their victory:

the passover will come, the night that widens the fjord
until then, you suffer, you march you wait (p. 7)

'Sophistry' (p. 9) once again deplores hypocrisy of the religious ministers, the judiciary and the surprising silence of the populace. He calls upon the prophet Jeremiah and a martyr of Sierra Leone nationalism, Bai Bureh, to liberate and redeem his country from men with 'silver-back of snakes, hyena-sweet of tongue'.

The state of the country is summed up in 'The Diaspora' (p. 10). It is pictured as sick and dying, having transformed itself into shame and disgrace in which her nobility and honour have been thrown to the dogs, and even her history can only be recounted in tears. It is indeed, in a later stanza, 'a corpse' where there is mixing up of values where 'truth is imprisoned in the tissues of our dying world'.

A strong autobiographical element appears in some of the social poems such as 'Childhood' (p. 64), 'The Artist' (p. 63) and particularly in 'Sonata and Rain' (p. 22) which gives a touching portrait of the poet's father plunged into adulthood at sixteen, struggling to bring up a family with only his organ for consolation.

Father, sometimes I see how you came
over youthfull boulders to the threshold

of man, in the infinite tenderness of woman
bearing the loneliness of those years
coming on tranquil Sundays to your organ
where you played sonatas while singing
into the distant night, your distant dream

Similar touches describing family life, even in the midst of priva-
tion, are a welcome contrast to the harshness with which the rest
of society is treated particularly in the political poems:

when moulding the earth we bake our bread
drink a glass of rum before the hour
for putting out our flame with our fate (p. 22)

The poet's isolation from the political trends in his country draws
him to figures like Agostinha Neto whom he obviously admires and
identifies with. Such lonely men, poets and seers, are the hope of
the masses in Africa. They produce

the poetry that transformed slaves into men
and mistresses polluted by plantation blood
return hoping to be mothers once more
bearing the dark sons of your name. (p. 31)

The cost of such leadership is often suffering, imprisonment and
even death as exemplified in the life and death of Steve Biko, the
South African writer, poet and freedom fighter. Such 'Prisoners of
Conscience' endure the pains of solitude and confinement, the filth of
faeces in bucketfuls, the beatings, the use of force and deadly weapons of torture. His own sufferings unite him not only with other poet
heroes of the past but unfortunately with thousands yet to suffer:

The magistrate has freed me
from this cell but the two thousand cells
of others open and close in the prison of my soul! (p. 39)

The overall picture of his country and indeed, much of the world,
is bleak, but the collection *The Blood in the Desert's Eyes*, is not
entirely without its glimpses of hope.

NOTES

1. Syl, Cheney-Coker, *Concerto For An Exile* (London: Heinemann, 1973
   and 1980).
   Syl Cheney-Coker, *The Graveyard Also Has Teeth* (London: Heinemann
   1980).
   Syl Cheney-Coker, *The Blood in the Desert's Eyes* (London: Heinemann
   1990).
2. *English Verse*, Vol. III, ed. W. Peacock (London: Oxford University
   Press, 1943): 486.

'New Worlds, New Wholes': Kojo Laing's Narrative Quest for a Social Renewal

Pietro Deandrea

Major aMofa Gentl was feared in Achimota City for his gentleness, since it was this quality that won the first war for the golden cockroach, the emblem of the city. And this emblem, accompanied by his friend the silver mosquito, would shed its symbolic nature and become a real city cockroach crawling about looking for truth. The war was won against Torro the Terrible Roman, the only man in the universe who could stand frontally and sideways at the same time.

In an essay published in 1983, Charles E. Nnolim complained quite straightforwardly about the lack of daring in Nigerian literature, mainly because Nigerian novelists still appeared to be enclosed in smothering narrative genres, such as social realism, folktale *et al.* (Nnolim: 37)

In recent years some refreshing attempts to break open those cages seem to have been made by a new generation of narrators from Nigeria and other African countries: authors like Ben Okri and Syl Cheney-Coker managed to pave new, still untrodden paths for West African literature, and ended up being branded with the theoretically vague definition of 'magic realism'. The one novelist whose work should strike the literary critic as unique and groundbreaking is the Ghanaian Kojo Laing, and the opening of his latest novel – employed here as introductory epigraph – is a case in point: Laing's writing performs an utter and uncompromising dismantling of every expected relation between objects or concepts. The passage quoted at the beginning is not a metaphorical or symbolic rendering of a familiar reality – it is *the very reality* of the book, the foundations on which the actual plot of the novel is built: kindness wins a war, a symbol materializes to become one of the main characters, another character is ubiquitous.

It is extremely surprising, then, that most critics have largely ignored the three novels he published from 1986 to 1992, and that Heinemann (Laing's publisher) has in stock only half a dozen cuttings reviewing his books, one of which considers *Major Gentl* 'awful' and 'silly', closing an avalanche of academic virulence with a 'Pfah!' (Waters: 22) One of the few critics that soon recognized Kojo Laing's importance is Robert Fraser, who considers *Search Sweet Country* 'the finest [novel] ever written in Africa ... his novelistic venture can perhaps most helpfully be seen as an attempt to break intellectual and literary moulds which set hard twenty years ago.' (Fraser: 9)

The principal aim of this essay is to trace a chronological development of Laing's 'novelistic venture' through his three novels; such a main intent will necessarily imply a net of comparisons with the other African authors mentioned above, and an attempt to verify whether critical labels such as 'magic realism' could possibly be applied to any of them.

My analysis, however, will try to go far beyond Laing's formal innovations; his impressive display of creativity, in fact, is employed only as a tool towards the literary shaping of a new Ghanaian society; notwithstanding his revolutionary style, Laing still belongs to that descent of African artists who have brought to the fore their preoccupation with the state. The main theme of his writing could be summarized in one question: how could a new Ghana – and, consequently, a new world – be built? Although Laing's anti-realism and problematization of history might easily be assimilated by some postmodern or post-colonial critics, the pervasive national project supporting his style cannot be traced back to the constant dismantling of such projects theorized by postmodernist academics like Homi Bhabha, and vehemently opposed by the critical works of, among others, Aijaz Ahmad and Arun P. Mukherjee. The latter's fear of a postmodern/post-colonial theory 'which erodes or elides this difference in our [the ex-colonies'] historical or material circumstances' (Mukherjee: 2) seems to me more than legitimate. On the other hand, both Laing's socio-political quest and stylistic influences succeed in going far beyond any Ghanaian or African boundary, therefore rejecting any potential label of 'nativism'.

That is, in my opinion, the greatest quality of his literary achievement: an innovative post-colonial writing grounded on the local at the same time, successfully overcoming that sterile impasse feared by many which Kwame Anthony Appiah calls 'the binarism of Self and Other', where 'To one side lies parochialism; to the other, false claims of universality' (Appiah: 251, xiv).

I The title of Laing's first novel, *Search Sweet Country* (1986), includes all the main facets of the book in its three words. Set in a colourful and multifarious Accra from 1975 to 1977, the plot is deployed through the evolution, or 'search', of a wide range of characters who often cross or run into one another. What all of them are after is a meaning to their existences, each in his/her own way, a meaning inextricably linked with the future of Ghanaian society – 'a quest,' as Robert Fraser writes, 'for a meaningful and self-renewing Ghanaian identity' (Fraser: 9), right in the worst years of Ghanaian post-colonial history when Colonel Acheampong's National Redemption Council was draining both the nation's coffers and hopes. The presence of a collective pre-occupation is pervasive throughout the book, even between loving couples:

> But does your head really live in Ghana? ... don't speak of love yet, innocent people like you shouldn't speak of it. You have to do something first, you have to find some of that new Ghana you speak of! (pp. 110, 112)

says the trader Araba Fynn to her naive lover Kojo Okay Pol. According to M.E. Kropp Dabuku, in this novel 'there can be no retreat from public failure to private concerns' (Kropp Dabuku: 27).

The pivotal scene of the book takes place at Kotoka Airport, where the principled Okay Pol has been sent to supervise an illegal importation of racehorses officially supporting the government's plan of agricultural production. The whole operation falls apart when the boxes break and the horses start galloping through the airport, creating havoc all around. A panic-stricken Okay Pol resorts to threateningly warning the gathered crowd:

> I must warn you that what you are seeing here is not true ... the government needs your support ... you are in the name of law asked to remain here until further notice ... you may continue to look but don't pass water – I mean don't pass judgement. (pp. 40–1)

Other main characters are consequently brought in; the day-dreamer Kofi Loww, 'the man who walked with the sky in his eyes' (p. 9), refuses to be intimidated, because 'he would not be told when to leave an airport in his own country'; he is saved by the timely intervention of the preacher Osofo Ocran, founder of the Church of the Smiling Saint: 'Stop stop stop all you gentlemen, three times stop. Remember the trinity, in the name of the Lord, not the law' (p. 42). Pol will eventually manage to silence the whole crowd by offering them drinks: 'Beer is served, all you kind people that don't see what you see, you can have free beer . . . Long live Ghana!' (p. 46)

The same chapter is closed by Beni Baidoo, who arrives just in time to enjoy the beer and whose role in the novel deserves more attention than any other character's. He seems to be omnipresent throughout the book, opening and closing several chapters with his sudden, sometimes slapstick appearances, linking all the characters together and apparently playing a great variety of roles. He may seem a beggar, to start with, since he is always asking for money to make his personal dream come true – the founding of a village, a search epitomizing the other characters' quests because 'The search of a fool touches other lives' (p. 1). He could appear to be a fool, in fact, given his odd behaviour and language, but it would be a mistake to interpret him as if he were a living character like the others; he is rather a collective thread among them, since 'he watched others as he did not watch his own life . . . flowed with his one obsession in and out of the lives he met' (pp. 1, 2); he seems, in other words, to embody the soul of the town: 'Beni Baidoo was Accra, was the bird standing alive by the pot that should receive it, and hoping that, after being defeathered, it would triumphantly fly out before it was fried' (p. 1).

The sweetness mentioned in the title of the novel is a fairly obvious hint of the utter lyricality of the language describing the characters' searches, both in their own words and in the omniscient descriptions in third person: 'Araba's smile was a market: it brought in everything and gave out everything, the warmth being at the edges and only for the few' (p. 96). The lyrical dimension of Laing's narrative is also supported by a wide range of typically poetical devices, like rhymes ('Where is the church that began this search?', p. 136) or alliterations ('his lap was like the sound of the sea in a shell', p. 216). Such devices clearly show how much Laing's writing is affected by oral narrative style in general, and Akan poetic style in particular (Okpewho: 220–6; Kropp Dabuku: 23)

Other cases in point could be Laing's graphic experimentations ('She must Must MUST give me sons!', p. 163), emphatic exclamations ('All that stagnation around him bogged him down, Ah', p. 142), onomatopoeia and ideophones ('Gasps and OOOooos varied the air, tilted Pol's fez in consternation', p. 39). The graphic innovations may be considered as remnants of his poems, later collected and published by Heinemann under the title *Godhorse* in 1989; Laing combined in them the influence of the Concrete Poets' technique and 'the techniques of figurative speech characteristic of formal language use in Akan' (Kropp Dabuku: 19). Language, then, being conferred a physical substance, is brought back to its oral dimension, something Amos Tutuola had already tried to achieve with the use of capital letters in *The Palm-wine Drinkard* (Tutuola: 21, 118; Lasagna: 33-4). The use of exclamations, too, seems to be affected by oral influences; the reader feels compelled to ask him/herself whether the 'Ah' quoted above comes from the character or the narrator. I think that such a distinction would not help to find an answer, though; that 'Ah', in fact, could be traced back to what Isidore Okpewho calls 'climactic alerts' of the oral bard, when he communicates to the crowd the 'momentous points' of his narration. It is common for the artist in oral literature 'to weave his personality into that of his characters ... that it is difficult to tell where narration ends and dialogue resumes'. Such an authorial empathy, according to Okpewho, would be unacceptable in written literature 'for its failure to make the right distinction between its characters' – an analysis that would not apply to Laing's writing (Okpewho: 211–14, 238).

All those oral stylistic influences in *Search Sweet Country* are a striking evidence of how Laing may be located in a mainstream tradition of post-colonial Ghanaian literature which has been deeply affected by ancestral patterns. During my research in Ghana in 1993*, I noticed a great predominance of poets over novelists, and most Ghanaian poets conceive their poetry as oral deliverance, considering it a communal act much more akin to theatre than to the novelistic genre. And this predominance of poetry, in any case, can be detected in most Ghanaian novelists as well, who have rarely been affected by plain social realism as the Nigerians generally have: Ayi Kwei Armah's experimentations with a diversity of narrative viewpoints in his first novels and his later attempts to confer an oral dimension to his narrators; Kofi Awoonor's overwhelmingly lyrical Ewe ancestry in *This Earth, My Brother*; Ama Ata Aidoo's short stories recuperating the oral collective voice and her novel *Our Sister Killjoy* interspersed with verses – all traditionally-influenced attempts to make the boundaries between literary genres blur, to recover that continuum of verbal discourse on which traditional performances were rooted. Between traditional narratives and poetry, after all, the distinction is 'based more on the circumstances of the performances than on any formal elements' (Andrzejewski: 141). 'The heart of the matter,' the critic and writer Kofi Agovi told me, 'is that poetry is very strong in this society; we are lyrically poetic people, very conscious of speech styles, even in everyday social intercourse'; 'our normal people,' agreed Efua Sutherland, 'mother' of

Ghanaian literature, 'are very poetic: it is our natural use of language'.

Laing started as a poet, in fact, and later moved to the novel, but not completely: 'I wrote the novel partly in the same way I would write the poems. Sometimes you will find whole lines within the novels which have come direct from the poems, they're quotations,' he told me. It is notable that the same method of novelistic composition has lately been used by Ben Okri, (Deandrea: 82) another young author whose 'magic realism' is associated with Laing's (Innes: 5–6).

The richness of Laing's English, in addition, is increased by the insertion of a lot of Ghanaian words and cultural references, a constant feature in his novels which all have a final glossary – a way of looking for an 'authentic' language, as Kropp Dabuku would say, which on the other hand does not neglect the employment of other sources, such as Scottish words or a Steinbeckian reference ('but the third generation *of men of mice* had come to Araba', italics mine, p. 99). Laing's Ghanaian English is authentic in so far as it bears all the Ghanaian cultural influences, beside being extremely realistic in dialogues. This sensitivity to the multiplicity of his heritage is probably the main drive leading him to a constant creative effort to change the clichés of language: 'There's a gap between written history and oral history,' he said to Adewale Maja-Pearce. 'That gap should be the source of an original thrust in ideas, in inventions, in creation.' (Maja-Pearce 1987: 28) His own use of that gap is palpable in his prolific coinage of neologisms (such as 'logologo' for genitals or 'zagazogo' for wild man) and in the abundance of puns:

> Sally Soon . . . was an English witch sent over on a secret assignment against Ghana, but she had now fallen in love with Ghanaians, and had almost neutralised her own powers: the weaker she became the more she became Sally Sooner, the weakest she became the more she became Sally Soonest. She usually travelled the degrees of her surname. (p. 124)

The humour of *Search Sweet Country* is often raw and popular, sometimes almost gross, another similarity with the traditional oral performance (Okpewho: 202–8). Beni Baidoo appears to embody this feature:

> And let me tell you a secret: when I get money, I intend to sneak toward Libo and pay for a touch of woman's softness. I will pay for softness to exercise my own hardness. I will pay for a resurrection of the past, for a little exercise for my popylonkwe [male organ]! (p. 131)

The definition of Beni Baidoo's role gets more and more complex: why does this character take to the extreme all the characteristics of Laing's language? The figure of an African trickster or of a mythical Ananse come soon to the reader's mind, because of their wicked humour, their penchant for tricks and taboo-breaking which Baidoo certainly shares (Pelton: 31–6). When he suddenly materializes in the back of Professor Sackey's car and then steals its keys, he really seems to assume a supernatural dimension (pp. 150–1). Moreover, Baidoo acts as a diviner, an explainer of others' lives, since he often knows the subject of their streams of thought and what their future will be like. Trickster – or perhaps Shakespearian fool – could be valid terms of comparison, given also the implicitness and ambiguity of his language:

> If I say herbs herbs herbs herbs herbs herbs herbs herbs herbs; then I say Lord lord lord lord lord lord lord lord lord; then, I divide this ten-ten draw with very fresh palm-wine, equally, what chance would I have of being thought a holy Ghanaian? (p. 218)

The West African trickster – and Ananse in particular – is said to act against the rigidity of tradition, continuously redrawing its boundaries 'not so much in defiance as in a new ordering of their limits' (Pelton: 35). In *Search Sweet Country* tradition is also synonymous with supernatural, thanks to the presence of the witches Adwoa Adde and Sally Soon, and to $\frac{1}{2}$ Allotey's contacts with the spirits of his village. Even the academic Professor Sackey does not limit his search to rational enquiry: 'There is no territory between the supernatural and the purely factual,' he says (p. 240). On the other hand nothing, not even the supernatural dimension, is immune to change. $\frac{1}{2}$ Allotey has to leave his village 'because of his impudence, his constant questions, and his own idea about the rituals'. (p. 199)

The author's idea of new society, then, bears the same multi-cultural characteristics as the language on which it is built: a middle way between 'the narrow Eurocentrism' (p. 235) and 'the weight of our past' (p. 241). Professor Sackey, Allotey and Kofi Loww embody different attempts to overcome an apparently inescapable dichotomy: 'you either live fragmented and half yourself, half your heart, or you keep slow, and whole, and die!' complains Sackey (p. 79–80).

Such a new way is far from being easily attainable on a collective level, and Laing's disillusionment with the present state of Ghanaian political structures is quite evident in *Search Sweet Country*. That is probably the reason why the only political enterprise of the novel is led by the preacher Osofo Ocran, whose ideal of church is another way of combining different cultures: 'near his knees the herbs of the fetish priest appeared without warning, and joined Jesus Christ in giving his life meaning' (p. 47). Osofo decides to lead a procession for miles and miles, to the centre of town, and it will become a joyous, musical, overwhelmingly massive march fuelled by Baidoo's endless witticisms. Osofo's intentions are overtly political, because he wants to march to the seat of the government, and the huge crowd seems to stand by him, at first: 'ONE WHOLE COUNTRY CANNOT FIT UNDER A SOLDIER'S CAP! ... 'Ampara!' [true] was the refrain.... Ghana was a photocopy country, and they wanted the original truth!' (p. 222). But the whole spirit is channelled elsewhere by a group of policemen offering food to everybody; Osofo's search, being too mystical and not down-to-earth enough, has no chance to succeed politically – 'he's one of those zagazogos who can't discuss God without going off into a spiritual fury. He can't last in Ghana!' (p. 226).

What is left to do, then, after the march's failure? Rejecting any political solution, Laing brings to the fore the individual's power: 'All the ordinary people were real people: they lived beyond the slogans, outlasted the politicians' (p. 244). That is where the author's hope resides – in the creativity of the ordinary:

> It looked as if each space given to each person to walk in was a source of art: the movement of people was nothing less than a series of abandoned dances controlled marvellously in the most ordinary, most triumphant ways ... Thus the universe was danced in all the walking of Ghana. (p. 16)

The ending of the novel is actually rather despondent, but it cannot be said to be in tune with Armah's inescapable corruption and decay in *The Beautyful Ones Are Not Yet Born*: 'I felt that his exposition of the Ghanaians' and Africans' world didn't do enough justice to their humanity. My first novel was partly a reaction against that,' Laing told me.

II Thanks to its poeticized reality and supernatural presences, *Search Sweet Country* could be associated with other African authors' works where different worlds co-exist. Stephen Slemon considers magic realist texts as containing a battle between two oppositional systems 'locked in a continuous dialectic', never succeeding in arranging themselves into any kind of hierarchy' (Slemon: 11). Ben Okri's *The Famished Road* (1991) and its sequel *Songs of Enchantment* (1993) apparently apply that principle through the narration by Azaro, an abiku ('spirit child', according to Yoruba beliefs) who can perceive both natural and supernatural reality at any given moment. Some comparisons with Latin American magic realists are certainly traceable, particularly with those who founded their writing on autochthonous cultural myths which are lived through on an everyday basis, as theorized by Alejo Carpentier: the concept of *real maravilloso* in his introduction to *The Kingdom of This World* (1949) is based on indigenous and African world views.

On the other hand, there exist Latin American authors (such as Gabriel García Márquez) who developed supernatural dimensions having vaguer connections with indigenous beliefs (Chanady: 50). The Sierra Leonean poet Syl Cheney-Coker appears to be more influenced by this strand in his first novel, *The Last Harmattan of Alusine Dunbar* (1990), a book bearing some resemblance to Márquez's *One Hundred Years of Solitude*. Those different instances of Latin American and African magic realism have one common feature: 'In an attempt to draw the reader's attention to the richness of their continent, they often poeticize it', Chanady writes on Latin Americans (Chanady: 52), and the same is easily said about Okri and Cheney-Coker.

Nevertheless, African magic/marvellous realism certainly deserves to be critically outlined on its own, without any intercontinental justification. Kole Omotoso's was one of the first to draw the necessary distinctions: his *marvelous realism* is composed of 'the juxtaposition of the belief system of one archaic and economic social system side by side with the belief system of another economic and social system, this time capitalism'. According to him, *marvelous realism* is not to be considered as a literary import, but 'has to be seen in relation to ... the ontological disposition of the African mind undistorted by the Western concept of order and reality'; the African version of this novelistic genre should not be escapist, but 'has to be seen side by side with the material condition of his characters'. (Omotoso: 26, 25, 57) He seems to be afraid, in other words, of a *marvelous realism* not realist enough, of what Jacques-Stéphen Alexis defined, when theorizing a Haitian *réalisme merveilleux*, as 'recherches surréalistes à froid' (Alexis: 264).

Omotoso's theoretical category, in my opinion, weakens when he tries to apply it to particular novels (Omotoso: 57–70), but it can work usefully for Okri and Cheney-Coker: both artists never forget the material lives out of which their magic arises, ranging from Okri's contemporary ghettos to Cheney-Coker's struggle of the Black Pioneers who went back to Africa after the American

Revolution. Omotoso could not possibly include novels written ten years after his essay, but he should have mentioned Ali Mazrui's *The Trial of Christopher Okigbo* (1971), set in a dimension called 'After-Africa' inhabited by the ancestors. Its imaginative setting, though, singled out as an example of narrative courage by Charles Nnolim (Nnolim: 37), is mainly a pretext to build a rich novel of ideas on the problems of real Africa.

Kojo Laing's second novel, *Woman of the Aeroplanes* (1988), appears to move some steps beyond all the narrative bulk mentioned above, being set in a dimension which is neither our real world nor an ancestral spirits' abode, a place where temporal and spatial relations follow their own unpredictable rules. Tukwan, the place in question, is an invisible place which has been banished – and is still persecuted by – the real Ghanaian town of Kumasi. It would be difficult to say where it is situated:

> this town was near enough Kumasi to be far enough away never to be seen by residents of that city, except rarely; and if it had not been situated over one hundred miles from Accra but was nearer Koforidua than Ho, you would not have seen how far it was from Bolgatanga. (p. 8)

Those are all Ghanaian towns, but a map of the country would not help much. Its inhabitants, once again a great number of characters, have been kidnapped to live there, and are all immortals. Their hopes and aspirations are basically human, but their lives disrupt any kind of realistic expectation. Every page is, for the reader, a game 'of finding and continually adjusting ... the very idea of "meaning"', as Stewart Brown writes about Laing's poems (Brown: 97). In Tukwan laughter can be collected by tractors, people can photograph dreams and meet one another when dreaming, and Pokuaa is 'the mistress of two small aeroplanes which both stood at the level of her lips: one at her upper lip and the other at her lower lip. She perfumed her aeroplanes every morning with frangipani lavender' (p. 6). Such planes will carry people to Scotland, later: they are not a metaphor, but the actual world of the novel, inexplicable by our ordinary physical perceptions; as Laing told me, 'That is the whole impetus behind my language; cubism, expressionism and other aspects of modern art seem to be propounding a world that I feel already exists for me on a day-to-day basis.'

Thus *Woman of the Aeroplanes* cannot be defined as 'magic/ marvellous realism', since the dismantling of our real world's functioning is total, and there is no co-existence of different worlds. Even Levensvale, Tukwan's twin town in Scotland, 'had rejected all the usual categories of life and thought' (p. 91). Time is disrupted as well: the two cities 'are both towns out of time' (p. 153), sharing a 'manoeuvrability of time' (p. 66) so wide-ranging that, when it comes down to business deals, they have to choose in which year: 'How can we calculate in the same economic year when we are children of eternity?' (p. 95).

The greatest disruptions are created by Kwame Atta, a wicked inventor/scientist who, like his twin brother Kwaku de Babo, is in love with Pokuaa. His creativity is necessary for Tukwan to go on: besides slipping 'in and out of raindrops without getting wet' (p. 3), he invents (amongst other things) a stupidity machine by putting truncated worms in a basket; the same machine will help the town, becoming a talking character. Thus Atta is the mischievous critical spirit, often disrespected: 'He would say to the scorners: know me! For if they wanted him to lead them from the back, then some of the values too would come from the back' (p. 39). His wickedness makes him a kind of trickster, but different from Beni Baidoo; Atta, in fact, talks less and acts more, and seems more prone to practical pranks than ambiguous monologues.

The novel's reality is conveyed through a language containing the same rich variety of formal devices as *Search Sweet Country's* – alliterations, rhymes, multifarious vocabulary, puns, humour, emphatic authorial exclamations. The language is still rendered physically on the page, with graphic innovations ranging from the use of the fractional line ($\frac{meet}{meat}$ me there!' says Dogo the khebab seller, p. 20), to a whole page of words and numbers arranged in mathematic formulae (p. 196).

In the unknown dimension where Tukwan and Levensvale are situated, things work and time runs according to their own rules; every page creates a series of perceptive displacements in the readers' minds, so many that Adewale Maja-Pearce writes: 'This was fantasy for its own sake, as if the author had simply fallen into a mannerism' (Maja-Pearce, 1989: 23). Behind all this, though, the characters share human hopes and aims; like those in *Search Sweet Country*, they are after a new Ghanaian society, for better or for worse. *Woman of the Aeroplanes*, therefore, could be considered neither as magic/marvellous realism nor as pure fantasy. *Fantastic realism* may represent a more suitable definition, with the usual reservations due to the theoretical ambiguity of any critical label.

That ideal Ghanaian society longed for by most characters is, once again, an unavoidable combination of ancestral and western values: 'new things were as wise as the old in Tukwan, and ... the opposition between the two was welcome and controllable'

(p. 36). When they meet in Levensvale, Ghanaians and Scots face a similar world view: David Mackie is convinced of the worthiness in exchanging ideas: 'they take some of ours and we take some of theirs, that's the way to the new toughness of the world ...' (p. 130), while Tukwan had been banished from Ghana 'for refusing to listen to *all* the songs of the ancestors' (pp. 1, 2). It is a common feature in contemporary Ghanaian culture, after all, that 'when it comes to town and village communal development, people who were originally regarded as strangers become the leading champions' (Assimeng: 94). That is a clear change in attitude, with respect to the traditional folktales where a girl marrying a stranger of her own choice always ended badly. Ghanaian authors have either reproduced the same pattern, as Ama Ata Aidoo did in *Anowa* (1970), or changed it in favour of a new openness of traditions: Efua Sutherland's *Foriwa* (1967) brings a new life to her village thanks to her unusual marital choice.

As regards hybridity in post-colonial Africa, Appiah writes that 'if you postulate an either-or choice between Africa and the West ... your home must be the otherworldly, the monastic retreat' (Appiah, p. 251). Such a seclusion could apparently apply to *Woman of the Aeroplanes'* unknown dimension, but Tukwan's people vehemently try to regain their mortality in the most diverse ways – breaking the barrier of 99 houses which is a gods-imposed limit, flying abroad for profit and change 'so that the gods were giving Tukwan a final choice: the more change it made, the more mortal it became' (p. 41); and mortality is attained, at last, when someone dies without resurrecting, Pokuaa gets pregnant, more houses are built and profits are made. Tukwan's utopian society is taken back into reality. The new society must be lived concretely on earth, then, trying to employ elements of both dimensions ... Maja-Pearce's remarks about the novel's sterile fantasy sound less and less convincing.

The choice between mortality and immortality (present throughout the book) is simply another way of facing the dilemma which opposes the 'monastic retreat' mentioned by Appiah to a new multicultural society. Nevertheless the contact with real life ends up being dangerous, carrying within it all the implications of neo-colonialism: 'the first invasion [by Kumasi] was physical and it failed; this second one ... is more subtle ... it is a phantom: ignore it and you look a fool, fight it and you look outdated' (pp. 234–5). Taken aback by the threat of having one's consciousness narrowed, Tukwan makes a final effort to obtain 50 years more of immortality; as in *Search Sweet Country*, the new society is not ready yet to be built in our world. What is left, for the moment, is once again the collective creativity. Having been its chronicler, Kwaku de Babo is well aware of the dangers looming ahead:

> if you allow the experience and memory of the ordinary person to disappear before the dead-end of politics or stagnation or both, then you are left with a mind that may retain its anatomical size, but it will be a mind that will either grab at straws of meaning, or create an easy spiritual mush over everything ... (p. 239–40)

The importance of individual creativity is also stressed when Laing deals with the theme of political power, a subject he develops further in his third novel. Actually Tukwan has a traditional chief, Nana Bontox, stubbornly fond only of traditional ways, but his lack of cultural flexibility makes him appear 'unwiser than anyone else ... Nana did not disappoint his people: he continued to make a fool of himself as often as possible' (p. 10). Sometimes Laing's parody of the uselessness of frozen ancestral customs ventures to the pillars of Akan history: Bontox, for instance, owns a golden ring he claims belonged to Okomfo Anokye, the legendary divine messenger who gave Asante people the Golden Stool still believed to contain the soul of the Asante nation (Assimeng: 111). The rest of Tukwan seem to strive after a different kind of political decision-making, on the other hand. Apart from Bontox, there are three more recognized 'bosses': Kofi Senya, the spiritual guide of the town, Pokuaa with her beauty and down-to-earth entrepreneurship, and the lake (probably a reference to Lake Bosomtwe, sacred for the Akan because it embodies one of their twelve patrilinear groups) which can be moved closer to a public meeting by pulling its ripples (Rattray: 54–76; Asare Opoku: 98). Resolutions are taken collectively quite often, and the meeting about the journey to Scotland narrated in 'Class Two' (the second chapter, pp. 18–38) is a case in point. Tukwan's complex political structure (contorted, some would say) explodes the stereotype of African traditional power as extremely autocratic, just as *The Trial of Christopher Okigbo* does through a less imaginative but conceptually erudite writing. In Mazrui's 'After-Africa', politics implies the active participation of all residents, with an Assembly of the Ages as legislative body independent from the Almighty. The novel quotes Julius Nyerere, too, who saw Africa and Greece as societies in parallel evolutions, where the collective decisions of small communities constituted 'the appropriate setting for the basic, or pure, democracy' (Mazrui: 112).

A lake being one of the town bosses, anyway, is only the tip of an iceberg supporting the whole novel, since life in Tukwan is experienced as much as possible through a harmonic contact with natural life. The reader finds sacred ducks, talking vultures, creative goats and intelligent termites, while 'long artistic yawns' (p. 8) are valued in order to attain a more natural life rhythm, opposed to the sheepish rationality of those characters who are after political power for its own sake such as Lawyer Tay, whose 'perception wasn't as sharp as his logic' (p. 11). This symbiosis with nature is supposed to involve Western borrowings of any kind, too, like the plane seats made of dried moss; even inventions are no exception, being made of organic materials 'so that the renewal of these parts led to the addition of some soul, some vulnerability before the intimidating neutrality of your own [Western] invention' (p. 198).

After his first two novels, Laing might be considered as a pessimist about the possibility of attaining on earth his ideal of new society. His third novel, however, seems to succeed exactly where Tukwan partly failed.

III In the year 2020 AD, the Ghanaian town of Achimota has incorporated the neighbouring Accra and Tema, while the rest of the nation has mysteriously vanished. Achimota City has just won the first War of Existence against Torro the Terrible, thanks to the kindness of Major aMofa Gentl, who owns two rooms on the moon, and to the craft of Nana Mai the Grandmother Bomb, who can sew up the sky and lives in a satellite 'which had a sexy booster tail to charm the galaxies with' (p. 44).

In *Major Gentl and the Achimota Wars* (1992), as in his previous novel, Laing recreates the world by disrupting any expected connection between things: in Achimota City Gentl's shadow is promoted to the rank of sergeant, a sax can play on its own, a bike acts as the talking referee of a football match, and a man is killed by being put *inside* a bullet. Rather than a world made of flesh and blood, the reader may sometimes feel as if he were experiencing an animated cartoon, where everything is possible, 'disestablishmentarianism' being the law. When the two opposing leaders happen to dream the same dream at once, it is consequently impossible to distinguish this from the rest of the novel. This time, though, Laing does not employ a different dimension; his plot develops on our very planet, in a Ghanaian town, about 30 years after when he is writing. Genre definitions become increasingly difficult … is this another case of fantastic realism – a further projection of Stephen Slemon's conception of magic realism where 'enabling strategies for the future require revisioning the seemingly tyrannical units of the past in a complex and imaginative double-think of "remembering the future" ' (Slemon: 21) – or the first example of African *science fiction*?

Whatever label one chooses to adopt, the pivot of the whole novel resides once again in the dismantling function of Laing's language. As mentioned at the beginning, the cockroach changes from being a symbol to a real character: 'I've always believed that the metaphor or symbol sometimes cheats, in terms of concentrating more on the message than on the components making the image,' Laing told me. It is by tapping ancestral devices that the ordinary categories of written literature are rendered much more dynamic. African traditional art, in fact, 'avoids the use of representation of objects as if they were symbols'; just like an individual's ego, an object cannot be 'spoken of as a discrete unit and given a label' (Duerden: 10–11).

Such a dynamism of Laing's writing, in turn, drives to compelling extremes other oral characteristics; like in a folktale everything, from animals to object, is portrayed as alive and thinking. Beside the formal mechanisms already present in his first two novels, the author reminds me of a bard-like figure especially when establishing a relation with his readership/ audience, saying 'I *swear*' (p. 44) when facts become too unreal, emphatically inciting some characters to act, or addressing the reader directly, as at the bottom of page 66: 'And would you be so kind as to hold your page while one elder went to the toilet, thought the troublesome rabbit'. The fact that some of such passages are written in italics is to me a little perplexing, since Laing should not need to be so explicit about his attempt to stress the transforming power of the word. He is extremely effective, for instance, in changing the characters' names according to the context – the golden cockroach is also called Mr Cockgold, Mr Cee, Mr Cockroach, the golden cee or Roach-the-cock. Another sign of Laing's tendency to be more explicit, in *Major Gentl*, is his introductory note, where he justifies his polyglot lexis as 'usual in Ghana' and states he intends 'to internationalise the English', 'to create one gigantic language'.

The author's 'linguistic project', as Kropp Dabuku calls it when analysing *Search Sweet Country*, is symbiotic with the idea of a new post-colonial society, with 'the need for an all-encompassing change' (Kropp Dabuku: 33); the two main sides of that change proceed together, as one of his italics affirms: '*If the life had to be backwards before you won it, then so be it, so be the language*' (p. 124). Laing's new society keeps being founded on a blend of ancestral and Western values, where the living can meet the dead but also have 'computers of the African kind which were soft to touch'. (p. 16) A credible alternative vision of post-colonial Africa, in fact, would necessarily imply the establishment of indigenous research structures, as recommended by the scholars who took part in the 1987 BEYOND HUNGER PROJECT: their vision included a 'capitalism ... with a "humane face" ' based on a 'locally derived science and technology'. (Achebe: 94, 89)

Given all this, *Major Gentl* may really be considered as a prototype of African *science fiction* novel. On the other hand, the magic realist concept of 'remembering the future' mentioned above seems particularly pertinent if one thinks that Achimota, the city where the novel's language is developed in all its richness, is a Ga term meaning 'speak no name', having been a place where runaway slaves took refuge (Therson-Cofie: 4). Both hypotheses are effectively unified within the image of the three trains

> rolling among the people. They were the type of trains that automatically laid out their own tracks as they moved, and then picked them up from behind to reuse in the front again. Train, train, train the duellists, for the engines gave an atmosphere of past and present that brightened the future immeasurably. (p. 116)

Such trains cannot but bring to one's mind the Akan ancestral image called Sankofa, the bird walking on while picking food from behind (Kayper-Mensah: 4).

Major Gentl's new society, anyway, could not be understood by applying Fredric Jameson's well-known definition of 'national allegory' (Jameson: 69). After the fruitful international collaboration between Tukwan and Levensvale in *Woman of the Aeroplanes*, Laing definitely moves the focus beyond the national boundaries, taking into consideration the Western ideology trying to subdue Achimota and that only Achimota can save by setting a pattern for our whole planet: 'they may need our help!' Gentl thinks (p. 166). The Wars of Existence, after all, are to be considered as a narrative rendering of a Western neo-colonial attempt to impose itself on the rest of the world. Torro's invisible bosses are after something other than conventional warfare ('Direct wars were too out of date with the bosses abroad, subtle extinction being preferred', p. 7), trying to control Africa's resources and seeing its people as expendable. Even Torro seems to be a victim of that attitude. He is said to love Achimota, but the ideology within which he has been fostered (he has a touch of Italian Mafia and South African apartheid, being born in both places) drives him to subjugate Gentl's people. His 'spaghetti English', by the way, adds another nuance to Laing's linguistic variety:

Mama mia, dear Major, I'm losing my Roman accent, I do not comprehendo. My dear belly is shaped just like one of the eastern hills in your dear city, and I do nothing but let wind escape in any direction. Diavolo! I theenk I have the serious ulcers, noo! (p. 10)

Westerners are described as 'physically fast but spiritually snails' (p. 70), driving 'the new car whose fastest gear is the reverse gear' (p. 41). Nevertheless, the subtle power of their ideology has been charming multitudes of Ghanaians, and that is exemplified in the novel (once again very dynamically) by the rest of the country which Achimota has lost. When a piece of the national soil suddenly reappears from the sea there is only one man on it, a moping individual who would like to support Torro: 'A tiny house had been made for him, and they almost built it on his back because he had refused to move from the appropriate spot for it. His favourite occupation was refusing' (p. 123). This 'been-to', then, seems to recoil from the external world just as Herman Melville's *Bartleby, the Scrivener* did, paralysed by 'the sterility of a spiritless society' (Marcus: 112). It is notable that Melville described his character as 'absolutely alone in the universe. A bit of wreck in the mid-Atlantic.' That tiny house, too, cannot but remind the reader of the screen that Bartleby's employer puts around him (Melville: 493, 475).

The strategy suggested by the novel in order to face the Western ideological onslaught and to save the world is composed, first of all, of an unexpected sympathy and kindness Torro cannot handle, and also of a general flexibility up to the point of nominating Torro, the enemy, as Minister of Defence. But, most of all, the Achimotans are shown to have regained a real contact with nature, whereas the Western bosses have built a totally self-referent culture where people 'taste only the recurring substance of their own tongues' (p. 155), and end up declaring that 'there is no difference between existence and non-existence' (p. 166); their-contact with physical reality, therefore, has fallen apart, a loss symptomatized in the book by a widespread difficulty in remembering the names of Western towns.

In Achimota the bond with nature is intact again: creative termites 'continued to change the architecture of Government House when they wanted, with their inspired saliva plus earthen engineering' (p. 66), 'Fruit was law' (p. 3) and fish are given a Ministry to support their rights.

The novel in general, more than any particular character, is full of scatologic and phallic images, and owns a coarse quality as if it were inhabited by tricksters, by several Ananse. Drawing his own conclusions from Eliade and Turner's works, Robert D. Pelton associates the Ananse tales' vulgarity with the liminal state of shamanic transformations, where religion dives into biology and nature in order to re-emerge as regenerated and invested with a recreative power for societal needs (Pelton: 31-6). The method employed by Gentl to attain his 'series of fast intuitions' is rather similar: 'Gentl had to crawl to think, sharing the ground with frogs, lizards, crow dung, cricket droppings, the shit of wise sparrows, and worm tunnels' (p. 144).

Besides having to fight for its own survival, then, Laing's Achimota is a sort of utopia, a harmonic place that has 'achieved something harder that the ancestors could offer at that time ... but the ancestors too were learning, were changing' (p. 160). I am doubtful whether a comparison with New World utopias and their individual's solitary retreat into nature would hold, though, given the urban and collective setting of *Major Gentl*. At the same time European dis/utopias and their state-dominated individuals are not similar to Laing's either, since 'You could speak your mind koraa [completely] in Achimota City, and even talk to the Government while sitting on the toilet' (p. 74). Such Government is constituted by three extravagant Elders who used to confer power to citizens in rotation, until Pogo Alonka Forr the carrot millionaire refused to continue the tradition. This character's view on power clashes with the general opinion: Pogo loves and desires power for its own glamour and in fact, to emulate Gentl's lunar rooms,

he had faithfully cultivated the sun to see whether an arrangement could be worked out there in a serious and solar manner; bamboozle the sun with attention and you could even end up having a hotel in it, burning ambition, he said. (p. 12)

But in Achimota blind adulation is not tolerated: its political structure appears to be based on a principle of 'decentralised centralism' as Max Assimeng defines the complex traditional Ashanti system (Assimeng: 98); for the Achimotans power is a burden, not a pleasure, just like it used to be in their ancestral society (Duerden: 34-5). The political project developed by Laing's narrative, then, seems to follow the paradigms set by those African intellectuals who are depicted as being deeply dissatisfied with the democratic model imposed by the colonizers. Kole Omotoso, for instance, writes: 'in a situation where social change – economic policies which would reward rather than exploit the labour of the majority ... – meaningful social change is the goal, another form of democracy must be found' (Omotoso: 71). The inspiration for that other form is likely to be found, if anywhere, in traditional structures, if one takes into consideration the high degree of democracy implied in ancestral practices such as the destoolment of kings, which was the apex of a particular conception of power where nobody is above public scrutiny and criticism.

The final victory of Achimota, toward which armies of diverse animals have given a great contribution, leaves Major Gentl jobless and satisfied, followed by a crowd of children who have been acting a playful parody of the adults' war:

> it was seen clearly that Achimota City was the standard they all had to follow, a place where power was the last resort, and humanity and invention allowed even the smallest human being to open out into the trees and into the universe, to see the whole, to touch the inner. (p. 180)

> It so happens that creativity is the highest instance of human intelligence at work ... This is plain and logical. But for the Western critic of African literature it constitutes a problem.
> (Armah, 1976: 2)

This essay does not intend to underline literary standards; unlike Homi K. Bhabha, I do not think that 'Magical Realism' – or *fantastic realism* or African science fiction or whatever – 'becomes the literary language of the emergent post-colonial world' (Bhabha: 7). Completely different kinds of fiction can be as effective and compelling as Laing's.

Nevertheless, what I hope I have managed to stress are the groundbreakingly unique characteristics of his style. If I have, the question posed at the beginning remains unanswered: why that general indifference on the part of the critics, why does Harold A. Waters write 'I certainly didn't care' about *Major Gentl* whereas Larweh Therson-Cofie considers it 'creative, courageous, ... simple and quick-reading'? Maybe the answer is to be found in another question, asked forty years ago by Jacques-Stéphen Alexis: 'Comment se pourrait-il que les hommes du vingtième siècle ne se rendent pas compte que les genres sont à peine entrés dans leur adolescence?' (Alexis: 262)

* Funded by the Piedmontese Center for African Studies.
Special thanks also to the CSA (Center for African Studies, Turin), Claudio Gorlier (University of Turin), Kofi Agovi (University of Ghana) and Paul Gready (SOAS, London).

BIBLIOGRAPHY

Fiction & poetry
Aidoo, Ama Ata, *Anowa* (London: Longman, 1970).
Aidoo, Ama Ata, *No Sweetness Here* (New York: Doubleday, 1971).

Aidoo, Ama Ata, *Our Sister Killjoy: or reflections from a black-eyed squint* (New York: Nok Publishers, 1977).

Armah, Ayi Kwei, *The Beautyful Ones Are Not Yet Born* (Boston: Houghton Mifflin, 1968).

Armah, Ayi Kwei, *Fragments* (Boston: Houghton Mifflin, 1970).

Armah, Ayi Kwei, *Two Thousand Seasons* (Nairobi: East African Publishing House, 1973).

Armah, Ayi Kwei, *The Healers* (Nairobi: East African Publishing House, 1978).

Awoonor, Kofi, *This Earth, My Brother* (New York: Doubleday, 1971).

Carpentier, Alejo, *The Kingdom of This World* (London: André Deutsch, 1990). Translated by Harriet de Onís.

Cheney-Coker, Syl, *The Last Harmattan of Alusine Dunbar* (London: Heinemann, 1990).

Kayper-Mensah, Albert W., *Sankofa – Adinkra poems* (Tema: Ghana Publishing Corporation, 1976 (1978)).

Laing, Kojo B. *Search Sweet Country* (London: Heinemann, 1986).

Laing, B. Kojo, *Woman of the Aeroplanes* (London: Heinemann, 1988; Picador, 1989).

Laing, Kojo, *Godhorse* (London: Heinemann, 1989).

Laing, Kojo, *Major Gentl and the Achimota Wars* (London: Heinemann, 1992).

Márquez, Gabriel García. *One Hundred Years of Solitude*. (London: Jonathan Cape, 1991).

Mazrui, Ali A., *The Trial of Christopher Okigbo* (London: Heinemann, 1971).

Melville, Herman, *Bartleby, the Scrivener* (New York: 1856). Edition employed: 'The Portable Melville'. (New York: The Viking Press, 1952 (1970)).

Okri, Ben, *The Famished Road* (London: Jonathan Cape, 1991).

Okri, Ben, *Songs of Enchantment* (London: Jonathan Cape, 1993).

Sutherland, Efua, *Foriwa* (Accra: State Publishing Corporation, 1967).

Tutuola, Amos, *The Palm-wine Drinkard* (London: Faber and Faber, 1952).

Books of literary criticism et al.

Achebe, Chinua et al. (eds), *Beyond Hunger in Africa. Conventional wisdom and a vision of Africa in 2057* (Nairobi: Heinemann; London: James Currey; Portsmouth: Heinemann, 1990).

Ahmad, Aijaz, *In Theory. Classes, nations, literatures* (London: Verso, 1992).

Andrzejewski, B.W. et al., *Literatures in African Languages. Theoretical issues and sample surveys* (Warsaw: Wiedza Powzechna; Cambridge: Cambridge University Press, 1985).

Appiah, Kwame Anthony, *In My Father's House* (London: Methuen, 1992).

Asare Opoku, Kofi, *West African Traditional Religion* (Accra: FEP, 1978).

Assimeng, Max, *Social Structure of Ghana* (Tema: Ghana Publishing Corporation, 1981).

Bhabha, Homi K. (ed.) *Nation and Narration* (London: Routledge, 1990 (1994)).

Duerden, Dennis, *African Art and Literature: the Invisible Present* (New York: Harper & Row, 1975; London: Heinemann, 1977).

Okpewho, Isidore, *The Epic in Africa. Towards a poetic of the oral performance* (New York: Columbia University Press: 1975 (1979)).

Omotoso, Kole, *The Form of the African Novel* (Akure and Ibadan: Fagbamigbe Publishers, 1979).

Pelton, Robert D., *The Trickster in West Africa. A study in mythic irony and sacred delight* (Berkeley: University of California Press, 1980 (1989)).

Rattray, R.S., *Ashanti* (New York: Clarendon Press, 1923; Negro University Press, 1969).

Essays

Alexis, Jacques-Stéphen, 'Du réalisme merveilleux des Haitiens', *Présence Africaine* 8-9-10 (June–November 1956): 245-71.

Armah, Ayi Kwei, 'Larsony or fiction as criticism of fiction', *Asemka* 4 (September 1976): 1-14.

Chanady, Amaryll, 'The origins and development of magic realism in Latin American fiction', *Magic Realism and Literatures – Essays and Stories. Proceedings of the conference on magic realist writing in Canada* Ed. Peter Hinchcliffe and Ed Jewinski (Waterloo: University of Waterloo Press, 1985): 49-60.

Innes, C.L., Introduction to *The Heinemann Book of Contemporary African Short Stories* (London: Heinemann, 1992).

Jameson, Fredric, 'Third world literature in the era of multinational capital', *Social Text* 15 (Fall 1986): 65-88.

Kropp Dabuku, M.E., '*Search Sweet Country* and the language of authentic being', *Research in African Literatures* 24.1 (Spring 1993): 19-35.

Lasagna, Laura, 'The logos of the African Trickster', *Africa America Asia Australia* 16 (1994): 29-40.

Marcus, Mordecai, 'Melville's Bartleby as a psychological double', in *Bartleby the Inscrutable*. Ed. M. Thomas Inge. (Hamden, Connecticut: Archon Books, 1979): 107-13.

Mukherjee, Arun P., 'Whose post-colonialism and whose postmodernism?', *World Literature Written in English* 30.2 (1990): 1-9.

Nnolim, Charles E., 'The Nigerian tradition in the novel', *Commonwealth Novel in English* 2.2 (1983): 22-39.

Slemon, Stephen, 'Magic realism as post-colonial discourse', *Canadian Literature* 116 (Spring 1988): 9-24.

Reviews & interviews

Brown, Stewart, 'Dreams, godhorses and vultures', *Planet: the Welsh Internationalist* (June–July 1990): 96-8.

Deandrea, Pietro, 'An interview with Ben Okri', *Africa America Asia Australia* 16 (1994): 55-82.

Deandrea, Pietro, Unpublished interviews with Kofi Ermeleh Agovi, Kojo Laing and Efua Sutherland.

Fraser, Robert, 'Kojo Laing – profile and extract', *Wasafiri* 3 (Autumn 1985): 9.

Maja-Pearce, Adewale, 'Interview with Kojo Laing', *Wasafiri* 6-7 (Spring/Autumn 1987): 27-9.

Maja-Pearce, Adewale, Untitled review of *Woman of the Aeroplanes, Wasafiri* 10 (Summer 1989): 23.

Therson-Cofie, Larweh, 'Life is war in Achimota City', *People's Daily Graphic* 9 (September): 4.

Waters, Harold A., Untitled review of *Major Gentl and the Achimota Wars, World Literature Today* (Spring 1993): 22.

Index

Lightning Source UK Ltd.
Milton Keynes UK
UKHW010229291122
413003UK00003B/85

9 780852 555200